The Social Psychology of the Primary School

The Social Psychology of the Primary School

Collaboratively edited by
Colin Rogers and
Peter Kutnick

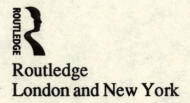

Routledge
London and New York

First published 1990
by Routledge
11 New Fetter Lane, London EC4P 4EE

Simultaneously published in the USA and Canada
by Routledge
a division of Routledge, Chapman and Hall, Inc.
29 West 35th Street, New York, NY 10001

Typeset by LaserScript Limited, Mitcham, Surrey
Printed and bound in Great Britain by
Biddles Ltd, Guildford and King's Lynn

British Library Cataloguing in Publication Data

The social psychology of the primary school.
   1. Great Britain. Primary schools. Students. Socialisation
   I. Rogers, Colin II. Kutnick Peter
   372.181
   ISBN 0-415-02400 5

Library of Congress Cataloging in Publication Data
The social psychology of the primary school / edited by Colin Rogers and
Peter Kutnick.
      p.   cm.
   Includes bibliographical references.
   ISBN 0-415-02400-5
   1. Education, Elementary——Social aspects. 2. Social psychology.
   3. Interaction analysis in education. 4. Classroom environment.
   I. Rogers, Colin, 1950–   . II. Kutnick, Peter.
   LC192.3.S57 1990
   372—dc20   90–32016
                                                                        CIP

This volume is dedicated to our children
Lauren and Hazel
Sam and Laura

Contents

Contents

Figures and tables

Contributors

Paul Croll, Department of Education, Bristol Polytechnic.

Derek Edwards, Department of Social Sciences, Loughborough University.

Jane French, Department of Education, University of York.

David Galloway, Department of Educational Research, Cartmel College, University of Lancaster.

Maurice Galton, School of Education, University of Leicester.

Peter Kutnick, Institute of Continuing and Professional Education, University of Sussex.

William Maxwell, Grampian Regional Council Education Department, Aberdeen, Scotland

Diana Moses, Department of Education, Bristol Polytechnic.

Colin Rogers, Department of Educational Research, Cartmel College, University of Lancaster.

Dale H. Schunk, School of Education, University of North Carolina, USA.

Robert E. Slavin, Centre for Research on Elementary and Middle Schools, The Johns Hopkins University, Baltimore, USA.

Peter K. Smith, Department of Psychology, University of Sheffield.

Acknowledgements

Irrespective of the order in which our names have finally appeared on the cover of this volume, the editorial work represented here is the result of a collaborative enterprise. We accept equal responsibility and (if any is forthcoming) equal credit for this work.

We take this opportunity to thank all the numerous colleagues and friends whose help has been invaluable during the production of this book. We are naturally particularly indebted to the contributors of the original work contained here and thankful for their promptness in dealing with our numerous requests.

Peter Kutnick
Colin Rogers

Chapter one

Process and structure in the primary school

Peter Kutnick and Colin Rogers

Introduction

In this edited book we bring together a number of concerns and interests which will be relevant to teachers and researchers of the primary school. The book is a product of current research and practice in the primary school, and many of the themes pursued here could not have been undertaken until this point in time. The book acknowledges that classroom practice has come a long way from the traditional teaching strategies criticized in the Plowden Report (1967). We rarely find excessively formal classrooms which have been linked to stratified results (such as discrimination by social class, gender and stature of primary school). Yet current studies show that the move to action-oriented and child-centred classrooms has not (unambiguously) led to expected successful results (of equal educational enhancement for all pupils). In analysing and explaining this ambiguity, discussion has shifted to classroom processes which may affect the quality of the educational product.

In relating social psychology to educational practice in the primary school we are mindful to take a 'balanced view'. The balance draws upon descriptions of educational practice, social psychological theory, analytic tools and processes in social psychology, and the malleability of the classroom (the ability to experiment and change practice). The timing and presentation of this book will be apparent as it draws upon recent studies of classroom practice and educational concerns in Britain. It cannot present all practice and all theory, but focuses on up-to-date concerns of grouping, social interaction, classroom talk, motivation and development of the child. Social psychological issues are chosen to represent classroom processes in a social context; even though the product of schooling is usually presented in terms of the individual pupil, that product cannot be divorced from the social processes of the classroom.

The current educational climate dictated by the Educational Reform Act (1988) establishes a national curriculum and diagnostic testing of individual attainment of that curriculum. We fear that teachers may become overwhelmed with concerns of integrating and establishing the new curriculum. But the curriculum can only be applied through processes of teaching and learning. While the Education Reform Act has a distinct product in mind, teachers will still be reliant on grouping strategies and patterns of teacher–pupil and peer interactions to achieve the curricular products. Classroom processes are common to all of the separate curricula being pursued in the Act.

In the past we would have referred to processes as blending the overt and hidden curriculum of the classroom which affect intellectual and social outcomes of the classroom. Now we refer more specifically to types of task demands within the curriculum (roughly identified in research by Bennett, *et al.* 1984 and others as cognitive enhancement, practice, application and so on) and the range of classroom groupings that may enhance or hinder self-concept and learning. We wish to balance the effects of 'curriculum-led' schooling by understanding effective processes to support curricular innovations. We do not wish to see a repeat of classroom problems of management/control which have hindered teachers' matching of individual pupil's educational need to specific levels of developmental curricula, limited effectiveness of groupings in class, the association of low motivation and self-esteem with failure, and so on.

Each of the following chapters presents a general or specific focus on processes in the primary classroom. As a totality, the book also represents a reassessment of the role of social psychology in the classroom. In recent years social psychology of education concerns have been expressed in selective studies and chapters. We must look back to the 1970s to find coherent volumes published in Britain concerning social psychology and schooling (see Morrison and McIntyre 1969, 1971, 1972). Since that time certain issues as the relation of theory to practice have remained. New concerns have also been introduced, concerns such as consideration of the developing abilities of the child in the classroom (including intellectual development and social sensitivity), academic attainments promoted or hindered as related to self-concept, and the role of social context in inducing type and quality of classroom understanding. There is now a greater body of classroom descriptions (generally atheoretical) telling us about activities related to outcomes in the classroom. Classroom descriptions (found especially in studies undertaken by the ORACLE team as presented by Galton – Chapter 2 in this volume) point out problems and possibilities of social interaction, groupings of pupil and teacher strategies. The descriptions provide useful backgrounds upon which more theoretical analyses can be pursued and explained. In a repeat of history, some of the concerns pursued here were first introduced in the 1920s and 1930s. At that time educators and psychologists pursued studies into collective (and co-operative) learning, social bases to cognitive development, social discourse between child and teacher, and the relation of context and classroom structure to learning. Expositions in this book draw upon some of those preliminary studies, but bring current perspectives to bear.

With current classroom descriptions and advances/recapitulations of theory, we become aware of the variety of developments and potential problems that may occur in the classroom. Awareness and analyses of classroom processes can occur at the broad macro level and the narrow micro level; each involves separate methodologies for study and these will be commented upon throughout the text. From these analyses four separate themes recur: a questioning of whether the real focus of development in the classroom should be on the individual or the social group; how the context of the classroom and the various types of interactors (teacher, pupil, peers) affect development; that classroom actions, whether planned or simply allowed to occur (through imposition of school ethos, and so on) in the classroom context, are always 'structured' and this structure can be linked to specific products; and that the teacher has a vital role to play in both structuring context and extending her/his accountability to include process as well as product. The four themes will be qualified by childrens' general development in the classroom. And development may be accounted for comparatively over the years of the primary school as well as within individual and group interactions in any particular year group.

Practice and theory

As social scientists intimately involved with education we are very conscious that practice and theory do not always fit well together. There have been a number of classic examples in which theory has dominated practice, leading, at times, to suspect results. Theory may work very well in small-scale experimental situations, but has limited transferability to the real situation of the classroom. On the other hand, there are many good descriptions of classroom activity which show effectiveness (or lack of effectiveness) of practice. Without theoretically induced tools of analysis or means of explanation, these descriptions may only be left at the here-and-now level; neither explaining the why's of effective practice nor offering alternative strategies to change practice. Some classroom descriptions actually imply a theoretical critique; hence there are examples which: qualify the (often noted) unequal power relationship between child and teacher as displaying genuine negotiation; note that the actual social climate of the classroom (whether competitive or co-operative, and so on) affects quality of learning and control; show that the term 'autonomy' is used variously by teachers, classroom observers and theoreticians. Thus descriptions tell us of the power relationships between teacher and pupils, the comparative role of peers for the pupil, and the *laissez-faire* versus structured organization of classroom interaction by the teacher. These descriptions also assert that the teacher is in the focal role of: defining how current and innovatory curriculum is undertaken in classroom process; planning for young childrens' potential movement from early dependence to establishing self-hood and autonomy; being the reflective exemplar of classroom behaviour.

The perspective presented here does not deny the central position of control into which teachers are often cast. Rather, we place greater emphasis on potential problems inherent in today's classrooms and use both descriptive and theoretical evidence to expand our understanding and provide future directions for classroom behaviour. We wish to see that the movement away from traditional practices with discriminating results remains a movement away, and not allow ourselves to be persuaded that this 'progressive' movement has failed in its educational products (as implied in recent announcements by the Secretary of State for Education. Indeed, from comparative information based on HMI reports (especially DES 1978) we should be aware that classrooms have lost their traditional physical layout of desks in rows, incorporated various methods of grouping pupils, maintained most teaching in the 'core' curriculum, and upheld academic standards). We do not wish to see the national curriculum and testing obligations of schools and teachers force a retreat in classroom process to pre-existing practice. Given our value-laden approach, the relation of theory and practice in this book is assuredly a relative one. In one sense, the theories which we cite have been 'grounded' and developed through observation of social practices (invariably of the pupil in the classroom). The theories drawn upon are also useful tools for analysis of practice and suggest alternatives to existing practice. Theory, except possibly in the chapter by Slavin (Chapter 13), does not dominate our perspective on future directions for practice. Even Slavin's chapter is derived from a critique of ineffective past classroom practices in the United States, and grounded experiences of effective working groups, to establish a model of co-operative learning. Thus our theoretical interests are bounded by practical constraints of existing classrooms from which models of current and projected practices can be analysed and recommended.

Accountability and the reflective teacher

Over the last decade teachers have been under an onslaught of cries for accountability which have culminated in the imposition of the

Education Reform Act. Accountability is undoubtedly of benefit to education generally and to classroom practice. Within the perspective of accountability teachers are frequently requested to explain the performance of their class and individual pupils to school administrators, parents and government. While we fully support this perspective, we also note that what is brought to account is generally the end-product of pupil performance. Generally, pupil product in the classroom is a limited unit of analysis. It does not allow for explanation in terms of a range of performances in the classroom, and does not focus on classroom process (which may be more or less effectively structured to enhance performance for all pupils).

A genuine concern of this book is to promote movement away from simple and end-product definitions by which teachers are held to account. We do not wish to see the curriculum (and diagnostic testing) 'tail wagging the process dog'. We know that a reliance on traditional means of accounting causes pressure to be placed on the teacher to use traditional means of classroom process. While traditional processes do provide consistent end-products of educational attainment, we are aware that the traditional product has been highly discriminatory and stratified (as explained in social class and gender analyses of '11+' results and limited entry into grammar schools of children of the working class and girls of high ability). To move away from traditional accountability pressures, products in education have to be tied to the processes that generate those results. The teacher must be in a position to know how to relate to pupils, understand their growth and develop- ment, and structure the experiences that are being offered in classroom. The teacher must reflect on classroom process as it relates to product.

In taking on this reflective role (which numerous practitioners have already adopted), there are a number of aspects for teachers to consider which are explored here. The aspects include the need to structure pupil groupings for particular classroom learning tasks, positive ways to instil classroom motivation and autonomy in pupils, the role of play and friendships in classroom planning, relationships between classroom actors (teacher and pupils), and tools with which to analyse the on-going processes of the classroom. All of these aspects are premissed on a movement away from the individual as the unit of teaching and learning and the assertion that the classroom is the social context of meaning and development for the pupil. There are a number of aspects of classroom practice which have been analysed previously, and which we do not need to repeat here. We are already aware that: traditional classroom process and products have been explored in numerous other texts and that pupil groups are frequently used in the classroom, although methods of grouping may range from *laissez-faire* (unplanned) to friendships to ability (homogeneous or heterogeneous) bases.

5

Competitive versus co-operative learning processes will produce various social and academic performance effects.

This book should enable the reflective teacher to draw upon a variety of models and considerations of classroom process in planning for classroom activity. The processes will relate to numerous curriculum subjects. We hope to expand classroom accountability from product to include process, and to legitimize that process is socially as opposed to individually based in the classroom.

Structure of the book

The planning and arrangement of chapters in the book fall into two sections. The sections are strongly linked to one another, and the links will become clear as one progresses through the book. The sections represent introductions and overviews of general issues initially, and focused/applied consideration of issues in the second half.

The first half of the book (Chapters 2 to 6) begins with a description of the group work and social interaction in the classroom. Consideration then moves to quantity and quality of social interaction between children and teachers with a special focus on discourse analysis. Development of the self is explored through self-concept, motivation and autonomy – each aspect drawing upon experimental, theoretical and practical studies of the classroom. These chapters have links among themselves and with the focused discussions in the second half of the book.

The second section is based on classroom realities; what has been done and what can be done. Of prime concern are the relationships engendered in the classroom. The quality of hierarchical and collaborative relationships generated in Piaget's consideration of moral development are made relevant to the classroom. Activities of young children in school and the role of teacher- induced structuring of activity are taken up in play and friendships. Distinctions between the behaviour of boys and girls provide insights into the potential of gender differentiation and disruption in the classroom. The section culminates with an amalgamation of process and curriculum concerns by citing an American model of co-operative learning (which strongly substantiates that academic and social products can be enhanced by consideration of specific grouping and learning processes which teachers may structure) and a critique of the integration of children with 'special educational needs' into the normal classroom.

General issues

The chapter on 'Grouping and Group Work', by Maurice Galton, (Chapter 2) is reflective of the ORACLE observations of process and product in junior schools. Groups are a convenient and much-used method for organizing children in classrooms. Group work has been strongly supported by HMI and government reports. But the effects of using groups in the classroom are not always clear or advantageous. Teachers need to plan/structure their groupings rather than simply 'allowing them to happen'. Group size, composition and task demand are all considerations that ought to be brought to bear on classroom organization. This chapter sets a background for ensuing concerns in the book, especially motivation (Chapter 6), autonomy (Chapter 7), friendships (Chapter 10), and co-operative learning (Chapter 13).

With a background into the use of groups, a more focused look at the intimacy of classroom interactions is explored in the chapter by French (Chapter 3). This chapter is important in that it qualifies distinct and meaningful actions in the classroom which may benefit or hold back development of learning and express particular gender bias. A discussion of social interaction notes that both teacher and children have rights and meaningful positions in the classroom. The interactions focused upon and explored will be limited by the perspective of the social scientist and the methods chosen for study. The importance of this chapter is immediately exemplified in discourse (Chapter 4), provides tools of analysis for self-concept (Chapter 5), autonomy (Chapter 7) and play (Chapter 9). Themes in this chapter are further explored in the discussion of gender/sex roles in the classroom (Chapter 11).

The study of classroom conversation and its relationship to the development of knowledge reminds the reader that learning is the result of a social process. This chapter critically assesses the role of the individual in classroom learning, and explicitly shows that this learning takes place in a social context (the classroom). The type of knowledge generated in this context is dependent on the quality of social relationships that are structured to take place between interactors. Knowledge, in short, is a process of shared meanings in a climate of specific power relationships. The discourse analysis used in the chapter is an example of a social interactional methodology (from Chapter 3), and has direct links to classroom activity in the development of classroom autonomy (Chapter 7), the relationship between teacher and pupil (Chapter 8), and peer relations in co-operation (Chapter 13).

More focused exploration of the development of the child's self-concept and its correlation to achievement is reviewed by Schunk in Chapter 5. He reminds the reader of the child's active role in the learning process and how classroom performance is strongly linked to the learning context itself. This chapter is premised on past research showing that the child's self-identity is established through social interactional and evaluational processes by which primary school classroom life is made meaningful for the child. Discussion leads directly to further consideration of classroom motivation (Chapter 6), friendships generated through schooling (Chapter 10), and possibly in themes identified in special needs (Chapter 12).

The pupil's motivation to enhance school-based learning and/or social relationships is introduced by Schunk but more fully explored by Rogers in Chapter 6. This chapter draws upon studies of classroom practice and social theories of identity. Pupils' approach to classroom work is strongly related to the social and interactional climate structured by the teacher. The resultant quality of interaction structured in the classroom will depend on the understanding of autonomy drawn upon by the teacher (Chapter 7), specifically alludes to the relationship between teacher and child (Chapter 8), and poses an alternative practice to promote motivation amongst the whole class taken up in co-operative learning (Chapter13).

The general issues section is completed by providing some in-depth consideration about the social development of the child. Social development is discussed in terms of the type and quality of relationships within which the child interacts. Archetypical relationships with adults and peers are described as the roots of autonomy, and are significantly affected by the structured relationships and motivational concerns of the classroom. While theoretical in nature, this chapter draws on the role of groups (Chapter 2), relationships (Chapter 8), friendships (Chapter 10), and co-operation (Chapter 13) in the classroom.

Focused issues

Derek Wright has been involved in the study and classroom implications of moral education for many years. Do not mistake this chapter (Chapter 8) as a curriculum issue, as it is based upon practical concerns and the importance of relationships between teachers and pupils. Themes recurrent in this book are made relevant here, especially the qualities of hierarchy and collaboration that the teacher may structure in classroom life. The practicality of this chapter is complimented by theoretical and structural concerns in the previous chapters on motivation (Chapter 6) and autonomy (Chapter 7).

The role of play in the classroom again combines curricular and practical considerations. Peter K. Smith has researched the complexity of this subject over many years. Readers may be aware that issues presented here (in Chapter 9) are immediately relevant to pre-schools and early infant classes. Nevertheless, these issues describe the active roles played by both teacher and pupil in their own development, and that teachers must consider the careful structuring of play as essential to their classroom process. Issues in this chapter are taken up in all of the succeeding chapters, especially those on friendship (Chapter 10) and sex roles (Chapter 11).

Maxwell's consideration of friendship in Chapter 10 integrates developmental and social concerns, and lays an important issue before the classroom teacher. Much of children's time will be spent developing, extending and altering friendships. In one sense children display 'natural' tendencies towards certain types of friendships. On the other hand we must be aware that friendships are often structured by the culture and interactional experiences offered to children. This chapter picks up themes of social interaction (Chapter 3) and play (Chapter 9), and the importance of structuring relationships is further explored in co-operative learning (Chapter 13).

Sex roles in the classroom is a hotly debated and debateable issue. Here we need basic information, minimally to move away from common prejudice. While it has often been assumed that girls perform more poorly in schools than boys, this is not so in primary schools, and we shall need to place strict qualifiers around the statement. There may be distinct patterns of interaction that differentiate between boys and girls in primary schools. Some of the interactional differences may not be characteristic of boys or girls generally, but may be magnified by particular teacher-based concerns (especially of disruption). Issues raised in Chapter 11 are derived from social interaction (Chapter 3), discourse analysis (Chapter 4), and motivation (Chapter 6). That some of these sex differences may be the result of inadvertent teacher structuring is discussed in Chapter 12 on special needs (including disruption). Some of these behaviours may be changed in processes such as co-operative learning (Chapter 13).

Consistent reports identify that up to 20 per cent of children in school may present themselves as having special educational needs at any point in their schooling careers. Galloway, who has researched the generation and identification of classroom disorders, considers in Chapter 12 the role of teacher and classroom structure in coping with the integration of a large number of special needs children in the normal classroom. A central dilemma for the teacher is how to structure 'normal' classroom processes to include the child with special needs. Social dynamics of pupil groups in the classroom may, if allowed to structure themselves, result in discrimination and separation of pupils from one another. Other classroom structures as co-operative heterogeneous groups have produced significant movement towards integration and enhanced motivation of all pupils (see Chapter 13).

The final issue chapter in this section is the one most consistently referred to throughout the text. Robert Slavin, internationally known for his practical research into co-operative learning, brings together a number of issues. In acknowledging that traditional classroom structures and *laissez-faire* groupings produce genuine learning amongst pupils (but this is combined with discrimination), we ask how teachers may structure their classrooms more effectively to produce good results for all. The practice of co-operative learning, which has been explored for some years in the United States, draws upon the realization that learning is a social process. For learning to be effective at all, the teacher's role in structuring learning tasks, groups and assessment is essential. This chapter (Chapter 13) will draw upon themes of co-operative learning and report on its practical usage and results.

The final chapter of the book (Chapter 14) reviews a number of issues discussed. In so doing, the intention is not to provide a summary. The chapter will take the issues and focus upon models for classroom structuring that the teacher may initiate. As stated in the opening of the book, our intention is to draw upon current and up-to-date classroom studies and social psychological concerns. The integration of these issues provides a solid background for the assertion that processes of classroom interaction should be studied and structured in teaching. Teachers and schools should not be held to account solely for curricular-based results. The reflective practitioner will plan for process concerns of the self, motivation and autonomy in the relationships and grouping approaches of the classroom, and these concerns will apply to all of the subjects in the national curriculum.

References

Bennett, S.N., Desforges, C., Cockburn, A. and Wilkinson, B., (1984) *The Quality of Pupil-Learning Experiences*, London: Lawrence Erlbaum Associates.

Department of Education and Science (DES) (1978) *Primary Education in England*, London: HMSO.

Education Reform Act (1988), London: HMSO.

Morrison, A. and McIntyre, D. (1969) *Teachers and Teaching*, London: Penguin.

Morrison, A. and McIntyre, D. (1971) *Schools and Socialization*, London: Penguin.

Morrison, A. and McIntyre, D. (eds) (1972) *The Social Psychology of Teaching*, London: Penguin.

Plowden Report (1967) *Children and Their Primary Schools*, 2 vols. Report of the Central Advisory Council for Education in England, London: HMSO.

Chapter two

Grouping and group work

Maurice Galton

Editors' introduction

Maurice Galton's brief was to provide a review of research into group work within the classroom. This he has done by drawing attention to a number of central dilemmas that group work can invoke.

Central to these concerns are the issues of pupil autonomy and teacher control. Galton demonstrates how the study of group work can lead to a consideration of issues relating to pupil motivation and self-concept. Pupils are required to negotiate their way through the often conflicting demands made upon them both by their teachers and by their peers. Pupils are seen to be striving to develop a sense of 'ownership' over their work while at the same time seeking to avoid having to accept responsibility for work that is judged to be less than adequate by their teacher or peers. Group work can liberate the pupil from undue teacher control, enabling ownership and encouraging the development of autonomy. At the same time, the more closely involved with the group the individual pupil becomes, the more public his or her efforts will be. Group work can thus aid the pupil in the quest for ownership but also increase the threats implicit in increased peer evaluation. The application of group work strategies cannot therefore be considered unproblematic but must also be seen as potentially rewarding.

The issues introduced here will be returned to on a number of occasions throughout the book, but, in particular, common threads will be found in the chapters on self-esteem (Chapter 5), pupil motivation (Chapter 6) and pupil autonomy (Chapter 7). A related perspective on group-based approaches to learning can be seen in the chapter on co-operative study methods (Chapter 13).

Introduction

One of the most striking changes to have taken place in the post-war decade at primary level has been the change in the pattern of organization and the use of more informal seating arrangements. For example, writing about the late 1950s, Donald Jones provides an account of a Leicestershire classroom where, according to the teacher, 'We used to have classes of over fifty in such tight rows that nobody could leave the room until somebody stood up' (Jones 1987: 35). Yet by the beginning of the 1970s most junior school classrooms in the same authority used some variation of group seating arrangements (Bealing 1972). The organization of pupils into groups was one of the distinguishing characteristics marking the move away from rigid streaming, following the abolition of the 11+ and reorganization of secondary education along comprehensive lines. By the time the ORACLE survey reported (Galton *et al.* (1980), over 90 per cent of the classes visited were using some kind of group arrangement to seat pupils with less than 1 per cent retaining the traditional patterns of rows of desks.

Definitions of group work

When questioned by the ORACLE observers, however, many of these teachers looked upon group work as little more than a form of seating organization, particularly in mathematics, where children were seated in homogeneous groups according to ability. Even where groups were heterogeneous, to a large extent there was little emphasis on instituting joint tasks and even less on allowing children to help one another with their work. Beyond these seating arrangements group work then had a range of meanings. At one extreme was *joint group work* where pupils were engaged on specific tasks which then contributed to an overall theme. For example, children might be mounting a wall display in the classroom as part of an environmental study of the local surroundings. Some children might be projecting a transparency of a map of the area on to the classroom wall and colouring in various sections while others would be engaged in mounting specimens of material collected during the field trip and locating these at the various places where they were found. For the most part decisions concerning who did what task would have emerged during joint discussion with the teacher. Joint group work is therefore characterized by the setting of individual tasks linked by a common theme and contrasts with seated group work where the children sit at the same table but engage in similar but unrelated tasks. For example a group of children may be on the same mathematics worksheet but they will be expected to complete the questions on their own.

At the other end of the scale is co-operative group work, where children are expected to pool their ideas as part of a joint presentation. One example, taken from the ORACLE study, concerned a group of children who were engaged in a cloze procedure exercise. The children were expected to pool their ideas in order to decide on the missing words. Co-operative group work therefore has a joint outcome to which all members of the group have, at one time or other, contributed.

The use of group work in the primary classroom

In the ORACLE study it was common to see examples of joint group work in most classrooms involving common tasks but individual assignments. These joint activities, however, were seldom used for teaching basic skills of computation and English or for science, but were largely restricted to art and craft or general studies where there was a practical element. Less than a quarter of the teachers who made use of joint group work did so for more than one curriculum area (Galton 1981). In a more recent investigation of curriculum provision in small schools, the PRISMS study (Galton *et al.* 1987), similar patterns were observed in both infant and junior school classrooms. Here there was greater teacher interaction with groups than in the ORACLE study (12.6 per cent in infant classes, 15.8 per cent in junior classes compared to 9.4 per cent in ORACLE classes). This was, in the main, a consequence of the fact that in most classes in small schools the age range of the children is wide and pupils tend to be seated and taught in groups of the same age. In these groups, when the teacher was not present, pupil–pupil talk was less than in ORACLE (13 per cent as against 19 per cent). However, unlike ORACLE, in PRISMS 55 per cent of these pupils' conversations were task-related compared to only 20 per cent in the ORACLE study. In the PRISMS analysis, however, a wider range of curriculum activities (including games, dancing and drama) were included. Nevertheless, the overall patterns of working showed that 79.1 per cent and 81.2 per cent of observations in infant and junior classrooms involved a pupil working alone within the group (seated group work). When children were involved in collaboration then 3.5 per cent and 4.2 per cent of all activity of infant and junior-aged children respectively was in pairs compared to 4.8 per cent and 5 per cent in larger groups. This suggests that, overall, the amount of collaborative work in small schools was not much greater than in ORACLE. Further evidence for this conclusion comes from recent studies conducted in the Inner London Education Authority, at infant level (Tizard *et al.* 1988) and at junior level (Mortimore *et al.* 1987). Here again, for the most part children sat in groups but worked individually. According to Mortimore *et al.* (p. 82) 'Not a great deal of collaborative work was observed' although:

> there was some evidence that where pupils worked on the same task as other pupils of roughly the same ability or when pupils worked within the same curriculum area but on different tasks at their own level, the effect on progress was positive.
>
> (Mortimore *et al.* 1987: 230)

Differing prescriptions of good practice

In the last twenty years there have been continuous calls to include more collaborative group work within primary pedagogy. Her Majesty's Inspectors' survey (DES 1978) defined groups in terms of seating pattern rather than teaching strategy and argued that the main advantage of such grouping was to enable teachers to provide work of an appropriate level of difficulty (para. 8.32). The inspectors called for more direct teaching of groups, particularly in mathematics, arguing that this was a more efficient way of introducing new aspects of the subject to children. Groups were therefore seen by the inspectors as a way of increasing the amount of contact between teachers and pupils, particularly if the work involved thinking at higher levels of abstraction. They argued, for example, that in teaching mathematics: 'challenging questions and quick recall of numbers and facts, including multiplication tables often required a lively sustained contact between the teacher and a group of children' (DES 1978: para. 5.65).

The inspectors' view of grouping, therefore, seems to give tacit support to their finding that over 70 per cent of teachers place children in ability groups for mathematics, since in such groups 'children were doing more challenging work and the teacher was able to inject more pace'.

This suggests that, for basic skills, groups should be set up where pupils are able to undertake work of a similar level of difficulty – a view supported by Mortimore *et al.* (1987).

This viewpoint, however, concerning the functioning of groups, differs markedly from the prescription to be found in the Plowden (1967) Report. The report placed great emphasis on the individualization of the learning process but acknowledged that in a typical sized classroom this meant that only limited amounts of teacher–pupil contact were possible. Collaborative group work was a way of overcoming this problem and was recommended, in particular, for science activities. According to the Plowden prescription, teachers could economize on their time 'by teaching together a small group of children who are roughly at the same stage' (para. 754).

This was not a recommendation for streamlining within the classroom since the Plowden Committee recommended that 'the groups should be based on interest or sometimes on achievement, but that they should change in accordance with children's needs' (para. 824). The organization of pupils into groups in this way, however, was advocated by Plowden not only to allow more efficient use of teachers' time but so that the number of contacts between pupils and teacher could be increased. Collaborative grouping also performed a pedagogic function since the report claimed that within such groups children 'make their meanings clear to themselves by having to explain it to others and gain some opportunity to teach as well as learn'. Group interaction of this kind was thought to help the timid child who might be 'less shy in risking hypotheses in a group', while apathetic children 'may be infected by the enthusiasm of the group while other children benefit from being caught up in the thrust and counterthrust of conversation in a small group of children similar to themselves' (para. 757–8).

The Plowden view of group work was therefore in marked contrast to that suggested by the inspectorate who appear to have seen its use as a means of teachers' directing work more efficiently and stimulating the group to higher levels of thinking. Plowden, on the other hand, argued that the teacher has 'missed the whole point if he tells the children the answers or indicates too readily or completely how the answers may be found' (para. 669). Class discussion should be introduced towards the end when the individual pupils' contributions are complete so that 'the pieces of the jigsaw can be fitted together...or seen not to fit' (para. 760). Thus the use of groups in Plowden's sense involved co-operative working between children which continued even when the teacher was engaged elsewhere. The teacher's role was to promote enquiry with the twin objectives of stimulating pupils' thinking and developing communication skills.

Many of the same outcomes are endorsed by Kerry and Sands (1982). They argued that the main advantage of collaborative group work is that it helps pupils to work together co-operatively and allows them to learn from each other, thus removing the stigma of failure for slow learners. Pupils are given a chance to work at their own pace and become less teacher dependent. Group work, according to Kerry and Sands, also improves individual pupils' self-image in that by working in groups the children come to respect each other's strengths and weaknesses. For the teacher the advantages were said to be two-fold. First it provides an opportunity for the teacher to circulate and correct individual work while other children are collaborating actively within groups. Second, it enables the teacher to tailor a range of tasks which are more appropriate to the children's needs and abilities. These aims are also endorsed by Yeomans (1983).

Criticisms of group work

These views are not universally shared among those writing about current primary practice. Robin Alexander, for example, takes to task those local authority advisers whom he claims, following the ORACLE findings, convey to teachers the message that 'unless pupils are inter-acting and collaborating within their groups, there is little point in grouping them' (Alexander 1988: 178).

Alexander goes on to describe the work of a group of teachers who place children into collaborative group situations, to engage in problem-solving, while they themselves continue to instruct other pupils individually although these latter pupils are seated in groups. This is exactly the pattern recommended by Plowden. Alexander claims that the teachers' interpretation of the prescription for grouping requires everyone in the class to be working in groups at the same time and, in so far as this is attributed to ORACLE influence, it is incorrect. ORACLE, like most other studies of primary classrooms, has persistently called for the use of mixed organization strategies although, as has been argued elsewhere the use of individual instruction coupled with children working on their own collaboratively in groups is itself problematic (Galton 1989a).

There are others, however, who actually question the use of grouping as part of a 'mixed economy' of primary practice. Wheldall *et al.* (1981) found a significant increase in on-task behaviour when children were seated individually in rows, and that levels of distraction increased when children returned to seating in groups. Wheldall's study has been replicated by Bennett and Blundell (1983). They used the quality of the work as an additional dependent variable as well as 'time on task'. They found that the quantity of work increased when children were moved from groups to rows and that there was no decline in quality. In the United States, among those making similar criticisms of group practices, there is a grudging acceptance that some form of group participation may be required when the class consists of vertically-aged cohorts. Writing in the third *Handbook of Research on Teaching*, Brophy and Good (1986) argue that:

> The small group approach requires well chosen assignments that the students are willing to engage in and able to complete successfully, as well as rules and procedures that enable students to get help (if confused) or direction (about what to do if finished) without disrupting the momentum of the teacher's lesson. Teachers...may find it takes too much effort to be worth the trouble.
>
> (Brophy and Good 1986: 361)

Thus, in this country, despite the interest in group work which has developed over the last twenty years at primary level, there is still little agreement about the methods teachers should use when attempting to develop collaboration and co-operation within their classrooms.

Research into group work and grouping in the United States

In the United States there has been much work on aspects of collaborative working in groups, with somewhat different conclusions emerging according to the different focuses of these studies. Much of the American research has its origins in the investigation of earlier researchers into the merits of co-operative, competitive and individualistic goal structures. Thus the emphasis in most American studies is on the effect of these different 'goal structures', on group productivity and achievement. Unlike the United Kingdom, there have been fewer studies of a descriptive nature where the interactions between pupils within such groups have been observed.

By far the largest body of research has emerged from the work of Slavin and his colleagues (reported in chapter 13 of this volume). Slavin's model of group working in the classroom is based upon a team games approach (Slavin 1983, 1986). Just as in the sporting analogy, class teams are made up of high, average and low-performing students, boys and girls, and, where appropriate, pupils with different racial or ethnic backgrounds. As far as possible each team is representative of the whole class structure. Team members have to accept responsibility for the learning of all individuals within the team and not just their own progress. While the pupils can help each other during team practices, they have to take the test, on which the group score is based, on their own. Individual scores of team members are then combined to form the team score. There are also other versions of this procedure known as the student teams achievement divisions (STAD), involving team games tournaments (Devries and Slavin 1978) and team-assisted individualization (Slavin *et al*. 1984).

In an analysis of some thirty-three studies in both elementary and secondary classrooms it is claimed that twenty-two showed a significant positive effect on student achievement, particularly when the study involved student team-learning techniques. It is also claimed that such arrangements improve intergroup relations particularly with students of different ethnicities. Grouping was also said to improve self-esteem (Slavin 1983), particularly when a team-learning approach was combined with a jigsaw arrangement where each student was given the opportunity to become an expert on some aspect of the work (Aronson *et al*. 1978).

In this type of programme pupils who had to master the same area of expertise were brought together in a group to pool ideas. They then returned to their own teams to teach the other pupils what they had learned in the expert group. As in the STAD programme, each pupil then took individual quizzes and these were aggregated into team scores. The essential characteristic of Slavin's approach to group work, therefore, is that it involves some group reward incentive structure. A summary of this work is given by Bennett (1985).

A different strategy has been developed by Johnson and Johnson (1976). The Johnsons' model is based upon the definition of collaborative group work used earlier. Unlike Slavin's approach, where individuals complete the assignment by themselves and the scores of individuals are then aggregated, the Johnsons recommend that the outcome of the groups' activity should consist of a single assignment sheet, as in the earlier example of cloze procedure. In addition, the groups are judged not only on how well they do on the group task, but on how well they have worked together in carrying out the assignment. In an analysis of a number of studies, Johnson and Johnson (1980) have claimed that such co-operative structures promote higher achievement at all age-levels and in all subject areas on tasks demanding a range of skills such as concept attainment, predicting and evaluating. Johnson *et al.* (1981) claim that the evidence demonstrates the clear superiority of co-operation in promoting achievement and productivity although these conclusions have been attacked by other researchers such as Cotton and Cook (1982). These writers are particularly critical of the fact that many of the studies cited by Johnson *et al.* were of very short duration (less than two weeks) and were not carried out under normal classroom conditions.

A number of studies have also been carried out in Israel with the aim of improving the performance of pupils in science (Sharan 1989). These researchers claim that working co-operatively in groups improved self-esteem, the learning environment and student achievement. Student achievement was measured by using standardized tests and the learning environment by means of an inventory developed by Walberg and Anderson (1968). Self-esteem was assessed by means of a question-naire, based on an earlier version developed by Aronson *et al.* (1978). These Israeli studies were, therefore, more concerned to test the hypothesis that collaborative working in the classroom led to an improvement in student outcome measures rather than attempting to explain the mechanism by which working in groups facilitated such outcomes. This latter objective can only be achieved by a study of pupil and teacher behaviour within the classroom during group work supported by the teacher's and the children's explanations for their observed behaviour, rather than the use of rather crude questionnaires as in the majority of American and Israeli studies. Explanations based upon this kind of analysis make up the remaining part of this chapter. At present most of these conclusions remain tentative and require further empirical testing. They do, however, offer a framework for developing effective pedagogic strategies for group work.

Effective group work in the primary classroom

The starting point for further discussion requires consideration of the follow-up project to ORACLE, *Effective Group Work in the Primary*

Classroom. The main findings are described briefly in Galton (1987, 1989b). The project was conceived because of interest in a particular teaching style identified during the ORACLE study. A small group of teachers appeared to follow the HMI recommendation in DES (1978) and engage children in joint group work. These teachers were called group instructors. Associated with the use of this teaching strategy were a group of pupils who worked together in groups. However, an examination of their interaction patterns showed that, while they did collaborate together, this collaboration generally involved sharing materials and did not extend to conversation. This group of pupils were therefore described as quiet collaborators. Given that the ORACLE study had demonstrated that collaborative group work in the primary classroom was a 'neglected art' (Galton 1981), teams of teachers were set up charged with extending this 'quiet collaboration' into areas where conversation about ideas, and so on, was required. These teams of teachers then attempted to improve the practice of a group of colleagues using a 'team-training approach' which is currently in vogue for the development of new TGAT (Task Group on Assessment and Testing) initiative (Black 1988). For a period of one term this second group of teachers were observed when attempting to implement these new group strategies. Their performance was compared with a control who had followed a more conventional in-service course designed to improve aspects of individualized and whole-class teaching.

Initially the results obtained from the first systematic observation of the experimental and the control group were encouraging. The proportions of lessons involving extended discussion in the experimental group was 35.5 per cent compared to only 19.2 per cent in the control group. In both cases the teacher was present with groups for approximately the same amounts of time so that it appeared from this evidence that the children in the experimental study were collaborating together more frequently. Time on task, the degree of distraction and the amount of time waiting for teacher were all lower in the experimental group employing the collaborating group work strategy. This result therefore was in accord with the findings of Johnson and Johnson (1976). However, when the second set of observations were carried out some two to three weeks later, these differences had all but disappeared. While discussions in the control group remained around 20 per cent, in the experimental group they dropped to around 24.6 per cent and distraction rose in both groups to around 18 per cent. At the same time there was increased teacher involvement with the experimental groups. Thus after only a short time the patterns of interaction within both groups were remarkably similar to those which had been found earlier in the original ORACLE study and which have since been confirmed in other studies such as PRISMS (Tizard *et al.* 1988 and Mortimer *et al.* 1988).

Further analysis of this data revealed an interesting pattern. An examination of the original observations, where the experimental group had increased the amount of collaborative activity between children in groups to around 36 per cent, showed that there were large differences according to the curriculum area involved. Most striking was the fact that nearly 71 per cent of all collaborative interactions during this initial visit to the classroom involved the use of materials within the experimental group, compared with only 40 per cent in the control group. When correlation co-efficients were calculated between pupil behaviour and different curriculum activities during the first observation session the reason for the high level of group work in the experimental group and its decline by the second set of observations became apparent. In the experimental group discussion was negatively correlated with reading (– 0.129), writing (– 0.385) measuring (– 0.351) and arithmetical computation (+ 0.278) but, positively correlated with the use of materials (+0.541). The main difference between the two groups initially, therefore, was that the experimental group had made much greater use of materials and hence obtained higher levels of collaboration. Once the topic was under way and there was less use of materials and a need for more writing, reading, measuring and discussion, the pattern of both groups became strikingly similar, with a marked reluctance on the part of the pupils to work together in the absence of the teacher.

Pupils' perceptions of collaborative group work

The next stage of the project was to examine the pupils' reasons for this reluctance to work collaboratively. Rather than make use of questionnaires a projective technique involving the use of cartoon pictures was devised in the hope that pupils would then 'say what they felt' rather than what they thought the interviewer required. The cartoon pictures showed pupils in various classroom settings. Fuller details are given in Galton (1987). Of special interest were two cartoons, one which showed children talking to each other in a group without the teacher present and the other portraying children talking with the teacher with a tape recorder being used to monitor the discussion. The pupils were asked to say which were their favourite cartoons and to describe the conversation which was taking place. The children had to choose two pupils from the group in the cartoon picture and describe what these two children were either saying or thinking.

For the most part there was a strong rejection of collaborative group work. In particular the pictures where no teacher was present accounted for 30 per cent of all rejections. The least popular picture (17 per cent) involved the pupils' tape recording. Children gave various reasons for their lack of enthusiasm for group work.

'My friends make me silly'.

'There's no teacher. You're worried if you get things wrong'.

Only in one class of 12-year-olds, among some fifty studied, was there a strong positive response to the pictures where children were working on their own without the presence of the teacher. This group of pupils had very positive feelings about collaborating together.

—'Its good to work things out with the teacher. You can have a laugh when you discuss'.

Some put it even more strongly:

'I would like to work with my friends and discuss things on our own because when you work with teachers they always stop you'.

'One can learn more from each other when there is no teacher to nag'.

When the children in all the classes, including the one with a positive attitude to co-operation, described what teachers were saying when they came to a group there was an overwhelming perception that most comments were likely to be negative, to do with the teacher's attempt to get them to work properly. Repeated remarks included such things as,

'Look at the picture, get on!'

'Now listen to me."

'You'll not leave this room until you've finished'.

The contrast between the typical response presented by the pupils in the sample and the children in the one class favouring group work led to an extended case study of the latter, culminating with the author going to teach in the school for a six-week period. Much of the analysis of this experience is contained in *Primary Teaching* (Galton 1989b). Here, however, I wish to concentrate on some of the dilemmas which emerged as a result of the analysis of these case studies. These dilemmas centre round three particular contradictory features of primary classrooms which can be extended to other issues besides group work. They are particularly relevant, however, to the latter activity because, as I shall argue, group work provides pupils with very little opportunity to engage in the standard 'avoidance' strategies which are commonly used to deal with more typical classroom situations where children are taught individually or as a class.

Ownership and risk during group work

The first dilemma centres around the conflict between the pupils' desire for public acknowledgement of their contribution to the group effort and their concern that when the teacher and other pupils acknowledge their contribution there is also the risk of a 'public' failure with corresponding loss of self-esteem.

Fear of failure is an extremely strong element in the primary classroom as documented by other writers such as Pollard (1985) and Woods (1980). Pollard describes how pupils' 'interests at hand' lead them to develop what Measor and Woods (1984) call 'knife-edging' strategies of avoidance in order to develop a safe 'working consensus in the classroom'. In the ORACLE studies Galton *et al.* (1980) also described similar strategies. Pupils interviewed as part of the follow-up study to ORACLE, *Effective Group Work in the Primary Classroom*, likened activities such as classroom discussion to 'walking on a tightrope' (Galton 1987).

Thus the dilemma which faces pupils when working in groups concerns the tension which exists between their desire to own their ideas and the risk which such public acknowledgement carries of appearing to fail in the eyes of their peers and of the teacher. Case studies carried out, not only during the group work project, but in a more recent study of children's writing, suggests that children want the work they do to be acknowledged and to be seen as 'theirs'. As Pollard (1987) argues: 'children learn best when they feel in control of their own learning and interpretive sociologists reinforce this from a motivational point of view'.

Pupils lose this sense of 'control' when teachers seek to impose some order on the children's thinking. Here, for example, is a sequence taken from an interview with pupils during the project.

Effective group work in the primary classroom

The group are explaining why it is they like working in groups

Pupil 1:	When you are in groups you can discuss it, can't you, instead of working on your own. It's better working on your own than working with the class.
Pupil 2:	I think it is best when the teacher comes because they don't want you to mess about. Because when you are on your own you are always talking about other things but when you are with the teacher you start working harder.
Pupil 3:	Yes, the teacher helps you. She gives you different ideas.

Pupil 1:	I think the teacher wants to put her view into what you are thinking which might make you change your mind about something. You know, instead of keeping to your own idea.
Interviewer:	Is there anyone over here? Come on.
Pupil 4:	Teachers stop you if you are right, Say you get, say your answer's right and they think it is wrong well they will stop you and put what they think they want you to do. They don't like you to do your own work but sometimes they do.
Pupil 2:	When you have to do something, like we have had that before and you have got to do a certain number of things, when the teacher comes up telling you you've got a right good idea you go away and do it and they will come back and alter it all and they will make you do something else and (tell you) it's got to be like this.
Interviewer:	Now, why do you think that is?
Pupil 1:	Because they think it is best.
Interviewer:	Because they think it's best?
Pupil 1:	Because they think it can be improved.
Interviewer:	Does that stop you putting your ideas as well?
Chorus of pupils:	No.
Interviewer:	You can still put your ideas forward then?
Chorus of Pupils:	Yes.
Interviewer:	O.K. So what do you feel like if you think your idea is a good idea and then it happens like you say and the teacher comes and changes it?
Pupil 2:	You feel a bit upset. You have put all that work into it and then the teacher suddenly changes it.
Pupil 3:	You get a bit mad with her.
Pupil 1:	You don't feel it is your piece of work. You feel as if it is the teacher's. When you have done everything to it and you think, that's my piece of work and no-one else has done owt to it. But when the teacher has done something to it it don't feel as good.

Studies suggest that the idea of guidance which lies behind many of the interventions by teachers which produce the above perceptions in pupils come from what might be termed a 'two-stage' theory of pedagogy. Initially the teacher attempts to support and extend the pupil's tentative ideas in the belief that this support will encourage the pupil, increasing their confidence so that they will then continue working independently. From the point of view of many pupils, however, it would appear that this initial guidance is seen as a 'take-over bid' where the pupils feel they are no longer in a position where they think that the ideas are their own. As a result enthusiasm and motivation decline and the work produced is what the teacher is thought to want rather than what the pupil wished to do.

However, this desire for ownership has another dimension, since it carries with it a public risk of failure. This is particularly so when working in small groups where an individual's contribution is open to close scrutiny by both the teacher and one's peers. As the beginning of any new group activity, therefore, each participant's self-esteem is at considerable risk. Pupils with low 'self-concepts' will either be content to accept the teacher's intervention because it allows them to pass ownership back to the teacher, or else they will attempt to persuade another more competent member of the group to take over the teacher's role. During the initial stages of group work, therefore, these pupils welcome the teacher's intervention because they prefer to be dependent on the teacher and thus escape the responsibility of ownership. These are the pupils who disliked the cartoon picture when the teacher was not present because their friends 'made them silly' or 'they were worried about getting things wrong'.

There are other pupils, like pupil no. 4 in the interview, with healthier 'self-concepts' who appear to resent the teacher's intervention because it denies them the opportunity to demonstrate ownership of their ideas. In the initial stage, however, they are not sufficiently confident to wish to express these ideas in public. The two-stage theory of guided discovery seems to offer the worst solution to both kinds of pupils in that it encourages dependence in one group and produces resentment in the other as demonstrated by the transcript of the interview. An alternative two-stage theory is, therefore, required whereby the teacher limits their interventions initially during the 'incubation' period until the group members are sufficiently confident in their own ideas to expose them to the teacher. One reason for the success of the jigsaw arrangement whereby the pupils begin their discussions in pairs is that it minimizes the risk of failure in front of peers and the teacher. When such groups finally come together it is very difficult for any member apart from their initial partner, to know the extent of an individual's responsibility for the ideas which are presented.

Teacher interviews and evaluations

A second dilemma facing teachers relates to the framework which they use to evaluate the success or failure of a group activity. We saw earlier that the use of group work could be justified on a number of grounds, including the improvement of understanding among slow learners, the development of teaching skills among their peers and general development of social cohesion and collaboration within the group. At any one point in time during a lesson the teacher may have all of these objectives in mind. However, when intervening within a group in order to provide feedback, or some other form of evaluation, teachers tend, naturally, to base this judgement on some specific criteria appropriate to the particular situation. Thus some children may be praised because they have shown social responsibility in that they reduced the amount of disruptive behaviour while others might be criticized because they did not produce a sufficiently coherent outcome. Teachers make these judgements on the basis of their individual knowledge of children, knowledge which other members of the class or the group may not share.

Thus from the child's point of view the situation may seem to be one of confusion. For children to understand the teachers' evaluation they must be party to the criteria upon which the judgements were based. It seemed strange therefore, in our studies, to find that although teachers emphasized the processes of group work and were usually effective when explaining what the children were required to do by way of tasks, they rarely explained why the children were required to do the task in a particular way. Indeed, many teachers told us that they thought that children 'of this age don't need to know why they are doing things' whereas the pupils, when interviewed, said that 'if I knew why I was doing it I wouldn't mind, but I don't know *why* I'm doing it and I can't see the point of it'. In the school where children rated co-operative group work more highly teachers had carried out a careful analysis of the roles of children within the group. In addition to leadership roles such as identifying goals, allocating work and summarizing viewpoints, children were identified as willing followers who sometimes carried out tedious tasks such as tidying up and generally keeping things going by acting as gatekeepers. Other pupils helped to resolve disputes, and attempted to bring the discussion back to the point. These teachers defined effective group work as the capacity for every child, at one time or another to act out all these roles. Children were thus very clear on the criteria by which they were being judged within the group, and much of the teacher's evaluations concerned the extent to which they had consciously taken up these different roles.

Learning and behaving during group work

The third dilemma involved in group work concerns the ambiguity which exists within many primary classrooms concerning learning and behaviour. One of the main reasons for pupils continuing to reject the opportunity to work co-operatively with their peers is contained in the remark of the pupil quoted earlier: 'My friends make me silly'. Almost all teachers interviewed during the effective group work project saw a clear distinction in their role as 'the teacher' and as 'the facilitator of children's learning'. Elsewhere I have written of the pervasive message of the primary classroom which preaches to children the fact that when it's learning 'you do as you think', but when it's behaviour 'you do as I say' (Galton 1987). This sharp disjunction in the way in which learning and behaviour is dealt with in the primary classroom has important effects when children are asked to work together in groups. Teachers appear to recognize this dilemma between the role of the teacher as 'policeman' and the times when they have to be 'relaxed' in order to encourage informal learning (Nias 1988).

Unfortunately, while this distinction may be clear in teachers' minds, it is not understood by most pupils. When working in groups pupils are particularly vulnerable to the accusation (when the noise level rises in the classroom) that not all this noise is productive. Even if a teacher does not immediately reprimand the pupils for being noisy they are likely to intervene in the group to check on the level of purposeful activity, thus again creating in the children's minds the suggestion of a 'take-over'.

Other researchers, such as Rowland (1987), argue strongly that the tendency of pupils to 'play safe' out of 'fear of doing things wrong' is also closely related to the evaluation of children's work. Certainly in the study, *Effective Group Work in the Primary Classroom*, it was noticeable how frequently children, when responding to the cartoon pictures, associated evaluative comments with disciplinary ones. Thus the teacher would be described as saying, 'Get it right or you will not go out to play', or 'That's wrong, stop fooling and concentrate'. Rowland's way out of this dilemma is to place greater emphasis, particularly in the early stages of any activity, on the role of the teacher as critic where children are encouraged to comment openly on the teacher's ideas as well as on each others.

Towards a model of effective co-operative group work

In some of our case studies there were teachers who appeared, intuitively, to have a similar approach to Rowland. They reduced the risk to individual children by, initially, never commenting directly on a particular piece of work but by generalizing from a position of 'neutral' space within the classroom. In this context, 'neutral' space was defined as taking up a position which was outside the territory of any one particular group of pupils and, equally, was not seen as the teacher's space (that is, behind the desk). For example, one teacher (whose practice was approved by the children later in the interview described earlier) was observed, when visiting each group of children, to sit alongside the groups listening to their initial reactions to a writing stimulus. She appeared, deliberately, to convey to the children that she was not interested in contributing to the discussion by sitting with her elbow on the table facing slightly away from the group with one hand clamped firmly across her mouth! This body language appeared to convey to the children that she was there to listen and not talk. After visiting all the groups this teacher then moved to the centre of the carpeted area and said, 'While listening to what you have been discussing there have been a number of interesting ideas which I'd like to share with all of you. I'd also like to put one or two of mine and get your comments back'. Having done this she then revisited each of the tables and on this second occasion said to the children, 'Do you have any comments on what I have just said?'

Most of the descriptions by Nias (1988) of the teachers' attempts to develop informal approaches within their classrooms seem to imply, yet again, a 'two-stage theory' of teaching whereby one is firm at first and only relaxes once the class is under control. Although in most primary classrooms the teaching strategies used to obtain pupil co-operation are generally milder versions of the 'don't smile until Christmas' techniques used in the secondary school, there were numerous examples in the ORACLE study, particularly in the transfer to the age 9 to 13 schools, of how this two-stage theory of control operated. At the beginning of the school year teachers would talk about 'My way of doing things'. They would tell children that they were still 'behaving like infants' and would therefore have to be treated as such! More usually they would seek to capitalize on the advantage of the class–teacher relationship telling children that their behaviour had made them (that is, the teacher) feel 'sad' and that as a result they did not feel like going on with this particular exciting group activity. Instead children were required to do worksheets individually.

Nias's teachers seem to be searching for a model of a negotiated classroom which allows responsibility for learning and behaviour to be shared with the children. Writers such as Glasser (1969, 1986) have long been concerned with the development of such approaches which seek to confront children with responsibility for their teacher's needs as well as their own. For this to happen, however, children have to be aware of the teacher's needs; otherwise they cannot be in a position to accept their share of responsibility in meeting them. Programmes such as Thomas Gordon's (1974) Teacher Effectiveness Training seek to develop this approach to classroom behaviour as an alternative to the current two-stage prescription in which the teacher has first to exercise control either by power or persuasion. In this country we are only beginning to develop Inservice Educating Teachers (INSET) programmes which help teachers to negotiate, with their pupils, to create the kind of classroom climate which furthers collaborative working. Research into collaborative group work and other 'high risk' classroom activities, therefore, has wider implications for general primary practice.

References

Alexander, R. (1988) 'Garden or jungle: teachers' development and informal primary education' in A. Blyth (ed.) *Informal Primary Education Today: Essays and Studies*, Lewes: Falmer Press.

Aronson, E., Blaney, N., Stephen, C., Sikes, J. and Snapp, M. (1978) *The Jigsaw Classroom*, Beverly Hills, Cal.: Sage Publications.

Bealing, D. (1972) 'Organization of junior school classrooms', *Educational Research* 14: 231–5.

Bennett, S.N. (1985) 'Interaction and achievement in classroom groups', in N. Bennett and C. Desforges (eds) *Recent Advances in Classroom Research*, British Journal of Educational Psychology, Monograph series no. 2.

Bennett, S.N. and Blundell, D. (1983) 'Quantity and quality of work in rows and classroom groups', *Educational Psychology* 3(2): 93–105.

Black, P. (1988) 'National curriculum, task group on assessment and testing', *Three Supplementary Reports*, London: Department of Education and Science.

Brophy, J. and Good, T. (1986) 'Teacher behaviour and student achievement', in M. Wittrock (ed.) *Handbook of Research on Teaching*, 3rd edn, New York: Macmillan.

Cotton, J. and Cook, M. (1982) 'Meta-analyses and the effect of various systems: some different conclusions from Johnson *et al.*, *Psychological Bulletin* 92: 176–83.

Department of Education and Science (DES) (1978) *Primary Education in England: a survey by HM Inspectors of Schools*, London: HMSO.

Devries, D. and Slavin, R.E. (1978) 'Teams-games-tournament: review of ten classroom experiments.', *Journal of Research and Development in Education* 12: 28–38.

Galton, M. (1981) 'Teaching groups in the junior school, a neglected art', *Schools Organization* 1 (2): 175–81.

Galton, M. (1987) 'An ORACLE chronicle: a decade of classroom research', *Teaching and Teacher Education* 3 (4): 299–314.

Galton, M. (1989a, in press) 'Primary teacher training: practice in search of a pedagogy', in A. McClelland and V. Varma (eds) *Advances in Teacher Education*, London: Hodder & Stoughton.

Galton, M. (1989b) *Primary Teaching*, London: David Fulton.

Galton, M., Patrick, H., Appleyard, R., Hargreaves, L. and Bernbaum, G. (1987) 'Curriculum provision in small schools: the PRISMS project', *Final Report*, University of Leicester (mimeo).

Galton, M., Simon, B. and Croll P. (1980) *Inside the Primary Classroom*, London: Routledge & Kegan Paul.

Glasser, W. (1969) *Schools Without Failure*, New York: Harper & Row.

Glasser, W. (1986) *Control Theory in the Classroom*, New York: Harper & Row.

Gordon, T. (1974) *T.E.T. Teacher Effectiveness Training*, New York: Peter Wyden.

Johnson, D. and Johnson, R. (1976) *Learning Together and Alone*, Englewood Cliffs, NJ: Prentice-Hall.

Johnson, D. and Johnson, R. (1980) 'The instructional use of cooperative competitive and individualistic goal structures', in H. Walberg (ed.), *Educational Environments and Effects*, Berkeley, California: McCutchan.

Johnson, D., Maruyama, G., Johnson, R., Nelson, D. and Shaw, L. (1981) 'Effects of cooperative, competitive and individualistic goal structures in achievement: a meta-analysis', *Psychological Bulletin* 89: 47–62.

Jones, D. (1987) 'Planning for progressivism: the changing primary school in the Leicestershire authority during the Mason era 1947–71', in R. Lowe (ed.) *The Changing Primary School*, London: Falmer.

Kerry, T. and Sands, M. (1982) *Handling Classroom Groups*, University of Nottingham, School of Education (mimeo).

Measor, L. and Woods, P. (1984) *Changing Schools: Pupil Perspectives on Transfer to a Comprehensive*, Milton Keynes: Open University Press.

Mortimore, P., Sammons, P., Stoll, L., Lewis, D. and Ecob, R. (1987) *The Junior School Project*, ILEA (Research and Statistics Branch), mimeo.

Mortimore, P., Sammons, P., Stoll, L., Lewis, D. and Ecob, R. (1988) *School Matters: The Junior Years*, Wells: Open Books.

Nias, J. (1988) 'Informal education in action: teachers' accounts', in A. Blyth (ed.) *Informal Primary Education Today: Essays and Studies*, Lewes: Falmer Press.

Plowden Report (1967) *Children and their Primary Schools*, 2 vols, Report of the Central Advisory Council for Education in England, London: HMSO.

Pollard, A. (1985) *The Social World of the Primary School*, London: Holt, Rinehart & Winston.

Pollard, A. (ed.) (1987) *Children and their Primary Schools*, London: Falmer Press.

Rowland, S. (1987) 'An interpretative model of teaching and learning', in A. Pollard (ed.) *Children and their Primary Schools*, London: Falmer Press.

Sharan, S. (1989 in press) (ed.) *Co-operative Learning: Theory and Research*, New York: Praeger.

Slavin, R.E. (1983) *Co-operative Learning*, New York: Longman.

Slavin, R.E., Leavey, M. and Madden, N. (1984) 'Combining cooperative learning and individualised instruction: effects on student mathematics achievements, attitudes and behaviours', *Elementary School Journal* 84: 409–22.

Slavin, R.E. (1986) 'Small group methods', in M. Dunkin (ed.) *The International Encyclopaedia of Teaching and Teacher Education*, London: Pergamon.

Tizard, B., Blatchford, D., Burke, J., Farquhar, C. and Plewis, I. (1988) *Young Children at School in the Inner City*, Hove and London: Lawrence Erlbaum.

Walberg, H. and Anderson, G. (1968) 'Classroom climate and individual learning', *Journal of Educational Psychology* 59: 414–9.

Wheldall, K., Morris, M., Vanehan, P. and Yin Yuk Ng (1981) 'Rows v tables: an example of the use of behavioural ecology in two classes of eleven-year-old children', *Educational Psychology* 1 (2): 171–83.

Woods, P. (ed.) (1980) *Pupil Strategies*, London: Croom Helm.
Yeomans, A. (1983) 'Collaborative group work in primary schools, Britain and the USA', *Durham and Newcastle Research Review* X (51): 99–105.

Chapter three

Social interaction in the classroom

Jane French

Editors' introduction

Social interaction is clearly central to the concerns of this book. Any developments that take place within the classroom context will do so as a result of interaction of some sort. This makes a chapter on classroom interaction necessary for any collection of readings concerned with the social psychology of schooling.

Yet, while the pervasive nature of interactional processes makes this chapter necessary, it also provides its author with a monumental challenge. The range of issues that could be attended to is so vast that selection is obviously required, yet the basis for that selection is never likely to be readily apparent.

Jane French has concentrated on an analysis of verbal interaction, and her intention has been to provide a practical introduction. The chapter does not set out to provide a step by step guide of the 'how to do it' variety, but it does seek to raise basic issues that anyone would need to attend to before starting to analyse some classroom interaction of their own. In doing so it illustrates the complexities involved in making full sense of even the most straightforward exchanges. Obviously it would be possible to add into this a concern with many other aspects of interaction. Non-verbal interaction (facial expression, gestures, posture, tone of voice and so on) remain an important but much neglected area of concern.

As will become apparent from a reading of the chapter itself, some of Jane French's own work involving the analysis of classroom interaction has been concerned with an investigation of the nature of gender effects. The reader will find some useful comparisons and contrasts to be made with Chapter 11 by Croll and Moses, and is also likely to find the discussion of 'Discourse' by Edwards (Chapter 4) a useful compliment.

Jane French

Introduction

Over the past twenty years a great deal of research interest has focused upon social interaction in classrooms. Perhaps not surprisingly, the area has become something of a point of convergence for the social science disciplines, with representation from sociology, psychology and linguistics, as well as from the field of education more generally. This has resulted in what now amounts to a considerable body of research, which, at its best, provides us with a rich source of information as to what, precisely, happens in classrooms.

In this chapter I shall draw, selectively, upon this material in seeking to explore two central issues:

1. The nature of social interaction in classrooms.
2. The problems involved in conceptualizing and studying it.

I shall begin by setting the field within a historical context, taking into account some of the social and disciplinary trends which led researchers into classrooms in the first place. I shall then move on to discuss selected aspects of classroom interaction: some formal properties of teacher–pupil talk, the working out of social role identities through interaction, and so on. Finally, I shall move on to consider some of the difficulties involved in collecting, analysing and presenting classroom interactional data.

The nature of social interaction in classrooms

Historical roots

Until the late 1960s very few researchers had mounted detailed studies of the school classroom.[1] In Britain there was a concentration on the underachievement of pupils in the lower socio-economic groupings. In America the overriding concern was the poor performance of black pupils in relation to their white counterparts.

But on both sides of the Atlantic attention was focused not on the school directly, but on what went *into* them, and what came *out* of them, after *x* number of years' compulsory schooling. As a number of observers were later to note,[2] the predominant approach adopted an 'input–output' model, with the school as a sort of unopened 'black box' between the two.

During the 1960s this emphasis began to change. As Delamont and Hamilton (1976) note, student unrest during this period extended to a profound dissatisfaction with the content and modes of working of academic disciplines as well as with existing economic and social arrangements. Within the social sciences this resulted in changes in methodology as well as investigative focus.

In sociology, for example, the 1960s saw an emergence of interest in, or, in some cases, a rediscovery of the works of figures such as Mead, Schutz, Husserl, Simmel and, more latterly, Blumer and Garfinkel.[3] The end result of the renewed debate which followed appears to have been, at the least, a heightened awareness of fundamental issues, and at the most, a change of direction by significant numbers of practitioners.

One of the perspectives which aroused increased interest, and was instrumental in leading sociologists into the classroom, was that of symbolic interactionism.[4] Its development over the years had already tended toward distinct psychological and sociological adaptations (cf. Rose 1962), and it has become even more fragmented since its absorption into contemporary British sociology. But it is built upon certain assumptions which were, and are, relevant to those involved in the study of interaction in classrooms.

There is an emphasis, for example, on the need to study language and interaction. Through interaction with, first, parents and family, then the wider community, children learn the shared meanings of our culture, and, over the course of time, become thinking, self-conscious human beings. As Edwards and Westgate (1987: 12) put it:

> It is largely through talk that we develop our concepts of self, as members of various social 'worlds' which can be brought into focus and in which we can locate ourselves and recognize the values, rights and obligations which permeate them. As we listen and as we talk, we learn what it is necessary to know, do and say in that area of social life or that setting, and can display the competence necessary to be accepted as a member.

Clearly the school classroom is a forum for this gradual process of socialization, with children learning through interaction with both peers and members of staff. But if the language of the classroom is to be studied, the survey data, questionnaires and coding sheets traditionally associated with the social sciences are clearly inadequate to the task: one cannot mount a serious study of communication in the classroom merely by asking teachers or pupils what they said or did, or by coding their utterances into pre-set categories. Detailed observation and recording of data, using modern audio and/or video recording equipment are required, both to capture and to reproduce for analysis the complexities of classroom communication. As Mehan warns, we must '[look] *at* the window of language and not just *through* it' (Mehan 1984: 181, added emphasis).

Thus, because of both theoretical principles, and the practical concerns of finding a research method adequate to the task in hand, educationists from various social science disciplines began to use a range of observational techniques which had hitherto been associated mainly with anthropology. These 'ethnographic' methods included prolonged observation and recording of the people under study, just as though they were members of a foreign culture, immersion in their habitual practices and customs, and, finally, the writing-up of research reports. Within education Edwards and Furlong (1978) note that the term 'ethnography' was first adopted as a descriptive label for a (psychologically-oriented) school-based study by Smith and Geoffrey in 1968. And Jackson's (1968) account of schooling in America, Hargreave's (1967) and Lacey's (1970) detailed studies of British secondary schools, and Nash's later (1973) report, all stand as good examples of the 'new' approach, which is summed up as follows by Edwards and Furlong (1978: 53):

> It was a wish to capture this view from the inside which drew sociologists belatedly into classroom research. Using the observational techniques of the anthropologist, they tried to portray the realities of classroom life as they appeared to the teachers and pupils involved.

Findings

So, having, albeit belatedly, gained entry to school classrooms, what did researchers find there? The early, more broadly-focused, studies provided an excellent foundation for later, more specific investigations. Through their prolonged involvement and painstaking observation, studies such as those of Hargreaves, and Lacey indicated some of the areas which might fruitfully be exposed to further inquiry. They also demonstrated, in a way which many of the subsequent, more narrowly-focused studies have failed to do, the enormous complexities of classroom life: the constellations of factors which influence children's relationships with one another, with their teachers, and with education in a broad, overall sense. It is with these complexities in mind that I shall try now to bring together some of the findings from classroom research projects which pertain specifically to the primary age child. Given the sheer volume of work now available, my account will inevitably be highly selective.[5]

For convenience of exposition, I shall consider the findings under the subheadings of the Instructional context and the Social context. It is an artificial distinction, for in practice the two categories are mutually constitutive and I must stress that they are separated here purely for ease of expression.

The instructional context

Most people would agree that pupils attend school with a view to acquiring specific forms of culturally approved knowledge. Thus it is that lessons are structured in ways which facilitate the orderly dissemination of that knowledge among comparatively large groups of people. A number of recent research projects, representing various social science disciplines, have considered both the transition of children from the home to the school environment, and the forms of social interaction which they can expect to find when they get there.

These studies have to be set against a background of concern specifically for the linguistic and cognitive development of children from the lower socio-economic groups, which permeated teacher-training from the late 1960s onwards. At this time the work of Basil Bernstein became highly influential in training colleges and departments and, subsequently, in schools. As I, and others, have argued elsewhere (cf. Edwards 1986; French 1987), the details of what was a contentious, ambitious and complex theory were filtered down and presented in a simplified form in the training institutions, with results which gave cause for concern.

It became apparent to many educationists that detailed information was needed about the home environment, where primary socialization occurs. In particular, there was a need to investigate the interaction which actually occurs there, as opposed to the interaction which might be supposed to occur there. By the same token, detailed material needed to be collected from school classrooms.

Bearing the linguistic deficit theory in mind, it is interesting to note that a number of studies remarked upon the lack of dissonance between the home and the school, at least in terms of interactional structure. MacLure and French (1981: 237) note that from the point of view of children:

> from whatever social background, there is little in the nature of the interactional demands which will be made of them in school that they will not already have become familiar with at home, at the level of conversational structure.

Willes (1983) also remarks upon the ease with which children adapt to the interactional requirements of being a 'pupil' rather than a 'child', learning the norms of teacher–pupil communication within a matter of weeks.

Yet these norms are different in terms of their distribution if not their actual character from what most children have grown accustomed to in the home. An obvious feature of classrooms as opposed to homes, for example, is the fact that classrooms have many more occupants, and potential conversational participants, than the average home!

This affects the structure of the interaction in a number of ways. It is clear, first, that teacher–pupil talk is informed by broadly two sets of assumptions concerning what we might call the participants' 'social identities' and the 'rights' that they enjoy by virtue of these identities.

Adult–child

On the one hand, the teacher is an adult, and the pupil is a child. And most pupils (as well as their teachers!) will have learned and come to accept long before they come to school that in conversation with adults, children have restricted rights (cf, Sacks 1966; Speier 1976). Specifically, adults control conversations in the sense that vested in their identities as adults are the rights to, for example, select topics, evaluate children's contributions, and bring talk to a close without the agreement of the other, child, party. Speier suggests that this common orientation by both children and adults is predicated upon the 'classical' view of children as pre- and in- competent adults. And, of course, this assumption is repeatedly, though often implicitly, relied upon within the school classroom.

Given the comparative lack of autonomy of children in out-of- school encounters with adults, it would not be surprising to find a yet more rigid adherence to these practices in the school setting, since the social identity 'teacher' combines the subcategories 'adult' plus 'instructor', with all its associated rights. Similarly, the identity 'pupil' combines 'child' and 'instructee'.

Multi-party talk

Within a subdiscipline of sociology known as conversation analysis (cf. Atkinson and Heritage 1984; Heritage 1984), attention has been paid to the means by which orderly conversations are made possible because participants share an unspoken adherence to basic and specifiable turn-taking procedures (Sacks *et al.* 1974). Clearly, while conversations between only two people present few problems as to who shall be the next speaker, multi-party conversation, as in the classroom, can potentially be problematic. That is, the presence of three or more participants opens up the possibility of competition for turns, the presence of four or more for the setting up of subconversations in parallel with one another, and so on. In addition, participants in informal conversation at least may choose whether and when they speak: that is, they may 'self-select'. They need not wait for another participant to select or call upon them to take a turn, as frequently happens in the classroom (cf. McHoul 1978).

Managing the class

The sets of assumptions concerning (1) adult–child identity, and (2) the organization of multiparty conversation come together in the context of the classroom in ways which bear upon the orderly structure of teacher–pupil interaction. For example, many references are made in the literature to the fact that, in classrooms, teachers do most of the talking and that they ask children a great number of questions (cf. Flanders 1966). Indeed, as Tizard and Hughes (1984: 249–50) observe, this lies in direct contrast to most homes, even those which educationists might categorize as the least enabling: 'Simply by being around their mothers, talking, arguing, and endlessly asking questions ... children ... (are) provided with large amounts of information relevant to growing up in our culture'.

In order successfully to 'manage' the larger-scale conversation of the classroom, teachers find it useful to organize what is actually multiparty interaction into interaction between two parties: the teacher, representing one party, and the class collectively as the other (cf, Payne and Hustler 1980).The techniques involved in effecting this transformation involve the teacher in maintaining a delicate balance between under- and over-participation by pupils, which in turn involves ensuring that: (a) in the main, one speaker speaks at a time, and (b) as many pupils as possible are involved in the answering of questions.

One of the ways in which experienced teachers perform this balancing act is through quick-fire question-answer-evaluation sequences which serve to involve large numbers of pupils, and are paced so as to keep their attention (cf. Hammersley 1974; Sinclair and Coulthard 1975; Mehan 1979, among others).

Example 1 below illustrates the way in which a series of such sequences might work:

Example 1

1. *Teacher*: How many people here can tell me what a square is?
2. *Pupils*:   (Raise hands. Teacher scans class and selects child with hand up.)
3. *Teacher*: Alex?
4. *Alex*:   It's got four sides.
5. *Teacher*: Good boy. And what are those sides *like*?
6. *Pupils*:   (Raise hands. Teacher again scans class and selects child with hand up.)
7. *Teacher*: Becky?
8. *Becky*:   They're straight.
9. *Teacher*: They're straight. Yes, they're not all wiggly and

bendy are they? They're straight. And anything else? (scans class) Yes, Katy.

10. *Katy*: They're the same length.
11. *Teacher*: Yes, good girl! They're all the same length. That's the important thing, isn't it? They're all the same length.

In this straightforward example we can see clearly the way in which the teacher is able to involve several children, who all have one short turn each. The teacher first sets up a pool of possible respondents by asking those who know the answer to raise their hands. This saves her from asking a child who does not know or is unwilling to answer, which may slow the whole lesson down, and involve her in repeating the question, rephrasing it, and so on (cf. McHoul 1978). Her questions are also designed so that pupils are able to answer with a short phrase, rather than a long, possibly rambling, series of phrases. The lesson is thus able to move along at a smart pace, involving several children, and, importantly, eliciting from them the information the teacher wants.

Of course, questions are not always designed so as to facilitate short answers. During 'news' sessions, for example, the teacher may select a pupil or pupils to speak at greater length (cf. French and French 1984), while realizing that the rest of the class may become bored, and taking steps to prevent or remedy this. In addition, lessons may not always go so smoothly. There may be problems, even in a short, 'rapid fire' session, so that the attention of one or more pupils may lapse, children may start whispering to one another, or one child may start calling out and quickly be followed by others. Experienced teachers sense potential difficulties, and can be seen to deploy a variety of techniques both to prevent their occurrence, and to repair them when they have happened. Payne (1976), for example, notes that collective forms of address are used, thereby, as he puts it, encouraging them to act 'as a unit, making their individual fates collectively interdependent' (Payne 1976: 54).

In addition, a story may be prefaced 'Now listen to this story because then I'm going to ask you some questions about it' (cf. Payne and Hustler 1981), or children may be asked to 'look this way', or to display in one way or another that they are paying attention. If these methods fail to obtain the desired result, teachers may move on to what have been termed 'problem statements' (cf. French 1985; French and French 1986; French and Peskett 1986): that is, they may state a problem, couched at first in generally addressed terms (for example, 'some people are still not listening'). Pupils are left to make the (albeit often obvious) inference as to what is required, and to modify their behaviour accordingly.

Alternatively, teachers may issue 'directives' (cf. French 1985) which explicitly instruct pupils on how to behave, (for example, 'Sit down please', 'Don't call out', 'Put your hands up'). Or they may use question-related techniques to 'trap' suspected non-attenders by deliberately addressing questions to them, or by recycling already answered questions so that the non-attender is shown to be precisely that (Teacher: What season is it John? John: Spring. Teacher: Right. *Mark, what season is it?*).

The social context

But, of course, lessons are not simply strings of empty forms. Teachers and pupils talk about things. During the course of lessons, knowledge is transmitted and, one hopes, acquired, via some of the practices described above, as well as through listening, reading, observing and doing. In addition, messages may be passed, through the interaction and largely unconsciously, about a range of factors known to influence both the school performance and self-image of the individual pupil. These may include the personal relationship of teacher to pupils, attitudes (displayed by teacher and/or pupils) towards, say, different races or to the sexes, or particular cultural, subcultural or religious beliefs (again by teacher and/or pupils). These sorts of factors typically underlie the interaction, informing it in subtle and sometimes non-subtle ways, and moving in and out of focus as topics shift and activities change.

Some teachers, for example, may find that their perceptions of pupils are affected by some of the linguistically related issues discussed earlier. Like other members of society, they may respond differently to people who speak with a pronounced regional accent, or who use local dialect forms. The increased provision of pre- and in-service courses in language and education has helped in this connection, perhaps particularly at the primary level. Most teachers are now aware that, say, South Yorkshire English or Afro-Caribbean English are as rule-governed and semantically complex as Home Counties or BBC English. By the same token, a local accent is simply a local accent, and not an indication *per se* of a deficient intellect.

However, and as the Cox Report (DES 1988) has recently noted, judgements are still formed on the basis of accent and/or dialect. Marked local accents or use of dialect forms still convey the message, in class conscious Britain, that a child is probably 'working class'. And this social identification tag may carry with it a number of expectations concerning the child's home life, the attitudes of his/her parents to schooling, and, consequently, the child's school performance. As Edwards (1986) points out, the legacy of the linguistic deficit theory may well have brought self-fulfilling prophecies back into play in the classroom.

Dimensions of social identity other than socio-economic class membership are also displayed in classroom interaction. Over recent years, for example, a great deal of attention has been paid to the ways in which the sexes signal gender identity through language as well as through the more obvious channels of mode of dress, hairstyle and so on (cf. Thorne and Henley 1975; Fishman 1978).

We know that the classroom acts as a forum where children both display and develop their competence in this capacity. It is well established that during the pre-school years, parents and other significant adults respond differently to boys and girls (cf. Block 1985; Hodgeon 1985; Grabrucker 1988). Thus, by the time they reach the age of compulsory schooling, most children have a good idea of gender identity, and the forms of behaviour which adults and other children find appropriate.

In a study conducted at infant school level, French and French (1986) found boys to be given and to take significantly more speaking turns than girls in classroom discussions. They also found that boys were more often the subject of teachers' 'control talk' than girls. And interestingly, in a subcategory of control talk known as 'directives', boys, but not girls, were more likely to have appended some sort of explanation (for example, 'Sit down David, so that the people behind you can see'). I discuss this finding at greater length in a later section of this chapter.

At the upper junior level, French and French (1984) analysed a single lesson in some detail, showing the ways in which a particular, dominant subgroup of boys was able to take up a disproportionately large chunk of the time available. Some of these included calling out, making extraordinary or 'newsworthy' claims so that the teacher invited them to speak at greater than average length, or exploiting opportunities provided by the teacher to contribute by being 'different' (for example, being the only child who thinks that Maths is an unimportant subject!).

These sorts of findings have also obtained in studies elsewhere in the world (cf. Good, *et al.* 1973; Schools Commission, Australia 1984; Sadker and Sadker 1985; Morgan and Dunn 1988), and at all levels of the educational system (cf. Stanworth 1983; Croll 1985; French and French 1986; Hodgeon 1985.

As Swan and Graddol (1988: 63–4) points out, there seems to be a 'consensus' among girls, boys and teachers as to what constitutes normal interactional behaviour for each sex, whereby:

an unequal distribution of talk is seen as normal. In particular, girls seem to have learnt to expect a lower participation level than boys, and boys seem to have learned that their fair share is a larger one. These are expectations that are brought to school by all participants, since such inequalities in the distribution of talk are commonplace amongst adults.

It is thus that the so-called 'hidden curriculum' of education is transmitted: the signalling of status, the communication of implicit approval or disapproval, the patterns of behaviour which we treat as natural and, more often than not, do not even notice let alone challenge. But whether or not we want to make changes, it is in interaction that the transmission of social 'messages' is to be found. For students or practising teachers who wish to consider any of these issues, or to examine the group dynamics of a particular class or group of pupils, the place to begin is in the practical world of everyday interaction.

Problems in conceptualizing and studying classroom interaction

Collection of data

The widespread availability of audio and, in some cases, video recording equipment nowadays has meant that many prospective and practising teachers are able to try their hand at classroom interaction analysis. While this can be an extremely valuable and satisfying exercise, directed to a variety of practical purposes, it can also bring home to would-be analysts some of the potential pitfalls and difficulties in both recording interaction, and interpreting what one finds.

In the first place, and at a practical level, classrooms are notoriously difficult places in which to record. They are usually comparatively large rooms, with children moving about between activities, and a high level of background noise. The difficulties of making good quality recordings which capture the flavour of lessons, particularly where children are spread out around the room engaged in group work, are considerable. It is for these practical reasons that professional researchers frequently focus narrowly on, say, teacher–class discussions or on single groups of children working. This goes some way to explaining why we know comparatively little about certain aspects of classroom life, and why some areas and issues remain unexplored and largely inaccessible.

Analysis and interpretation of data

The problems do not disappear, either, once data have been collected, for the process of analysis and the subsequent presentation of materials give rise to a number of issues concerning the status and reliability of findings. Obviously the practising teacher who wants to use classroom interaction analysis for essentially practical purposes cannot be expected to explore these issues in the same depth and detail as, say, a full-time post-graduate student. But if they are ignored altogether, then the quality of the individual's work will suffer, and its value will be questionable. I would also add that the capacity of that individual to be critical in relation to the work of him/herself and others will not properly have been developed.

Over-interpretation of data

One of the most common problems which arises, especially for the novice analyst, is the tendency to ascribe more significance than is, strictly speaking, justified, to impute unwarranted motives and intentions to participants, and then to put one's understandings forward, implicitly or otherwise, as the only possible ways of interpreting the data. It is important to balance evaluative or prescriptive interests with analytic rigour and integrity, and to advise caution in the interpretation of what is found. An example may help to make this point more clearly.

As noted at an earlier point in the present chapter, French and French (1986) found that in a subset of teachers' talk known as 'control talk', boys were more likely to have the rules and norms of classroom conduct explained to them than girls. Why should this be? They suggested four possible explanations (there may be more):

(i) First it may be connected with same-sex identification. That is, that teachers assume girl pupils, as females like themselves, know the rules and the reasons behind them.[6]

(ii) It may also be that girls are assumed to be more socially adept and mature, and that rules need not be explained. Boys, on the other hand, may be thought to need repetitive restatement.

(iii) Girls may be seen as more compliant. On this basis teachers may assume that they may safely dispense with explanations: the girls will comply anyway. Boys, however, may question the teacher's authority and, therefore, in the cause of expediency, explanations are appended.

(iv) The phenomenon may constitute evidence that teachers prefer boys and consider them more important than girls. Simply, boys are worthy of an explanation whereas girls are not.

(French and French 1986: 20–1)

As we go on to note, the possible interpretations listed above were all suggested by teachers with whom the issue was discussed. But it is important to recognize that although all of them are plausible interpretations, retrospectively assigned, no one of them necessarily provides a definitive account. Indeed, it is not always possible to provide as definitive an account as one would perhaps wish: classroom interaction analysis sometimes throws up intriguing findings which are difficult to explain. Because of a variety of factors, such as our common-sense knowledge of schools and teachers, our overall cultural competence or our individual biographies, we may be able to come up with explanations, but it is important to bear in mind that they are generally, as in the case of the example quoted above, among several plausible possibilities. They should not be given a privileged or elevated status, or presented as 'the truth' about this or that phenomenon. Rather, the limitations of this type of work should be acknowledged.

Coding of interactional data

The coding of interactional data is a perennial problem for analysts. In my view, the most detailed and elaborate scheme cannot be 100 per cent accurate, and I regard the categorizations made during the course of a research study as a useful shorthand form of representation rather than an impressive 'scientific' system.

Again, an example may help to clarify the point. During the course of interaction, in the classroom or elsewhere, participants might sometimes interrupt one another. We all 'know' in one sense when we are interrupting someone else, or when someone else is interrupting us, but how as analysts do we decide what, precisely, constitutes an interruption? A remark intended by a speaker as an 'aside' comment may be interpreted by a hearer as an interruption. Alternatively, a speaker may mistime an utterance so that his/her speech sounds like an interruption when it was not intended as such.

It is therefore clear that simple definitions of phenomena such as interruptions (that is, 'interruption' = overlapping talk) are unsatisfactory. It seems, moreover, that in interpreting talk as interruptive, conversational participants may use variable clusters of cues including prosodic features of speech (for example, pitch, height, loudness) (cf. French and Local 1983) and assessments as to the supportive or non-supportive character of the talk of the incoming speaker (cf. Bennett 1980). Students of interaction have long recognized that one cannot transform such complexities into coding criteria, and that the exercise of coding is always a matter, essentially, of common sense, based on the analyst's competence as a cultural member. As Sinclair and Coulthard (1975) admit, there are always and always will be marginal cases and arbitrary choices.

Some descriptive issues

Finally in this section I shall discuss some descriptive issues which arise during the course of any piece of research, and which merit serious consideration.

A number of analysts have drawn attention to the processes of selection which are inevitably engendered during the course of producing any descriptive account (cf. Sacks 1963).[7] In transforming experience into a written version of events, one is enabled only ever to record a partial version of events, which has undergone two basic forms of selection. First, the words used have been selected from what is, in theory, an indefinitely extendable list of possible descriptions. Second, and more important from the point of view of the present paper, the events to be described have been selected for recording at the cost of excluding others.

This has traditionally been an acute problem for those engaged in ethnographic work. Where data consist of observational field-notes, inevitably much is lost in that one cannot capture and recreate all that went on in the setting. The composition of field-notes constitutes a first process of 'filtering' from raw data to eventual account, which sets up a distance between the actual events giving rise to the account, and the readers of the account. And this in turn can mean that the only interpretation of events available to readers is the analyst's interpretation. The reader is not able to challenge the analyst's view because he/she does not have access to the material necessary to do so. This then raises questions as to the status of ethnographic accounts. Is the account purely a subjective view, or does it have aspirations to a more detached and 'objective' status? If so, how can the inevitable withholding of original data be justified?

The advent of widely-available audio and video recording facilities represents an important advance. The capacity of technology to reproduce data without significant loss means that analyst and audience (whether on a professional level, or in the roles of teacher-analyst and tutor, or lecturer and students) can have access to the same materials, and may re-run and discuss particular aspects of data as necessary.

However, the danger of selective presentation remains. There is scarcely more merit in presenting chosen extracts from tape-recorded materials than from field-notes. It is, in fact, in this connection that writers such as Mehan (1979) have spoken disparagingly of researchers presenting 'tidbits' of audio-visual materials or transcripts. In such cases, researchers could seek to 'prove' whatever they liked, within reason, about classroom interaction.

One solution to this problem is carefully to record data, and to allow audiences the fullest possible access to materials. In the context of seminars or lectures, this may involve the presentation of audio and/or video recordings together with verbatim transcriptions. In the case of written presentations, verbatim transcriptions have to suffice.

Conclusion

In this paper, I have sought to explore a number of issues pertaining to social interaction in classrooms. These have ranged from discussion of the complex character of classroom communication to the problems involved in collecting and analysing data. In my view they are important issues, for they affect classroom practice in several respects.

First, knowledge of and about areas such as social interaction informs and underlies one's approach to a class. It sensitizes and develops the critical faculties in much the same way that musical or literary analysis sharpens the understanding and appreciation of works of art. And once the seeds of knowledge have been sown, the student is enabled to 'see' teacher–pupil interaction in a different light: one begins to notice the mechanisms which lie beneath the surface of lessons, to appreciate their variety and the skills of the teachers who, largely unconsciously, deploy them.

For the beginner in particular, this can be an eye-opening experience. Although many training institutions now use video, it is often the case that students are instructed simply to watch, without being told specifically what to watch for. Yet many novice teachers crave practical knowledge. Indeed, one of the chief criticisms directed at teacher-trainers is that too much time is spent on theory and not enough on practical skills. While I am emphatically not of the school of thought which believes educational theory to be a useless irrelevance, it does seem to me that there is much to be gained from observing experienced practitioners. But in order to observe, in the strict sense of that term, one must first be taught both where and how to look. The student who has even these skills is at an immediate advantage.

Notes

1 Although see Waller (1932)
2 See particularly, Delamont and Hamilton (1976), Hammersley and Woods (1976), and, for an American point of view, Mehan (1979)
3 See Garfinkel (1967), Blumer (1969) and, for discussions of the influence of these and the other authors mentioned, see Rock (1979) and Leiter (1980).
4 For a more detailed exposition of symbolic interactionist theory see Rose (1962) and Rock (1979).
5 The selective focus of the paper has meant that, inevitably, much work of value has been left out. I would draw readers' attention in particular to the considerable contribution of those working within linguistics and its subdisciplines. Texts of especial relevance include Crystal (1976), Stubbs (1983) (2nd edition) and Stubbs and Hillier (1983).
6 The teachers in our sample were all female.
7 For further discussion of these issues see Atkinson and Drew (1979) and Heritage (1984).

References

Atkinson, J.M. and Drew, P. (1979) *Order in Court*, London: Macmillan.

Atkinson, J.M. and Heritage, J.C. (1984) *Structures of Social Action: Studies in Conversation Analysis*, Cambridge: Cambridge University Press.

Bennet, A. (1980) *Interruptions and the Interpretation of Conversation*, Tuscon: University of Arizona, mimeo.

Block, J. (1985) *Sex Role Identity and Ego Development*, San Francisco: Jossey Bass.

Blumer, H. (1969) *Symbolic Interactionism: Perspective and Method*, Englewood Cliffs: Prentice-Hall.

Croll, P. (1985) 'Teacher interaction with individual male and female pupils in junior-age classrooms', *Educational Research*, 27: 220–3.

Crystal, D. (1976) *Child Language, Learning and Linguistics: an Overview for the Teaching and Therapeutic Professions*, London: Edward Arnold.

Delamont, S. and Hamilton, D. (1976) 'Classroom research: a critique and a new approach', in M. Stubbs and S. Delamont (eds) *Explorations in Classroom Observations*, New York: Wiley.

Department of Education and Science (DES) (1988) *English for Ages 5-11: Proposals of the Secretary of State for Education and Science and the Secretary of State for Wales*, (The Cox Report), London: DES.

Edwards, A.D. and Furlong, V.J. (1978) *The Language of Teaching*, London: Heinemann.

Edwards, A.D. and Westgate, D.P.G. (1987) *Investigating Classroom Talk*, London: Falmer.

Edwards, J. (1986) 'Language and educational disadvantage: the persistence of linguistic "deficit" theory', in K. Durkin (ed.), *Language Development in the School Years*, London: Croom Helm.

Fishman, P. (1978) 'Interaction: the work women do', *Social Problems, 25 (4): 397–406*.

Flanders, N.A. (1966) *Interaction Analysis in the Classroom: a Manual for Observers*, Michigan, USA: School of Education, University of Michigan.

French, J. (1987) 'Language in the primary classroom', in S. Delamont (ed), *The Primary School Teacher*, London: Falmer.

French, J. and French, P. (1984) 'Gender imbalances in the primary classroom: an interactional account', *Educational Research*, 26 (2): 127–36.

French, J. and French, P. (1986) *Gender Imbalances in Infant School Classroom Interaction: Final Report to the Equal Opportunities Commission*, The College of Ripon and York St John, Lord Mayor's Walk, York.

French, P. (1985) 'Problem statements and directives: some aspects of control sequences in infant school classroom interaction', in J.C.P. Auer and A. di Luzio (eds) *Ergebrisse und Methoden in Moderner Sprachen Wissenschaft*, Koln: Narr.

French, P. and Local, J. (1983) 'Turn-Competitive incomings', *Journal of Pragmatics*, 7 (1): 17–38.

French, P. and Peskett, R. (1986) 'Control instructions in the infant classroom', *Educational Research* 28 (3): 210–19.

Garfinkel, H. (1967) *Studies in Ethnomethodology*, Englewood Cliffs, NJ: Prentice-Hall.

Good, T.L., Sykes, J.N. and Brophy, J.E. (1973) 'Effects of teacher sex and student sex on classroom interaction', *Journal of Educational Psychology*, 65: 1–27.

Grabrucker, M. (1988) *There's a Good Girl: Gender Stereotyping in the First Three Years of Life, a Diary*, London: The Women's Press.

Hammersley, M, (1974) 'The organization of pupil participation', *Sociological Review*, 1: 355–67.

Hammersley, M. and Woods, P. (eds) (1976) *The Process of Schooling*, London: Routledge & Kegan Paul with The Open University Press.

Hargreaves, D.H. (1967) *Social Relations in a Secondary School*, London: Routledge & Kegan Paul.

Heritage, J. (1984) *Garfinkel and Ethnomethodology*, Cambridge: Polity Press.

Hodgeon, J. (1985) *A Woman's World: Report on a Project in Cleveland Nurseries on Sex Differentiation in the Early Years*, Cleveland Education Committee..

Jackson, P.W. (1968) *Life in Classrooms*, New York: Holt, Rinehart & Winston.

Lacey, V.C. (1970) *Hightown Grammar*, Manchester: Manchester University Press.

Leiter, K. (1980) *A Primer of Ethnomethodology*, London: Oxford University Press.

McHoul, A. (1978) 'The organization of turns at formal talk in the classroom', *Language in Society*, 7: 183–213.

MacLure, M. and French, P. (1981) 'A comparison of talk at home and at school', in G. Wells (ed.) *Learning Through Interaction: the study of language development*, London: Cambridge University Press.

Mehan, H, (1979) *Learning Lessons: Social Organization in the Classroom*, Cambridge, Mass.: Harvard University Press.

Mehan, H. (1984) 'Language and Schooling', *Sociology of Education*, 57:.

Morgan, V. and Dunn, S. (1988) 'Chameleons in the classroom: visible and invisible children in nursery and infant classrooms', *Educational Review*, 40(1): 3–12.

Nash, R. (1973) *Classrooms Observed*, London: Routledge & Kegan Paul.

Payne, G.C.F. (1976) 'Making a lesson happen: an ethnomethodological analysis', in M. Hammersley and P. Woods (eds), *The Process of Schooling*, London: Routledge & Kegan Paul with The Open University Press.

Payne, G.C.F. and Hustler, D. (1980) 'Teaching the class: the practical management of a cohort', *British Journal of the Sociology of Education*, 1 (1): 49–66.

Payne, G.C.F. and Hustler, D. (1981) 'Stories and storytime in an infant classroom', in P. French and M. MacLure (eds) *Adult-Child Conversation*, London: Croom Helm.

Rock, P. (1979) *The Making of Symbolic Interactionism*, London: Macmillan.

Rose, A.M. (ed.) (1962) *Human Behaviour and Social Processes*, London: Routledge & Kegan Paul.

Sacks, H. (1963) 'Sociological description', *Berkeley Journal of Sociology*, 8: 1–16.

Sacks, H. (1966) Los Angeles: University of California, *Lectures*, spring (mimeo).

Sacks, H., Schegloff, E, and Jefferson, G. (1974) 'A simple systematics for the turn-taking organization of conversation', *Language*, 50: 696–735.

Sadker, D. and Sadker, M. (1985) 'Is the OK classroom OK?' *Phi Delta Kappan*, January, pp. 358–61.

Schools Commission, Australia (1984) *Girls and Tomorrow: the Challenge for Schools*, Canberra: AGPS.

Sinclair, J.McH. and Coulthard, R.M. (1975) *Towards an Analysis of Discourse: the English used by Teachers and Pupils*, London: Oxford University Press.

Smith, L. and Geoffrey, W. (1968) *The Complexities of an Urban Classroom*, New York: Holt, Rinehart & Winston.

Speier, M. (1976) 'The child as conversationalist', in M. Hammersley and P. Woods (eds) *The Process of Schooling*, London: Routledge & Kegan Paul with The Open University Press.

Stanworth, M, (1983) *Gender and Schooling: A Study of Sexual Divisions in the Classroom*, London: Hutchinson, with The Explorations in Feminism Collective.

Stubbs, M. (1983) *Language, Schools and Classrooms*, 2nd edn, London: Methuen.

Stubbs, M. and Hillier, H. (eds) (1983) *Readings on Language, Schools and Classrooms*, London: Methuen.

Swann, M. and Graddol, D. (1988) 'Gender inequalities in classroom talk', *English in Education*, 22 (1): 48–65.

Thorne, B. and Henley, N. (eds) (1975) *Language and Sex: Difference and Dominance*, Rowley, Mass.: Newbury House.

Tizard, B. and Hughes, M, (1984) *Young Children Learning: Talking and Thinking at Home and at School*, London: Fontana.

Waller, W. (1932) *The Sociology of Teaching*, New York: John Wiley & Sons.

Willes, M.J. (1983) *Children into Pupils: A Study of Language in Early Schooling*, London: Routledge & Kegan Paul.

Chapter four

Classroom discourse and classroom knowledge

Derek Edwards

Editors' introduction

'Classroom discourse and classroom knowledge' carries on from the previous chapters and adds new and critical focus to classroom process. From the previous chapters, Edwards acknowledges that there is an overwhelming tendency to teach the 'individual' in the classroom and that there are a number of 'hidden agendas' within the classroom concerning the structure of knowledge and power relationships between teacher and pupil. Even though the classroom may be structured in groups or draw upon groupings of children for economies of learning, teachers and curricula tend to focus on the individual as the point for, and point of, learning.

In his study Edwards draws upon a number of conversational extracts where learning takes place and reinterprets learning as a 'discourse' between people. The process of generating knowledge is a shared experience, whether between teacher and pupil or between pupils themselves. Reinterpretation of learning criticizes individualized developmental psychological theories that have informed the construction of many of the curricula now present in primary school classrooms, especially as the theories have characterized learning as an individual creation. It is interesting that the theorist most often cited as being responsible for individualization (Piaget) in the child-centred classroom is also the person who provides the most explicit rationale for the reinterpretation of learning and development as a shared process, and we are also made aware of the importance of Vygotsky. Classroom processes are seen as providing a social context for development as well as being formative of that process. The reader is made vitally aware that the relationships arranged within the classroom will direct the type and quality of knowledge engendered.

One final aspect of this chapter is the role played by the curriculum. Edwards has purposively chosen to research science and mathematics curricula. In investigating the curricula in general, he makes the point that scientific advances do not usually take place in a vacuum, but in a social (and usually collective) context. Actual extracts that Edwards provides show that at least two types of curricula-related learning can take place in the classroom, each dependent on the dialogue and quality of relationship in which the child participates: a socializational learning in which pupils apprentice themselves to the teacher's knowledge; and argumentation of self-constructed knowledge which takes place with peers. Socializational knowledge may be related to the imposition of the National Curriculum in which the end-products of learning become more important than the actual process. Argumentation is more clearly linked to understanding and process. In either case the teacher is the person responsible for structuring the classroom context so as to promote one or both types of learning.

Introduction

Educationists sometimes, though not always optimistically, turn to psychology for help in understanding the processes of teaching and learning. In particular, Piaget's classic studies of the development of children's thinking have helped to shape educational practice. The older, 'traditional', primary classrooms, all chalk and talk, discipline and rote learning, have largely given way to child-centred activity. Children are encouraged to develop their own understandings of things, to work individually or in small groups, learning from their own practical experience, rather than having ready-made conclusions thrust upon their unwilling ears. The legacy of this influence is a notion of children's learning that is highly individualistic. It stresses the importance of experience and action, playing down the significance of talk, of teaching, and of the ready-made curriculum. While social psychology might be the obvious place to look for insights into interpersonal relationships, patterns of communication, group structure and leadership, roles and friendships, and so on, it is to the psychology of individuals (learning and motivation, IQ tests, cognitive development, and so on) that we turn for insights into the processes of knowledge and learning, the development of conceptual understanding itself. Social factors may be thought to impinge upon such things social class, social context, social prejudice, parental encouragement, teaching styles, and so on, but the acquisition of knowledge is itself an individual process. Children learn from action and experience, process information, develop 'mental models' or theories of the world, to make sense of what they perceive, or of what happens when they act upon the world. At least, this is now the established view, the one that appears to prevail amongst teachers and the makers of educational policy (see, for example, the recent policy document issued by the Engineering Council and the Standing Conference on Schools' Science and Technology 1985).

This chapter will take an opposing view. It will draw upon some new developments in the social psychology of 'discourse' and 'rhetoric', and in the study of classroom education. It will look at the educational process from a social perspective, taking the view that the development of understanding is a communicative accomplishment, embodied in classroom discourse. Education is presented here as the development between teachers and pupils of shared understandings, shared experiences and procedures, and a shared conceptual vocabulary. Empirical studies depict classroom discourse as oriented mainly towards the achievement of a teacher-dominated consensus of understanding. We shall argue that this embodies an unnecessarily limited sense of shared knowledge. A different emphasis needs to be placed upon the importance of argument, disagreement, justification and criticism – in other words, a 'rhetorical' approach to shared knowledge. In view of the fact that scientific knowledge is often taken to be the most solid, best established, least vulnerable knowledge that can be taught, we shall concentrate our analysis upon science education, with groups of 9-year olds.

Towards a social psychology of educational knowledge

In the world of education, the currently dominant psychologies of conceptual development are individualistic. Piaget's major legacy has been the assumption that children are learners from experience, actively constructing their own understandings of the world, via how the world responds when it is pushed, pulled, grasped, poured, thrown and generally manipulated. The teacher's role is that of a supervisory provider of suitable materials and learning opportunities. Since the late 1960s, following the recommendations of such influential publications as the Plowden Report (1967), and the Nuffield Mathematics Project (Nuffield Foundation 1967), the Piagetian notion of individualistic learning-by-doing has been the major psychological underpinning for the 'progressive' movement in education. The Nuffield recommendation was embodied in the aphorism: 'I hear and I forget. I see and I remember. I do and I understand'. Teachers' words are for hearing and forgetting, unless they relate closely to the real source of understanding – practical activity. Piaget himself had declared: 'Each time one prematurely teaches a child something he could have learned for himself, the child is kept from inventing it and consequently from understanding it completely' (1970: 715). Similarly, in the recent educational policy document issued jointly by the Engineering Council and the Standing Conference on Schools' Science and Technology (1985), we are urged to accept that problem-solving projects are

51

particularly well suited to 'the ethos of the primary school', because 'the teaching is usually child centred and many learning experiences guided by the teacher start from activities with which the child is already familiar' (p. 8).

However, in the world of academic psychology Piaget's conception of the child is no longer predominant. Critiques of the Piagetian orthodoxy have appeared (for example, Donaldson 1978; Russell 1978; Butterworth and Light 1982; Walkerdine 1982; Carey 1985; Edwards and Mercer 1987). The view of the child as a 'lone organism' (Bruner 1986), constructing a succession of general models of the world as each new stage is mastered, is giving way to two new approaches. One of these is even more individualistic than Piaget's. It derives from the new field of cognitive science, and seeks the origins of mature conceptual thinking in ever younger children, even to the point of denying that any major conceptual changes take place at all, and that the main principles of human conceptual thought are pre-established in early infancy, and perhaps innately (for example, Fodor 1975; Carey 1985; Keil 1986). In fact this approach is new in surface details only; it is the doctrine of innate knowledge, at least as old as Plato, and essential to the rationalist philosophical tradition of Descartes and Kant.

The second 'new' approach is also at least as old as Piaget's, but is only now becoming a major influence in British and American developmental psychology. This is the work of the Soviet psychologist Leo Vygotsky and his followers, which emphasizes the social-cultural, linguistic origins of conceptual thinking, the importance of communicative social interaction in learning, and the roles of education and literacy in shaping what are often assumed to be natural, rational, objectively scientific modes of adult thought. In Vygotsky's perspective (see Vygotsky 1987 and Wertsch 1985; Wood 1988) mind is socialized and shaped through teaching and language. Education is formative of conceptual thought, rather than merely a practical context in which psychological theories and findings, derived from the experimental laboratory, can be 'applied'. Conceptual thought is derived from dialogue, and so must follow the rules and categories of discourse, of communicated symbols, and written text.

For example, in an extended treatment of this notion, David Olson (1984) has argued (controversially) that it is the invention and wide-spread use of written forms of language that has resulted in the development of rationality itself, of logical reasoning, of formal education, and of scientific thought. And it is the acquisition of literacy that is the key to how individuals and societies, in the modern world, also acquire those powerful modes of thought. The mere fact of having written text available to us for rereading, and repeated scrutiny, not only facilitates the creation of large cultures of formal knowledge and procedure (science, literature and education), but also encourages an analytic perspective on language and knowledge that differs fundamentally from common sense. We learn to isolate, examine and test statements for their truth value (science and philosophy), and their interrelationships. The form of language dictates the form of thought, such that 'what we call "intelligence" in our culture is little more than a mastery of the forms of literate uses of language' (Olson 1984: 238) – a far cry indeed from Piaget and practical action.

Clearly, it is the latter, Vygotskian approach which offers the most promise for a social psychology of educational knowledge. However, rather than offering a straightforward Vygotskian account of education, we shall enrich the analysis by drawing upon some recent developments in social psychology itself. There has been in recent years a discernible shift of interest in social psychology towards the study of language, and especially towards conversational discourse and text (see Billig 1987; Potter and Wetherell 1987; Billig *et al.* 1988). It is argued that much of the traditional subject matter of social psychology may fruitfully be studied in terms of the communicative work that people do in talk and text. Discourse analysis, and a concern with rhetoric (argumentation), are also at the heart of the new 'sociology of scientific knowledge' (for example, Latour and Woolgar 1979; Gilbert and Mulkay 1984; Woolgar 1988). These studies examine how scientists work together in laboratories, talk about their work, write about it in scientific journals, argue with each other, and generally 'construct' scientific knowledge as they do so. Scientific knowledge is studied as a socially constructed system of shared (and disputed) assumptions, understandings and procedures. For example, a contrast is often revealed between the official, 'scientific method', version of science, with its impersonal procedures and heroic, prize-winning individuals, and the social practices and communications through which scientific knowledge is created and established. Delamont (1987) has drawn attention to the lack of cross-fertilization between these new insights into the nature and workings of science, and the assumptions about science that prevail in the policies and practices of science education.

Alongside these developments in the analysis of discourse, rhetoric and scientific knowledge, there have been a series of studies of the discourse of classroom education itself (for example, Mehan 1979; Driver 1983; Edwards and Mercer 1986, 1987). Mehan's work is ethno-methodological (see Heritage 1984) in that its concern is with showing how the practical business of classroom education is accomplished – how the social order of the classroom education is accomplished – how the social order of the classroom is created and maintained over time, how teacher and pupils manage the moment-to-moment taking of turns at talking. As linguists have also discovered (Sinclair and Coulthard

1975), the pattern of classroom talk is highly organized, and even in apparently child-centred, 'progressive' sorts of classrooms, highly teacher-dominated. Teachers control the flow of conversation, ask most of the questions, determine who speaks when, and on what, and what the upshot shall be.

Rosalind Driver's studies (Driver 1983; Driver and Oldham 1986; Brook *et al.* 1988) are concerned more directly with knowledge than with properties of talk, with how children think, how they spontaneously explain things, and how they deal with the sorts of practical experiences out of which, in our modern Piagetian classrooms, children are meant to reinvent for themselves the findings and principles of science. She shows the process to be highly problematical. In the absence of any prior hypothesis or expectation, children simply do not observe what they are supposed to. They also offer reasonable but erroneous explanations: the time taken for a radio's sound to fade away means that there must be a very long piece of wire inside; the higher up something is, the greater the gravitational force exerted upon it; the denser a metal, the harder it should be for heat to penetrate it. Driver argues that it is quite wrong to imagine that children can work out for themselves, merely through observation and induction, what it has taken centuries of scientific research to establish. A better approach, she argues, would be for teachers to take a more active role 'as mediators between the pupils' experiences and understandings and that of the scientific community' (Driver 1983: 84) for example, by helping pupils to articulate the significance of their observations. Thus, 'by referring to the ideas and investigations of past scientists, some of the powerful ideas of young children can be explored in a way that treats them with respect' (p. 67).

Valuable as Driver's insights are, they are based upon two assumptions about the relationship between language and thought which pose difficulties for a social psychology of classroom knowledge. First, there is the assumption of a straightforward relationship between talk and thought. Children's talk is taken as a window upon their individual minds, as revealing how they think, how they solve problems, how they understand the world. Second, the view of science is one that pre-dates the new sociology of scientific knowledge; depicting scientific truth in the classical manner, as established, uncontroversial, arising from the proper application of hypothetico-deductive methods. This has been termed the 'storybook' account of science (Mitroff 1974), and has emerged as one amongst a series of 'repertoires' available to scientists for writing and talking about their work: a *post hoc* way of accounting for a preferred version of scientific truth, rather than an accurate description of how scientists actually talk, think and work (see, for example, Gilbert and Mulkay 1984; Potter and Mulkay 1985). So, while we should hardly expect children to reinvent in their classrooms the fruits of centuries of scientific endeavour, we may still be asking too much, that they should conform to an idealized version of scientific history and practice.

In *Common Knowledge* (1987), Edwards and Mercer offer an account of classroom discourse in which, rather than taking the talk as a window upon children's thought processes, they examine it as context-ualized dialogue with the teacher. The discourse itself is the educational reality, and the issue becomes that of examining how teacher and children construct a shared account, a common interpretative frame-work for curriculum knowledge, and for what happens in the classroom. This involves teacher and pupils in the moment-to-moment construction of 'context and continuity', the shared basis of talk and action upon which all subsequent talk and interpretation are built. Typically, this dialogue turns out to be no simple negotiation between equals but a process that is dominated by the teacher's concerns, aims, expectations and prior knowledge, via the teacher's control of the dialogue.

Examining classroom discourse

Investigating shared understandings and how they develop requires a close examination of classroom discourse. The first three extracts we shall examine are from a transcribed video recording of the last few minutes of a lesson on computer graphics. The teacher is coming to the conclusion of her first lesson on the subject with a group of 9-year-olds. They have been shown how to draw some straight lines and right angles on the computer screen, using commands from the computer language LOGO. Very briefly, this involves typing into the keyboard, instructions which move a point ('arrow') on the screen: 'FORWARD 100' moves the pointer 100 units in the direction it is pointing, drawing a line on the screen as it goes. 'RIGHT 90' makes the pointer turn clockwise through 90 degrees, and a further 'FORWARD 100' would draw the second side of a square. In extract 1 the teacher ('T') is talking the pupils through how to complete a 180° turn, subtracting 60° to leave 120° (normal punc- tuation is used here, with the addition of slashes for pauses, and some contextual notes italicized in square brackets).

Extract 1:—Doing a 180° turn

T:	You want to point that-a-way. You've got to turn from there/ right round to there. Can you tell me how many degrees?
Susan:	Measure it.
T:	You could measure it. Now how are you going to do that?

Susan:	With one of these [*Susan picking up a protractor*].
T:	Make sure you're measuring the right angle you're going to turn through. What do you turn it through?
Susan:	Ninety.
T:	Umm/ you're going to turn from that way right round to point that-a-way. This is your turn from here to there. Now you've got to measure the turn you're going to make. So what turn is that from there to there?
Susan:	A hundred and twenty.
T:	Now how did you get that? You're right Susan. How did you get a hundred and twenty? Any idea Lara?
Lara:	Sixty and sixty.
T:	Not sixty and sixty/no. It's got something to do with the sixty but not quite. If you imagine/ that line's continued/ now that angle's sixty. What do the angles/ what's a straight-lined angle? How many degrees in a straight-lined angle? If I turn there/ right round/ half turn or straight-line angle/ straight angle/ how many degrees have I turned? There's two quarter turns look. That's one. So one quarter turn is how many degrees? What's a quarter turn?[*T rotating her pencil through an angle of 90°, and then 180°*]
Lara:	Ninety.
T:	Ninety. Make another quarter turn. How many degrees would that be? Another/
Lara:	Half turn.
T:	It's a half turn but/ the first quarter turn is ninety. How many quarter turns do we need to make that half turn?
Lara:	Four.
T:	You think about it. We're pointing that way. OK we want to point this way. We want to turn our pencil right round so it's pointing this way/ one quarter turn which is how many degrees?
Lara:	Ninety.
T:	Again/ which is/ another quarter turn is/
Lara:	Ninety degrees.
T:	It's another ninety degrees. It's two quarter turns that way. If we do it one/ watch the pencil/ if we do one quarter turn/ it takes us to there. Yes/ that's ninety degrees.
Lara:	A hundred and eighty degrees.
T:	A hundred and eighty degrees. Right. And that is/ what that measures from there right round to there/ so

	if to there is sixty degrees what's that? It's a hundred and eighty altogether/ and that's sixty so what's that one?
Lara:	Forty a hundred and forty.
T:	Not a hundred and forty. What are you trying to do?
Lara:	Add them together.
T:	Not add them together. The whole lot is a hundred and eighty. The whole turn/ from there round is a hundred and eighty degrees. Yes/ that part of it is sixty degrees/ so what's that part going to be? Think about that. All right. Success [*T looking at what Lara has written onto the computer screen*]/ OK.

Extract 1 displays several of the features of classroom discourse that we have been discussing, and especially, the issues of control, and of the building of a context of shared understanding. The teacher is firmly in control, both of the flow of speech, of who takes turns at speaking, and also of its content. She does most of the talking, asks the questions that determine speaker and topic, and defines the points at which each question is satisfactorily answered. Her method is not simply to tell the pupils things; she could easily have told them outright, that a straight line represents 180°, and articulated the rule, for them to learn by heart, that to draw a triangle, you turn the 'arrow' through 180° minus whatever angle you wish to use (in the case of an equilateral triangle 180-60=120). Rather than that, she engages in the 'eliciting' style of progressive, child-centred education. She asks questions, and guides the pupils to the required answers by means of how her questions are couched, and by her responses, reactions, pauses, gestures and mimes. The pupils' pursuit of the angle of a straight line is progressively narrowed to working out, via the teacher's prompts and demonstrations with the pencil, what is twice ninety.

It is also a heavily contextualized piece of dialogue. One would need to be there to see what exactly they are talking about; even the video recording does not always reveal what people are looking at or referring to. The point is, of course, that the participants themselves are required to see and understand these things. But simply 'being there' is not enough. It is not merely a physical context that they are working with. The teacher is at pains to ensure that the significance of what is done and seen is understood by everyone, and can be used as the basis for proceeding with the lesson; the discourse of context and continuity is addressed to matters of shared understanding. So, once Susan comes up with the answer, 120°, the teacher switches to her partner Lara, and makes sure, not only that she also knows the answer, but that she can be guided towards working it out, with however much help, for herself.[1]

The teacher's questions are not oriented towards finding things out – at least not in the obvious sense. She does not need the pupils to tell her 'answers' that she does not know. Rather, they are oriented towards finding out what the pupils themselves know, serving to establish a commonality of understanding between herself and the pupils she is teaching. Teachers' questions also impart information, as well as requesting it, in that they are devices for introducing the formulations, conceptualizations and links between things that the pupils are meant to adopt ('One quarter turn which is how many degrees?')

Let us pursue this notion of establishing shared formulations. Extract 2 continues from where extract 1 leaves off. The teacher, having spent the last few minutes with the girls, now moves them over to where the boys are working at another computer screen. The teacher has already (earlier in the same lesson) worked through, with the boys, what an 'equilateral' triangle is, and how to draw one using LOGO, turning the screen pointer through angles of 120° to draw the required 60° angles.

Extract 2: Talking geometry

T:	OK will you come over and join this problem 'cause we've got a bit of a problem here/ and it's one I want you to think about for next week. We're going to try and draw a triangle. Now we've decided there's something different about it to what/ we've been doing. What do you think's different?
Mark:	The angles
T:	The angles are different aren't they.
Stuart:	Instead of ninety degrees you turn forty five.
T:	Well/ *DO* you?/ OK/ I want you to try for next week/ to draw a triangle. Now the girls have got an equilateral triangle here. How about you two [*Mark and Stuart*] doing an isosceles triangle?
Stuart:	What's that?
T:	To try/ what's an isosceles triangle? Tell him Mark. What's an isosceles triangle? [*Mark giggles, as T puts her hand on his head*]
Mark:	It's one with/ not all equal sides.
T:	Not all equal/ are any of them equal? Isosceles/ [*T holding up two figures*]
Mark:	Two.
T:	Two equal sides/ OK. One's got two equal sides/ that one's got three/ so what's that one called?
Mark:	Called equal/ [*T begins nodding her head*] equilateral.
T:	Equilateral.

The appeal to a continuity of shared understanding, the building from moment to moment of a context of common knowledge, is quite explicit in extract 2. The problem to be solved has a future orientation – it is one to pay special attention to, because it is to be taken up 'next week'. The starting point is the immediate past – the context of shared knowledge that has just been created – 'now we've decided there's something different about it...'. What previously was the explicit, acted-out and talked-about business of the lesson, is now offered by the teacher as part of an implicit common understanding, 'what we've been doing', the 'given' basis upon which new understandings can be built.

The teacher proceeds in the familiar, eliciting style ('What do YOU think's different?), together with clues, and prompts that signal when the answer is not the required one ('Well/ *Do* you?'). Then comes the introduction of new terminology, though again, apparently via elicitation ('What's an isosceles triangle. Tell him Mark'). Through the introduction of a common vocabulary, a common conceptual currency is established – joint terms of reference, by which teacher and pupils can express their common understandings, and also formulate these within the recognized language of geometry. For their part, the pupils appear to understand that, although they are being asked a question, the teacher will invariably provide them with clues to its answer. The teacher is understood to be in control of truth and definition. It having been defined, earlier in the lesson, what an 'equilateral' triangle is, Mark now offers the safe proposition that an 'isosceles' triangles must be something other than that – 'It's one with/ not all equal sides'. This is not acceptable. But rather than simply put him straight, the teacher proceeds to cue the required response, with words and gesture (the two fingers), and her well-timed nod then helps Mark to recall the term 'equilateral'. We have termed these uses of prompts, gestures, reformulations of questions and other devices 'cued elicitation' (Edwards and Mercer 1987). They serve, amongst other things, to maintain the appearance that knowledge and understanding are being elicited from the pupils themselves, rather than being imposed by the teacher. We shall discuss later, some educational problems that this subterfuge may create.

Extract 3 is the remainder of the lesson, beginning where extract 2 leaves off. The teacher is continuing to orient the pupils forward, to what will happen in the next lesson. The capitalized words are LOGO commands.

Extract 3: 'So, remember'

T: Equilateral./ What we're going to do for next week is/ you're going to go away and you're going to try and do it on your own/ right. You [*T addressing the girls*]

59

try and do a program for equilateral triangle. You two [*T looking at Mark and Stuart*]/ think about the turns you've got to make/ not the ones you've already got. That's a problem because we've gone LEFT NINETY haven't we [*T pointing to the diagram she has drawn on paper*]. FORWARD SEVENTY I think it was. Now we want to turn to point in that direction. We're trying to work out what our turn would be. We know that angle's sixty degrees [*pointing to an internal angle of the triangle*]/ but is that the angle we want to turn?

Susan: No

T: [*Turning to Mark*] Is it?

Mark: No.

T: No. We want to turn from there/ right round to there/ so we've got to decide the angle of turn. So remember that when you're writing your program/ you've got to write down the angle which you want the arrow to turn through/ not any of the turns you've already got. It's what you want it to turn through. So your problem [*T addressing the boys*] is an isosceles triangle/ doesn't matter about the length of the sides/ and yours [*the girls'*] is an equilateral triangle/ OK/ and we'll have a go at that next week/ and perhaps another thing/ if you manage to/ you suss out the triangles/ and we'll try and do our initials or something next week because/ this week you haven't taken the pen off/ the arrow off. What you've done is come backwards if you've needed to go in another direction. Next week I'll show you how to take the pen off/ as if you lift the pen off the paper [*T gesturing lifting her pen off a sheet of paper*]/ and how to put it back on again. OK/ so that's your problem this week/ equilateral triangles. Think you'll manage that?

Mark: Yes

T: OK/ fine.

The point about this future-orientation of the teacher's talk is that she is not merely providing information, or forward planning, about the next lesson. She is taking the opportunity to recap and reformulate what it is that the pupils are supposed to take away from this lesson, and bring back with them to the next. And it is not merely some homework. It is some shared understanding: 'So we've got to decide the angle of turn/ *so remember*...you've got to write down the angle which you want the arrow to turn *through* ... it's what you want it to turn through'. The words 'right', 'so', and 'so remember' mark out the upshot of the lesson, the point of it all, the knowledge to take away, think about, bring back, and be ready to build upon. The lesson's major point is made and repeated – to draw a triangle on the computer screen you have to turn the pointer not through the triangle's internal angle, but through its complementary one. In fact, teachers' recaps of what has been 'done' or 'covered' in lessons, are opportunities not only for repeating and reinforcing these shared understandings, but also, for tidying them up, redefining them in terms that better fit the teacher's preferred version of the knowledge in question. These 'reconstructive' recaps often occur at the beginnings and ends of lessons, but also during them, at moments when some doubt has arisen, that the required version of events is jointly understood (see Edwards and Mercer 1987; and in press, for a detailed examination).

Discourse, rhetoric and school science

The development of classroom knowledge is the development of a discourse, the creation of a shared conceptual framework, a common language for the interpretation and communication of thought and experience. We have seen that shared understandings are heavily contextualized in terms of the unfolding talk and activity, with the significance of experience and discovery being marked out in the talk, conceputalized, reformulated, and forming the basis for subsequent talk. Despite a superficial reliance upon pupils' own ideas and contributions, it is also very much a teacher-dominated affair. On close examination, classroom education looks much more like socialization, an inculcation of pupils into a predetermined culture of educated knowledge and practice, than some unfolding development of individual cognitions.

We may ask, therefore, what is going on, when teachers seem so much at pains to display education as '*e-ducare*', the classic definition, a matter of drawing out, leading out, or eliciting from pupils, thoughts and ideas ('cognitions'), that are latent within. Why do they overtly elicit everything from the children, while simultaneously gesturing, hinting at, implying and cuing the required answers? This sort of classroom discourse seems oriented towards the accomplishment of consensus, with pupils and teacher coming as soon as possible (if not immediately) to a shared understanding that accords closely with what the teacher already knows. Teacher and pupils appear to collude in this consensus, the content of which, while generally emanating from the teacher, is displayed as if emanating from the children. John Holt (1969) has documented a range of ways in which children learn to fake understanding, seeking to achieve recognized 'right answers', at the expense of any grasp of principle. It is important to emphasize that examining classroom discourse in terms of joint understandings does not mean that we must be solely concerned with consensual agreement. Shared understanding is the issue, not the assumption. We are interested in how teachers and children orient themselves in talk, to the issue of shared understanding, in how it is displayed or accomplished, or fudged, or ignored, or disputed. What we find, in the main, is that teacher and pupils strive to accomplish an appearance of consensus, avoiding resolved disagreements, and indeed, avoiding disagreements altogether.

Teachers are themselves trained and educated. They learn at college and university, and in teaching practice, the current educational theories and ideologies – the philosophy of *e-ducare*, of Piaget and Plowden, the inadequacy of teaching things to children that they are not ready to learn, that they may learn by rote but not understand. Teachers themselves can articulate the reasons, though not everything that they do is explicitly formulated. But the ideal of elicitation has to be practised against the requirement that the job gets done. There is an overriding practical concern with achieving order and control, both behavioural and cognitive, and with doing the curriculum. They are faced with the dilemma of having to elicit from children precisely what the curriculum determines shall be taught (these issues are discussed in more detail, in Edwards and Mercer 1987, and in Billig *et al.* 1988).

Another reason for all the subtle subterfuges may be that educationists are operating with an inadequate notion of the subject to be taught – of what doing 'science' is really like. We argued earlier that the popular view of science, and the one favoured even by scientists themselves when discussing their own, or some favoured work, is something of a 'storybook,' version. The lone scientist constructs knowledge through hypothesis and strict empirical method, the proposed theory being that which must be forced upon any rational mind by the evidence available. Other 'contingent' repertoires are available for accounting for what are considered to be false beliefs, opposing views and interpretations, misleading research, false trails and so on (see Gilbert and Mulkay 1984; Potter and Wetherell 1987). The point is, that science as it is practised is a social activity, a discourse amongst scientists that is oriented towards what is taken to be common knowledge. It has the character of a debate, and makes full use of the devices of rhetoric and persuasion (see also Yearley 1981, 1985).

Classroom science has some of the features of everyday scientific practice. It also is a communal, discursive activity, a construction of shared understanding, publicly communicated and embodied in shared symbolic forms – conversation, writing and text, diagrams, drawings and so on, with the same concern for establishing a common conceptual framework for the encoding of experience, method, observation and theory. The contrast lies in the lack of debate. Science has no 'teacher', no ultimate power and authority who knows all the answers in advance. There is, indeed, some of that quality in scientific practice. Events can go unobserved until some new theory gives them meaning, or even until some theory reifies them as observations at all – the development of science is full of instances of disputed observations, disputed phenomena, suspicions that the observed data of deepest space, of electron microscopes or of sub-atomic particles, may be more revealing of the equipment that produces them, than of the world they purport to measure. But what will prevail as the orthodox theory, or as an exciting alternative to it, or as an interesting or crucial discovery, has to be demonstrated, achieved, argued for, and accepted as such by other scientists.

The notion that pupils may be unable to understand what their individual cognitive development has not yet prepared them for, has an ironic parallel in classroom discourse. Readiness is indeed an issue, but what often occurs is that pupils come up with ideas that the *teacher* is not ready for. In their third lesson on computer graphics (two weeks later), the children decided that it would be a good idea to draw their names or initials on the screen (extract 4):

Extract 4:—'You can't do curves can you?'

Karen:	(to Lisa) ... The S is going to be a bit difficult/ though. You could just write LC if you wanted to.
T:	But you can't do curves can you? You can't do an S. We haven't learnt to do them ...
Lara:	We could do that [*finger drawing a boxed S in the air*].
T:	That's right ... box writing as long as it's got right angles/ as long as it's not curved/ you're all right. It can do curves/ but we haven't learned how to do them yet. So/ just use what you know. That's the best way.

Again, we have an explicit appeal to a continuity of shared knowledge that encompasses what has already been incorporated into their common understanding, and which extends into the future: '*you* can't do' what '*we* haven't learnt to do (yet)'. But here, it operates also as a constraint. The teacher's 'can you?' superficially elicits, but the teacher's own answer ('you can't') closes down the possibility of Lara's contradicting. Rather than following up the pupils' own thoughts and problem proposals, we have to settle for what, at a point near the scheduled end of the lesson, the teacher has taught so far.

The restrictions of teacher-dominated discourse point to the possibility that pupil–pupil dialogue may be able to offer some compensatory advantages. It was argued earlier that adult science is

more open-ended and uncertain than school science, more argumentative, free-wheeling, open to disputation and reformulation. This
suggests a role in the development of educational knowledge, for
children to argue things through with each other, without the teacher's
constant supervision and control over where the discussion has to lead.
Pupils do, ofcourse engage in such discussions. But one still has to
consider what their importance, if any, might be. Pupils' dialogues may
help to reveal how individual pupils think (this is the usual use of such
materials), but the possibility remains that they may be important also,
for the development of dialogical, argumentative forms of thinking.
Extract 5 is taken from the end of the third lesson on computer graphics.
The teacher has allowed the group to continue 'playing' with the
computer, while the researchers were packing up their recording
equipment. Stuart and Tracy continued to try to draw their names on the
screen. We left the camera running.

Extract 5: Arguing and thinking

Tracy:	RIGHT NINETY/ then we'll be there and I don't want to be there.
Stuart:	RIGHT NINETY/ is just here ... write your columns down here ... It's still not finished yet.
Tracy:	Then/ it's/ RIGHT SIXTEEN again. Put RIGHT SIXTEEN.
Stuart:	Where?
Tracy:	We're/ there we are. We're facing that way/ we want to go/ RIGHT SIXTEEN.
Stuart:	Then we want/ FORWARD.
Tracy:	No/ we don't want to be there. We're doing a RIGHT. Look. We go down there/ go back up there/ go down there.
Stuart:	FORWARD
Tracy:	Oh/ come on/ you do it (...)
Stuart:	NINETY/ that's your first (...) No that's wrong (...)
Tracy:	LEFT NINETY.
Stuart:	LEFT or RIGHT?
Tracy:	LEFT.
Stuart:	We'd be going that way then.
Tracy:	Tell you what/ we could go that way.
Stuart:	No we're going that way.
Tracy:	Over there/ you said/ RIGHT NINETY we'd be going that way. He don't' know his left and right. NINETY/ so then we'll be facing that way. FORWARD TEN. What's that supposed to be?

Stuart:	What/ who I mean?
Tracy:	TEN then we'll be here/ there then I want to go
Stuart:	Miss [*calling to the teacher*]/ what angle do we/ what are we (...) to be back up there again
T:	Where are you? You're there/ and you want to turn through that angle there?
Stuart:	No/ no/ we don't want to do that one Miss. We're going to do one of the smaller ones (...) was it LEFT or RIGHT?
Tracy:	See I told you.
T:	He's already done it.

It is clear that the children are not merely taking turns at thinking aloud, revealing for an observer's convenience, their processes of thought. Rather, they are engaged with each other in joint action and argument, such that what each says and does affects the other's next move. Furthermore, their verbal formulations of thought, are dialogical and argumentative in form, addressed persuasively to the difference between a proposed action or solution, and what the other person thinks or assumes – 'No/ we don't want to be there. We're doing a RIGHT. Look. We go down there ...' 'No that's wrong ... we'd be going that way then.') Argument is a form of thought, indeed many and varied forms of thought, irreducible to the mere adding together of individual cognitions that may happen to be put into words (cf. Billig 1987, from which the caption for extract 5 is borrowed). As with science proper, once we abandon the notion that there is some higher, pervasive authority that already knows everything, ideas have to be justified against criticism, supported by argument and evidence against possible refutation. They do not spring from the data, nor from some rigid logic, evident and undeniable. They do not arise merely out of the perception and cognition of individuals, finding form in words only as some final part of the process, for the purposes of teaching them to someone else. The common knowledge of science and of the school classroom is intrinsically social, framed in a common language, dialogical in form and process.

Ironically, given the powerful influence of Piaget upon the 'child-centred pedagogy' (Walkerdine 1984), it is Piaget who provides us with the clearest statement of the importance of argumentation between children, in the development of their thought:

What then gives rise to the need for verification? Surely it is the shock of our thought coming into contact with that of others, which produces doubt and the desire to prove ... The social need to share the thought of others and to communicate our own with

> success is at the root of our need for verification. Proof is the
> outcome of argument ... Logical reasoning is an argument which
> we have with ourselves, and which reproduces internally the
> features of a real argument.
>
> (Piaget 1928: 204)

The prevailing emphasis upon individual learning, individual cognitive
growth, coupled with the pervasiveness of teacher- dominated dialogue,
leads to some of the subterfuges and inadequacies of the sorts of
teaching we have examined here. There is a tendency in teachers to keep
their educational goals secret; pupils cannot be told too much, but have
to work things out for themselves. As Driver also observed:

> It is common to see science lessons which end with the clearing up
> after the practical work is finished. The time for the important
> discussion of how the important experiences gained relate to the
> new ideas is missed. Activity by itself is not enough. It is the sense
> that is made of it that matters.
>
> (Driver 1983: 49)

We might add that discussion is important throughout the lessons, and
that must include discussion between pupils, as well as with the teacher.
Our analyses of classroom discourse suggest that teacher–pupil talk and
pupil–pupil talk are both important, but often for different reasons.
There are overriding asymmetries between teacher and pupil, both
cognitive (in terms of knowledge) and interactive (in terms of power),
that impose different discursive patterns and functions. Teachers'
expertise lends itself to direct explanation and to assisted learning, of the
Vygotskian sort, in which the less competent child is helped
('scaffolded' is Jerome Bruner's term), towards increased competence.
But we should not ignore what pupils can learn from others who know
no more than themselves – the skills of disputation, the notion that all
knowledge is questionable, or in need of scrutiny and justification, that
we do not always have to agree. It is important that the teacher's
knowledge should not be immune from such an approach. Perhaps the
most difficult achievement is not to let children argue with each other,
but to open up the teacher's own understandings for scrutiny in the
classroom – her pre-established plans and assumptions, her aims and
methods, her own understandings and conclusions, for disputation,
without the whole exercise becoming merely another guessing game of
what the teacher wants us all to say. In any case, there is clearly an
important role for a social psychology of educational knowledge, which
emphasizes the social and communicative nature of knowledge, which
bases itself upon a sound understanding of the social and communicative foundations of the very knowledge ('science', for example) that

education seeks to impart, and which has as its empirical basis, the close examination of educational talk and texts.

Note

1 There is an intriguing similarity here between the teacher's elicitation of geometry from these pupils, and the famous sequence in Plato's *Meno*, in which Socrates, in a dialogue with a slave boy, appears to elicit from him a version of Pythagoras's theorem. Socrates claims that the boy must have known the theorem innately (see Billig *et al.* 1988, Chapter 4 for a full discussion of the significance of this parallel, its relevance to modern educational practice, and the doctrines of Piagetian learning and of innate knowledge).

References

Billig, M. (1987) *Arguing and Thinking*, Cambridge: Cambridge University Press.

Billig, M., Condor, S., Edwards, D., Gane, M., Middleton, D.J. and Radley, A.R. (1988) *Ideological Dilemmas: a Social Psychology of Everyday Thinking*, London: Sage.

Brook, A., Driver, R. and Johnston, K. (1988) 'Learning processes in science: a classroom perspective', in J.J. Wellington (ed.) *Skills and Processes in Science Education: a Critical Analysis*, London: Methuen.

Bruner, J.S. (1986) *Actual Minds, Possible Worlds*, London: Harvard University Press.

Butterworth, G. and Light, P. (1982) *Social Cognition: Studies of the Development of Understanding*, Brighton: Harvester Press.

Carey, S. (1985) *Conceptual Change in Childhood*, Cambridge, Mass.: Bradford Books/MIT Press.

Delamont (1987) 'Three blind spots? A comment on the sociology of science by a puzzled outsider', *Social Studies of Science* 17: 163–70.

Donaldson, M. (1978) *Children's Minds*, London: Fontana.

Driver, R. (1983) *The Pupil as Scientist*, Milton Keynes: Open University Press.

Driver, R and Oldham, V. (1986) 'A constructivist approach to curriculum development in science', *Studies in Science Education* 13: 105–22.

Edwards, D. and Mercer, N.M. (1986) 'Context and continuity: classroom discourse and the development of shared knowledge', in K. Durkin (ed.) *Language Development in the School Years*, London: Croom Helm.

Edwards, D. and Mercer, N.M. (1987) *Common Knowledge: the Development of Understanding in the Classroom*, London: Methuen.

Edwards, D. and Mercer, N.M. (in press) 'Reconstructing context: the conventionalization of classroom knowledge', *Discourse Processes*.

Engineering Council and the Standing Conference on Schools' Science and Technology (1985) *Problem Solving: Science and Technology in Primary Schools*, London.

Fodor, J.A. (1975) *The Language of Thought*, New York: Thomas Y. Crowell.

Gilbert, G.N. and Mulkay, M. (1984) *Opening Pandora's Box: a Sociological Analysis of Scientists' Discourse*, Cambridge: Cambridge University Press.

Heritage, J. (1984) *Garfinkel and Ethnomethodology*, Cambridge: Polity Press.

Holt, J. (1969) *How Children Fail*, Harmondsworth: Penguin.

Keil, F.C. (1986) 'On the structure-dependent nature of stages of cognitive development', in I. Levin (ed.) *Stage and Structure: Reopening the Debate*, New Jersey: Ablex.

Latour, B. and Woolgar, S. (1979) *Laboratory Life: the Social Construction of Scientific Facts*, London: Sage.

Mehan, H. (1979) *Learning Lessons: Social Organization in the Classroom*, Cambridge, Mass.: Harvard University Press.

Mitroff, I.I. (1974) *The Subjective Side of Science*, Amsterdam: Elsevier.

Nuffield Foundation (1967) *Nuffield Maths Project, I Do and I Understand*, London: W.& R. Chambers and John Murray.

Olson, D.R. (1984) 'Oral and written language and the cognitive processes of children', in A. Lock and E. Fisher (eds) *Language Development*, London: Croom Helm/The Open University.

Piaget, J., (1928) *Judgment and Reasoning in the Child*, London: Routledge & Kegan Paul.

Piaget, J. (1970) 'Piaget's theory', in P.H. Mussen (ed.) *Carmichael's Manual of Child Psychology*, New York: John Wiley & Sons.

Plowden Report (1967) *Children and their Primary Schools*, 2 vols, Report of the Central Advisory Council for Education in England, London: HMSO.

Potter, J. and Mulkay, M. (1985) 'Scientists' interview talk: interviews as a technique for revealing participants' interpretative practices', in M. Brenner, J. Brown and D. Canter (eds) *The Research Interview: Uses and Approaches*, London: Academic Press.

Potter, J. and Wetherell, M. (1987) *Discourse and Social Psychology*, London: Sage.

Russell, J. (1978) *The Acquisition of Knowledge*, London: Macmillan Press.

Sinclair, J. McH. and Coulthard, R.M. (1975) *Towards an Analysis of Discourse: the English used by Teachers and Pupils*, London: Oxford University Press.

Vygotsky, L.S. (1987) *Thought and Language*, Cambridge, Mass.: MIT Press.

Walkerdine, V. (1982) 'From context to text: a psychosemiotic approach to abstract thought', in M. Beveridge (ed.) *Children Thinking through Language*, London: Edward Arnold.

Walkerdine, V. (1984) 'Developmental psychology and the child-centred pedagogy: the insertion of Piaget into early education', in J. Henriques, W. Hollway, C. Urwin, C. Venn and V. Walkerdine *Changing the Subject*, London: Methuen.

Wertsch, J.V. (1985) *Vygotsky and the Social Formation of Mind*, Cambridge, Mass.: Harvard University Press.

Wood, D. (1988) *How Children Think and Learn*, Oxford: Basil Blackwell.

Woolgar, S. (1988) *Science: the very idea*, Chichester: Ellis Horwood.

Yearley, S. (1981) 'Textual persuasion: the role of social accounting in the construction of scientific arguments', *Philosophy of the Social Sciences* 11: 409–35.

Yearley, S. (1985) 'Vocabularies of freedom and resentment: a Strawsonian perspective on the nature of argumentation in science and the law', *Social Studies of Science* 15: 99–126.

Chapter five

Self-concept and school achievement

Dale H. Schunk

Editors' introduction

For many years social psychologists have been concerned with a study of the self-concept. Within a cognitive approach to social psychology this concern has led to the view that the individual is an active seeker of information, concerned with establishing a view of themselves that is consistent with their lives and that is centrally concerned with the degree to which they have control over important life events.

Within educational research there has developed a particular tradition that has seen self-concept as being closely involved with the individual's level of academic attainment. As Dale Schunk points out, while the relationship between self-concept and academic attainment exists, it is far from clear just what it means.

Schunk's case is based on the assumption that the self-concept is best regarded as being hierarchically organized. A general self-concept, our fundamental view of ourselves, can be regarded as the summation of a number of more particular beliefs relating to different aspects of our range of activities. It is these more specific self-concepts, Schunk argues, with which it is important for the teacher to be concerned.

Schunk's contribution illustrates how research into the operation of the self-concept, using the core notion of self-efficacy (one's beliefs in what one can achieve) leads into a number of practical implementations. The chapter is wide ranging in its scope and introduces concerns with the ways in which a teacher might use peer modelling and goal setting to further the development of pupils' self-efficacy and thereby enhance levels of attainment. The chapter, together with the following chapters by Rogers on motivation (Chapter 6), Kutnick on pupil autonomy (Chapter 7), and Slavin on co-operative learning strategies (Chapter 13), illustrates how concerns with the inner child can be seen to sit happily alongside a concern with classroom practices.

Introduction

Current theoretical accounts of learning view pupils as active seekers and processors of information (Pintrich *et al*. 1986). Learners' cognitions influence the instigation, direction, and persistence of achievement behaviours (Winne 1985; Corno and Snow 1986; Schunk, in press). Research conducted within various traditions emphasizes pupils' beliefs concerning their capabilities to control important aspects of their lives (Nicholls 1983; Covington 1984; Weiner 1985; Bandura 1986).

This chapter discusses the influence of the self-concept on children's motivation and learning in school. The self-concept comprises such dimensions as self-confidence, self-esteem, self-concept stability and self-crystallization (Rosenberg and Kaplan 1982). Much of the present discussion is focused on perceived self-efficacy, or individuals' perceptions of competence at academic tasks. Initially I give a brief theoretical overview of self-concept to include its development and differentiation. Research is reviewed that examines the influence of general self-concept on pupil achievement. I then present theory and research on domain-specific self-perceptions with the concentration on self-efficacy. The chapter concludes with suggestions of ways to enhance pupils' academic self-concepts.

Self-concept: development and differentiation

Self-concept refers to one's collective self-perceptions that are formed through experiences with, and interpretations of, the environment, and that are heavily influenced by reinforcements and evaluations by significant other persons (Shavelson and Bolus 1982). Self-concept is multidimensional. Self-esteem is one's perceived sense of self-worth – whether one accepts and respects oneself. Self-confidence denotes the extent to which one believes one can produce results, accomplish goals, or perform tasks competently. Self-esteem and self-confidence are related. The belief that one is capable of performing a task competently can raise self-esteem. High self-esteem might lead one to attempt a difficult task, and subsequent success enhances self-confidence.

Other dimensions of self-concept are stability and self-crystallization (Rosenberg and Kaplan 1982). Self-concept stability refers to the ease or difficulty of changing the self-concept. Stability depends in part on how crystallized or structured are one's beliefs. Beliefs become crystallized with repeated similar experiences. By adolescence people have relatively well-structured perceptions of themselves with respect to such characteristics as general intelligence, sociability and honesty. Brief experiences providing evidence that conflicts with individuals'

71

beliefs will not have much impact. In contrast, self-concept is readily modified in areas where people have ill-formed notions about themselves, usually because they have little if any experience (for example, ability to learn Swahili or perform mental rotations).

The development of self-concept proceeds from a concrete view of oneself to a more abstract one (Montemayor and Eisen 1977). Young children perceive themselves concretely: they define themselves in terms of their appearance, actions, name, possessions, and so forth. Children do not distinguish between overt behaviours and underlying abilities or personality characteristics. They also do not have a sense of an enduring personality. Children's self-concepts are rather diffuse and loosely organized. Children acquire a more abstract self-view with development and especially as a result of schooling. They develop separate conceptions of underlying traits and abilities and understand that behaviours do not always match capabilities. The self-concept becomes better organized and more complex.

Development also brings greater differentiation of the self-concept. Although most investigators postulate the existence of a general self-concept, recent evidence indicates that the self-concept is hierarchically organized (Shavelson and Bolus 1982; Marsh and Shavelson 1985) with a general self-concept located at the top of the hierarchy and specific sub-area self-concepts towards its base. Self-perceptions of specific behaviours presumably influence sub-area self-concepts (for example, English, mathematics), which in turn combine to form the academic self-concept. The general self-concept is formed by self-perceptions in the academic areas combined with those in non-academic (social, emotional, physical) domains.

The knowledge that children acquire about themselves occurs primarily through their social interactions (Mead 1934). School children receive many opportunities to evaluate their skills and abilities, and this evaluative information contributes to the formation and modification of their self-concepts. Performances are evaluated against absolute and normative standards. Absolute standards are fixed; normative standards are based on the performance of others. Both types are found in school. Pupils whose goal is to complete six workbook pages in thirty minutes gauge their progress against this absolute standard. Grading systems often are based on absolute standards (for example, A = 90-100, B = 80-89, and so on).

Social comparison refers to comparing one's performances with those of others. Festinger (1954) hypothesized that, where objective standards of behaviour are unclear or unavailable, people evaluate their abilities and opinions through comparisons with those of others, and that the most accurate self-evaluations derive from comparisons with those who are similar in the ability or characteristic being evaluated. The ability to use comparative information depends on higher levels of cognitive development and experience in making comparative evaluations (Veroff 1969). Festinger's hypothesis may not apply to children younger than age 5 or 6 because such children tend not to relate two or more elements in thought (for example, their performances with those of others) (Higgins 1981). This does not mean that young children cannot evaluate themselves relative to others, rather, they may not automatically do so. Children show increasing interest in comparative information in the early school years and by age 8 to 10 regularly use such information to help form self-evaluations of competence (Ruble *et al.* 1976; Ruble *et al.* 1980).

The meaning and function of comparative information change with development. Pre-schoolers actively compare at an overt physical level (for example, amount of reward). Other social comparisons involve how one is similar to and different from others and competition is based on a desire to be better than others without involving self-evaluation (for example, 'I'm the general; that's higher than the captain') (Mosatche and Bragonier 1981). Later on social comparisons shift to a concern for how to perform tasks (Ruble 1983). Early infants engage in peer comparisons, but these often are directed toward obtaining correct answers. Providing comparative information to young children increases their motivation for practical reasons. Direct adult evaluation of children's capabilities (for example, 'You can do better') seems more influential in helping children form self-evaluations of capabilities.

Recent research suggests that the self-concept is not passively formed through environmental interactions; rather, it is a dynamic structure that mediates significant intrapersonal and interpersonal processes (Cantor and Kihlstrom 1987). Markus and her colleagues (Markus and Nurius 1986; Markus and Wurf 1987) hypothesize that the self-concept comprises self-schemas or generalizations formed through prior experiences. These schemas process personal and social information much as academic schemas process cognitive skill information (Rumelhart and Ortony 1977). Self-schemas differ in various ways. Some are more elaborate (that is, include more information) than others; some refer to the present self, whereas others refer to past or possible future selves. Some schemas are positive, others are negative (for example, 'I'm no good').

The multidimensional nature of the self-concept is captured in the notion of working self-concept. Not all self-representations are equally active at the same time. Working self-concept refers to those self-schemas that are mentally active at the moment – one's presently accessible self-knowledge. This conceptualization allows for a relatively stable core (general) self-concept, surrounded by domain-specific self-concepts that are capable of being altered more easily. The latter are activated by task circumstances. For example, pupils working on mathematics problems have their mathematical self-concepts active, but once they switch to a different task (for example, reading), different schemas will be activated. Changes in domain-specific self-concepts that occur as a result of learning have an impact upon more general self-knowledge.

Self-concept and academic achievement

It is commonly believed that self-concept bears a positive relationship to school achievement. The thinking runs something like this. Pupils who are confident of their learning abilities and feel a sense of self-worth display greater interest and motivation in school, which enhances achievement. Higher achievement, in turn, validates one's self-confidence for learning and maintains a high sense of self-esteem.

Although these ideas are intuitively plausible, they have not been consistently supported by research. Wylie (1979) reviewed seventy-eight research studies examining the relationship of self-concept to academic achievement and ability. The average correlation between achievement measures (grade point averages) and overall measures of self-concept was +0.30. Correlation coefficients range from -1.00 through 0 to +1.00 and indicate the direction and strength of the relation between two measures. Positive coefficients denote a direct relationship: individuals high on one measure also are high on the other measure. Negative coefficients denote an inverse relationship: individuals high on one measure are low on the other measure. Coefficients at or close to zero indicate no relationship: individuals high on one measure are equally likely to be high or low on the other measure. Regardless of sign (plus or minus), the higher the number the stronger the relationship. For example, +0.10 is a weak positive correlation, -0.82 a strong negative correlation. Wylie's finding of +0.30 is a moderate positive correlation.

Correlations were somewhat higher when standardized measures of self-concept were employed, whereas they were lower (and often nonsignificant) with idiosyncratic, researcher-developed self-concept measures. Higher correlations – many around +0.50 – were obtained between grade point averages and measures of academic self-concept (self-concept of ability). That higher correlations were found between achievement and academic self-concept than between achievement and overall self-concept supports the hierarchical organization of self-concept (Shavelson and Bolus 1982). The highest correlations with academic achievement have been obtained with subject-area self-concepts (for example, English, mathematics).

Even assuming that self-concept and achievement are positively related, researchers have not agreed on the direction of influence (Scheirer and Kraut 1979; Shavelson and Bolus 1982). Different models have postulated that self-concept influences achievement, that achievement influences self-concept, that self-concept and achievement reciprocally influence one another, and that self-concept and achievement are each influenced by other variables (for example, teaching).

For various reasons, self-concept studies have typically not explored causal mechanisms. For one, many studies have not been based on theoretical models postulating causal dominance. For another, methods for exploring causal relations in correlational studies, until fairly recently, were not widely used. A third problem concerns the stability of self-concept. Given that general self-concept presumably is an enduring characteristic formed through many experiences over time, it should not fluctuate much as a result of relatively brief experimental interventions. Attempting to alter self-concept with a brief intervention to determine whether changes in self-concept affect achievement may be difficult. Similarly, changes in achievement may not have much immediate effect on perceptions of one's self-regard.

Bandura (1986) contends that general measures of psychological functioning cannot predict with accuracy what people will do in specific situations. Self-concept includes people's perceptions of their competencies (self-confidence) and their self-worth (self-esteem), both of which vary for performances in different domains. One might, for example, judge him- or herself highly capable in intellectual endeavours and feel a great sense of self-worth, moderately competent in social situations but feel inadequate, and low in competence in athletic pursuits but not feel inadequate. Variability is often found among different activities within the same domain. Within the intellectual domain, a pupil might judge his or her competence as high in science and mathematics, moderate in English and social studies, and low in French and Latin. Further, there is no necessary relation between self-confidence and self-esteem. Students may judge themselves competent in areas from which they derive no pride; conversely, low perceived competence does not necessarily result in low self-esteem.

As noted in the preceding section, self-concept researchers view the self-concept as being in dynamic interplay with the environment – reacting to it while simultaneously influencing it. This notion fits well with Bandura's (1986) contention that cognitions, behaviours and the environment reciprocally influence one another (triadic reciprocality). The best prediction of behaviour in a specific situation comes from people's self-perceptions within that domain, or their working self-concepts in different areas of human functioning.

Domain-specific self-perceptions

Domain-specific self-concepts are far less crystallized than is academic or general self-concept; therefore, the former are more readily modified by experimental interventions. In our own research, young people typically feel more self-confident about learning academic content after participating in a training programme that includes instruction and practice opportunities in the content. The training programme makes salient pupils' perceptions of their capabilities in that academic area. A broad construct such as academic self-concept is influenced by beliefs about many different skills. Unless the skill taught is general and affects many academic domains, academic self-concept is likely to show little change due to brief experimental interventions.

I will illustrate the influence of a particular type of domain-specific self-perception on school learning: perceived self-efficacy, or personal beliefs about one's capabilities to engage in activities necessary to attain designated performance levels (Bandura 1982). Self-efficacy is hypothesized to influence choice of activities. Pupils who hold a low sense of efficacy for accomplishing a task may avoid it, whereas those who believe they are capable should participate more eagerly. Self-efficacy also affects motivation and achievement. Especially when they encounter difficulties, pupils who believe that they are capable of learning ought to work harder, persist longer, and develop better skills, than those who doubt their capabilities (Schunk, in press).

People acquire self-efficacy information from their actual performances, vicarious (for example, observational) experiences, forms of persuasion, and physiological indices. In general, one's successes raise efficacy and failures lower it, although once a strong sense of efficacy is developed an occasional failure will not have much impact. In school, pupils who observe similar peers perform a task are apt to believe that they, too, are capable of performing it. Information acquired from vicarious sources will have a weaker influence on self-efficacy than performance-based information; when the two sources conflict, the former will be outweighed by the latter. Pupils also receive persuasory information from teachers (for example, 'You can do this'). Positive persuasory feedback enhances self-efficacy, but this increase will be short-lived if pupils' subsequent efforts turn out poorly. Children can also derive efficacy information from such physiological indices as heart rate and sweating. Anxiety symptoms before a test might signal that one lacks the skills to succeed.

Information acquired from these sources does not influence self-efficacy automatically, but rather is cognitively appraised (Bandura 1982). A self-efficacy model of cognitive skill learning is portrayed in Figure 5.1. This model is derived from different theoretical traditions including social cognitive learning, attribution, and instructional theory (Weiner 1985; Winne 1985; Bandura 1986; Corno and Snow 1986).

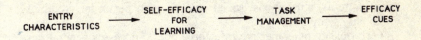

Figure 5.1 Self-efficacy model of cognitive skill learning.

I have discussed this model in depth elsewhere (Schunk 1985b, and in press). In this chapter I present the overall framework, along with some supporting research evidence. I then discuss evidence for the predictive utility of self-efficacy during cognitive skill learning. The article concludes with implications of the research findings for teaching and learning.

Self-efficacy and cognitive skill-learning

Pupils differ in aptitudes and prior experiences. Aptitudes include general abilities, skills, strategies, interests, attitudes and personality characteristics (Cronbach and Snow 1977). Educational experiences derive from such influences as prior schools attended, interactions with teachers and time spent on different subjects. Aptitudes and experiences are related. For example, skilled readers typically perform well on reading tasks, which earns them teacher praise and high grades. In turn, these outcomes lead pupils to develop greater interest in reading, which further enhances skills.

At the outset of a learning endeavour we may speak of self-efficacy for learning, acquiring knowledge, developing skills or mastering material. Aptitudes and prior experiences will affect pupils' initial beliefs about their learning capabilities. Pupils who previously have performed well in a content area are apt to believe that they are capable of further learning; those who have experienced difficulties may doubt their capabilities. At the same time, efficacy is not a mere reflection of aptitudes and prior experiences. Using pupils of high, average and low mathematical ability, Collins (1982) found children of high and low mathematical self-efficacy within each ability level. Pupils solved problems and could rework those they missed. Ability was positively related to skilful performance, but regardless of ability level, children with higher efficacy solved more problems correctly and chose to rework more than they had missed.

I discuss task engagement variables in a moment. While participating in learning activities, children derive efficacy cues that signal how well they are learning and that they use to assess efficacy for continued learning. In turn, higher efficacy for learning enhances motivation and skill acquisition. Some important cues are performance outcomes, outcome patterns, attributions, social comparisons, persuader credibility and bodily symptoms.

Performance outcomes are influential cues. Successes general raise self-efficacy and failures lower it; however, an occasional failure after many successes may not have much impact, nor should one success after many failures (Schunk, in press). Early learning is often fraught with failures, but the perception of progress promotes efficacy. Outcome patterns are important; efficacy will not be aided much if pupils believe that their progress is slow or that their skills have stabilized at low levels.

Attributions, or perceived causes of successes and failures, influence efficacy in important ways. Achievement outcomes are often attributed to such causes as ability, effort, task difficulty and luck (Frieze 1980; Weiner 1985; Rogers, this volume). Children view effort as the prime cause of outcomes. With development, ability attributions become increasingly important influences on expectancies, and the role of effort declines in importance (Nicholls 1978; Harari and Covington 1981). Success achieved with great effort should raise efficacy less than if minimal effort is required, because the former implies that skills are not well developed (Bandura 1982).

Children also derive cues from social comparisons. As stated earlier, Festinger (1954) hypothesized that, where objective standards of behaviour are unclear or unavailable, observers evaluate themselves through comparisons with others, and that the most accurate self-evaluations derive from comparisons with those who are similar in the ability or characteristic being evaluated. Pupils frequently compare their performances with those of their peers, and feel more (less) efficacious when they believe that they are accomplishing more (less) work. Peers are also important models, and observing models is a form of social comparison. Observing similar peers improving their skills instills a sense of efficacy for learning, whereas observed failures cast doubt on pupils' capabilities to succeed (Schunk 1985b). Similarity is based on perceived competence or on such personal attributes as age, sex, and ethnic background (Rosenthal and Bandura 1978).

Persuader credibility is important because pupils may experience higher efficacy when they are told they are capable of learning by a trustworthy source (for example, the teacher), whereas they may discount the advice of less credible sources. Pupils may also discount otherwise credible sources if they believe that the sources do not fully understand the nature of the task demands (for example, difficult for pupils to comprehend) or the effect of contextual factors (for example, too many distractions).

Bodily symptoms serve as physiological cues for appraising efficacy. Sweating and trembling may signal that children are not capable of learning. Children who notice that they are reacting in less-agitated fashion to academic tasks may feel more efficacious about learning.

Task engagement refers to pupils' cognitive activities (attending, rehearsing, processing and integrating information), along with their verbalizations and behaviours, that are focused on academic tasks (Corno and Mandinach 1983). While pupils are engaged in tasks, variables associated with the classroom instructional context give rise to cues that they use to appraise their self-efficacy for learning. Some influential task engagement variables are the purpose of instruction, content difficulty, methods and materials used in instruction, strategies taught to pupils, performance feedback, models, goal setting, attributional feedback, and rewards. Rather than discuss each of these in depth, I will focus on research investigating the effects of attributional feedback, goal setting, strategy training and peer models.

Research evidence

Attributional feedback.

Attributional feedback, which links pupils' successes and failures with one or more causes, is a persuasive source of efficacy information. Young children stress the role of effort. Although ability information becomes more important with development (Nicholls 1978), effort feedback motivates children of different ages. Being told that one can achieve better results through harder work (that is, effort feedback for prior difficulties) motivates one to do so and conveys that one possesses the necessary capabilities to succeed (Dweck 1975; Andrews and Debus 1978).

Effort feedback for prior successes supports children's perceptions of their progress in learning, sustains motivation and increases self-efficacy for continued learning. In an early study (Schunk 1982) children periodically received effort feedback as they solved problems during a subtraction instructional programme. Some children had their prior achievement linked with effort ('You've been working hard'), others had their future achievement linked with effort ('You need to work hard'), and those in a third condition did not receive effort feedback. Linking prior achievement with effort led to the highest motivation (rate of problem-solving during the instructional programme), post-test subtraction skill and self-efficacy.

The effects of ability feedback were compared with those of effort feedback using a similar methodology (Schunk 1983a). Children periodically received ability feedback for prior successes ('You're good at this'), effort feedback ('You've been working hard), ability and effort (combined) feedback, or no feedback. Children who received only ability feedback demonstrated higher post-test self-efficacy and skill compared with the effort-only and the ability-plus-effort conditions. The latter subjects judged their effort expenditure during training greater than did ability-only children. Children in the combined condition may have discounted some ability information in favour of effort. They might have wondered how able they really were if they had to continue to work hard to succeed.

Schunk (1984) tested the idea that the sequence of attributional feedback influences achievement outcomes. Children lacking subtraction skills received instruction and solved problems over sessions. One group periodically received ability feedback, a second group received effort feedback, a third condition was given ability feedback during the first half of training and effort feedback during the second half, and for a fourth condition this sequence was reversed. Ability feedback for early successes led to higher ability attributions, post-test self-efficacy and subtraction skill, compared with effort feedback. These results suggest that early ability feedback instilled higher expectations for continued learning.

Schunk and Cox (1986) explored how the sequence of effort feedback affected learning disabled pupils' motivation, self-efficacy, and subtraction skill. During an instructional programme, pupils received effort feedback during the first half of the programme, effort feedback during the second half, or no effort feedback. Each type of effort feedback promoted post-test self-efficacy and skill better than no feedback, but effort feedback during the first half enhanced effort attributions for success. Given pupils' learning disabilities, the effort feedback for early or later successes may have seemed highly credible, because they realistically had to expend effort to succeed. They may have interpreted the effort feedback as indicating that they were becoming more skilful and were capable of further learning. Over an extended period effort feedback might lower self-efficacy, because as pupils become more skilful they might wonder why they still have to work hard to succeed.

Goal-setting

Goal-setting involves comparing one's present performance against a standard. When children pursue a goal, they experience heightened self-efficacy for attaining it as they observe their goal progress. A sense of learning efficacy sustains task motivation. Goals exert their effects through their properties: specificity, difficulty level, proximity (Locke, *et al.* 1981; Bandura and Cervone 1983). Goals that incorporate specific performance standards are more likely to raise learning efficacy because progress toward an explicit goal is easier to gauge. General goals (for example, 'Do your best') do not enhance motivation. Although pupils initially may doubt their capabilities to attain goals they believe are difficult, working toward difficult goals builds a strong sense of efficacy, because they offer more information about learning capabilities than easier goals. Goals are also distinguished by how far they project into the future. Proximal goals, which are close at hand, result in greater motivation than more distant goals. As pupils observe their progress toward a proximal goal, they are apt to believe that they are capable of further learning.

To test the hypothesis that proximal goals enhance children's achievement strivings, Bandura and Schunk, (1981) presented children with a subtraction instructional programme over a number of sessions. The programme consisted of sets of material that included instruction and problems to solve. Some children pursued a proximal goal of completing one set each session; a second group was given a distant goal of completing all sets by the end of the last session; a third group (general goal) was advised to work productively. Proximal goals heightened task motivation, and led to the highest post-test subtraction skill and self-efficacy. The distant goal resulted in no benefits compared with the general goal.

These findings support the idea that when children can easily gauge their progress against a goal, the perception of improvement enhances self-efficacy. Similar results were obtained during a division instructional programme in which children individually solved problems over sessions (Schunk 1983b). Half of the children were given goals each session, whereas the other half were advised to work productively. This study also explored how providing social comparative information about other children's performances affected achievement outcomes. Within each goal conditions, half of the children were informed of the number of problems that other similar children had completed (which matched the session goal); the other half were not given comparative information. The comparative information was designed to convey that the goals were attainable.

Goals led to higher post-test self-efficacy; comparative information promoted motivation during the instructional programme. Children who received both goals and comparative information demonstrated the highest post-test division skill. These results suggest that providing children with a goal and information that it is attainable raises self-efficacy for learning, which contributes to more productive instructional performance and greater skill development.

Schunk (1985a) tested the idea that self-set goals promote achievement striving better than externally-imposed goals and no goals. The rationale for this study derived from the idea that participation in goal-setting raises goal commitment, which is necessary for goals to enhance performance (Locke *et al.* 1981). Children classified as learning disabled in mathematics received subtraction instruction and practice opportunities over sessions. Some children set performance goals each session, others had comparable goals assigned, and children in a third condition received instruction but no goals. Children in the two goal conditions judged their expectancy of goal attainment at the start of each session.

Self-set goals led to the highest post-test self-efficacy and subtraction performance. Although children in the two goal conditions demonstrated higher task motivation during the instructional sessions, children in the self-set condition judged their expectancy of goal attainment higher. The latter finding suggests that allowing pupils to set their learning goals enhanced their self-efficacy for attaining them.

Strategy instruction

Much research shows that pupils benefit from instruction on strategies, or cognitive plans oriented toward improving performance (Baker and Brown 1984; Paris *et al.* 1984). Strategy instruction also influences self-efficacy. The belief that one understands and can apply a strategy that enhances achievement leads to a perceived sense of control over learning outcomes and higher self-efficacy (Licht and Kistner 1986; Schunk, in press).

In learning a strategy, pupils benefit from verbalizing aloud the component steps while applying them to a task. Verbalization facilitates learning because it directs attention to important task features, assists strategy encoding and retention, and helps pupils work in a systematic fashion (Fuson 1979; Harris 1982). Verbalization is most beneficial for pupils who typically perform in a deficient manner, for example, impulsive, remedial, learning disabled or emotionally disturbed children (Borkowski and Cavanaugh 1979; Hallahan *et al.* 1983).

To test these ideas, Schunk and Rice (1985) presented language-deficient children in grades four and five (9- and 10-year-olds) with reading comprehension instruction. Within each grade, half of the children verbalize the steps in a strategy prior to applying them to passages; the other half received strategy instruction but did not verbalize the steps. This six-step strategy was as follows:

What do I have to do? (1) Read the questions; (2) read the story;

and (3) look for key words; (4) reread each question, and (5) answer that question; (6) reread the story if I don't know the answer.

Strategy verbalization led to higher reading comprehension, self-efficacy, and ability attributions across grades. The latter finding suggests that strategy verbalization may enhance self-efficacy through its effect on ability attributions, by leading to an increase in one's beliefs that one has the ability required for success.

Similar results were obtained by Schunk and Rice (1984). Remedial readers in the early years of schooling received instruction in listening comprehension. Strategy verbalization led to higher self-efficacy across grades, and promoted performance among the older children in the sample but not among the youngest (aged around 7 years). Perhaps the demands of verbalization, along with those of the comprehension task itself, were too complex for the youngest children. These children may have focused their efforts on the comprehension task, which would have interfered with strategy encoding and retention.

Subjects in the Schunk and Cox (1986) study received one of three verbalization treatments. One group verbalized aloud subtraction solution steps and their application to problems (continuous verbalization), a second group verbalized aloud during the first half of the instructional programme but not during the second half (discontinued verbalization), and a third group did not verbalize (no verbalization). Continuous verbalization led to higher post-test self-efficacy and skill than discontinued and no verbalization, which did not differ.

It is possible that when instructed no longer to verbalize aloud, discontinued verbalization children had difficulty internalizing the strategy; they may not have used covert instructions to regulate their performances. They may also have believed that although the strategy was useful, other factors (for example, effort) were more important for solving problems (Fabricius and Hagen 1984). We have found that emphasizing to children the value of the strategy as a means of improving performance produces greater increases in children's self-efficacy and comprehension performance compared with strategy instruction without information on strategy value (Schunk and Rice 1987).

Peer models

Models constitute a vicarious source of efficacy information. Perceived similarity of observers and models is an important cue. Models who are similar or slightly higher in competence provide the best information. Students who observe similar peers learn a task are apt to believe that they can learn as well (Schunk 1987). Peer models may exert more beneficial effects on self-efficacy than teacher models, especially among students with learning problems who doubt that they are capable of attaining the teacher's level of competence.

These ideas were tested with primary age school children who had experienced learning problems in mathematics (Schunk and Hanson 1985). Children observed videotapes portraying an adult teacher and a same-sex peer model. The teacher repeatedly provided instruction on subtraction with regrouping, after which the model solved problems. Other pupils viewed videotapes that portrayed only the teacher presenting instruction, and some pupils were not exposed to models. After viewing the tapes, children who had observed a peer model judged perceived similarity in competence to the model. All pupils assessed self-efficacy for learning to subtract, and then received subtraction instruction.

This study also investigated the effects of mastery and coping models: children exposed to a peer observed either a mastery or coping model. The peer mastery model easily grasped subtraction operations, solved all problems correctly, and verbalized positive achievement beliefs reflecting high self-efficacy, high ability, low task difficulty, and positive attitudes. The peer coping model initially made errors and verbalized negative achievement beliefs, but over time made fewer errors and began to verbalize coping statements (for example, 'I'll have to work hard on this one'). The coping model's problem-solving behaviours and verbalizations eventually matched those of the mastery model.

Observing a peer model enhanced self-efficacy for learning more than observing the teacher model or not observing a model; teacher model children judged self-efficacy higher than no-model children. Similar results were obtained on post-test measures of self-efficacy and subtraction skill. There were no differences on any measure between the peer mastery and coping conditions, which may have been due to pupils' prior classroom experiences with subtraction. Even though their successes had been limited to problems without regrouping, they none the less had these experiences to draw on and may have concluded that if the peer could learn to regroup, they could as well.

Follow-up research comprising two experiments further explored the effects of mastery and coping models (Schunk *et al.* 1987). Low achieving children observed videotapes portraying a peer model demonstrate either rapid (mastery model) or gradual (coping model) acquisition of skill in adding and subtracting fractions. These children had experienced little, if any, prior success with fractions. We expected that children would perceive the coping model's gradual learning to be more similar to their typical performances than the rapid learning of the mastery model, and thereby experience higher self-efficacy for learning after observing coping models.

Experiment 2 also investigated the effects of a number of models: children observed either one or three same-sex peer models display mastery or coping behaviours. Multiple models presumably increase the probability that observers will perceive themselves as similar to at least one of the models, which should enhance self-efficacy. Because subjects had encountered difficulties learning mathematical skills, we felt that they might be more likely to discount the successes of a single model than the diverse instances of successful learning displayed by multiple models.

In both experiments children who observed coping models judged themselves more similar in competence to the models than did children who observed mastery models. In Experiment 1, observation of a coping model led to higher self-efficacy, skill, and instructional session performance, compared with observation of a mastery model. In Experiment 2, children in the single coping model, multiple coping model and multiple mastery model conditions demonstrated higher self-efficacy, skill and instructional session performance, compared with children who observed a single mastery model. These latter results show that the benefits of multiple models did not depend on perceptions of similarity in competence. Similarity in competence may be a more important source of efficacy information when children are exposed to a single model and have a less-diverse set of modelled cues to use in judging self-efficacy.

Predictive utility of self-efficacy

The predictive utility of self-efficacy for learning is determined by relating this measure to the number of problems that children complete during the instructional sessions. Positive correlations have been obtained (range = +0.33 to +0.42), which indicate that the higher that children judge self-efficacy for learning, the more problems they complete during the sessions. More rapid problem-solving has not been attained at the expense of accuracy. Similar correlations have been obtained using the proportion of problems solved correctly. Self-efficacy for learning also relates positively to post-test self-efficacy and skill (range = +0.46 to +0.90).

The predictive utility of pre-test efficacy often is inadequate because students lack skills and judge efficacy low. In contrast, there is greater variation in students' post-test judgements and in their demonstrated skills. Studies have yielded positive correlations (range = +0.27 to +0.84) between post-test efficacy and skill.

We have also tested a causal model of achievement to determine the interrelationship of instructional treatment, self-efficacy, persistence and skill. Not surprisingly, we have found that instruction produces gains in pupils' skills and self-efficacy and that higher self-efficacy leads to greater skill and persistence.

Educational implications

The preceding results suggest that teachers help to promote children's self-concepts by structuring the curriculum so that pupils work on tasks they can accomplish and receive positive information from teachers and others (peer models) that they are capable of performing well. Teaching pupils to use learning strategies and to set challenging but attainable goals also fosters motivation, skill development and perceived competence.

Many of the procedures discussed in this article can be implemented easily in schools. For example, the strategy instruction procedures were applied in children's regular reading groups (Schunk and Rice 1984, 1985, 1987). Teaching pupils to use a comprehension strategy by having them verbalize steps fits well with the suggestion by researchers to teach strategies to pupils, especially those with learning problems (Borkowski and Cavanaugh 1979; Raphael and McKinney 1983; Brown *et al.* 1984; Paris *et al.* 1984).

Attributional feedback is easily delivered by teachers while pupils are engaged in seatwork activities. Feedback that signals progress in learning validates pupils' beliefs that they are acquiring skills and enhances motivation for further learning. It is important that the feedback be viewed as credible by pupils. Effort feedback for success at a task that they believe is easy may lead them to wonder whether the teacher thinks they are low in ability (Weiner *et al.* 1983). Pupils will discount ability feedback after they have had to struggle to succeed. Effort feedback is credible when pupils have to work hard to succeed, whereas ability feedback is credible when they succeed with little effort.

Goal-setting is incorporated by teachers with lesson goals for pupils. Contracts specify learning or performance goals. Goal-setting conferences, in which teachers meet periodically with pupils to discuss their goal attainment and to set new goals, enhance achievement and capability self-evaluations (Gaa 1973). Short-term goals are especially beneficial with young children, as well as with pupils with learning problems because they provide concrete standards against which to gauge progress.

Peer models are often incorporated into classroom procedures when teachers select one or more pupils to demonstrate a skill to other class members. The typical practice is to choose peers who master skills readily – mastery models. Among pupils who have experienced some learning difficulties, peers who also have encountered learning problems but who have mastered the present skill may make better models. Peers also could model such coping behaviours as increased concentration and hard work. While pupils are engaged in seatwork, teachers might provide social comparative information (for example, 'See how well Kevin is doing? I'm sure that you can do just as well'). Teachers need to ensure that learners view the comparative performances as attainable; judicious selection of referent pupils is necessary.

Peers also enhance observers' self-efficacy in small groups. Successful groups in which each member is responsible for some aspect of the task and members share rewards based on their collective performance reduce negative ability-related social comparisons (Ames 1984). Teachers need to select tasks carefully, because unsuccessful groups will not raise efficacy.

Strain and his colleagues have successfully used peers as social skill trainers with withdrawn children (Strain *et al.* 1981). Peers are trained to initiate social contacts with verbal signals and motor responses. Such initiations increase withdrawn children's subsequent social initiations and gains often generalize to classrooms. A less formal application involves pairing a socially competent peer with a less competent child to work on a task. The opportunity for social interaction within the dyad promotes the less competent child's social skills (Mize *et al.* 1985).

The use of peers as instructional agents is found in tutoring programmes. Despite some methodological problems in studies, research shows that tutoring results in academic gains by tutor and tutee (Feldman *et al.* 1976). Peer instructors are also helpful where their teaching strategies fit well with learners' capabilities or the skills being taught. Adult teachers typically employ verbal instruction and relate information to be learned to other material, whereas peer teachers use non-verbal demonstrations more often and link instruction with specific items (Ellis and Rogoff 1982). Peer instruction seems beneficial for students who may not process verbal material particularly well.

Given that diverse domain-specific self-concepts contribute to the general academic self-concept, we might expect that the development of self-confidence in one domain would show little transfer to other domains and have little impact on academic self-concept. One means of improving transfer is to teach pupils strategies that can easily be modified for use on different types of content. This point fits well with the suggestion that transfer is facilitated when pupils are trained using multiple tasks (Borkowski and Cavanaugh 1979). Pupils who believe that they have learned strategies that will improve their performance in different domains are apt to demonstrate higher achievement and hold higher academic self-concepts. Many task engagement variables (for example, goal-setting, attributional feedback) are general in the sense that they are not limited in use to only one academic domain.

References

Ames, C. (1984) 'Competitive, co-operative, and individualistic goal structures: a cognitive-motivational analysis', in R. Ames and C. Ames (eds) *Research on Motivation in Education: Student Motivation*, vol. 1, Orlando: Academic Press, pp. 177–207.

Andrews, G.R. and Debus, R.L. (1978) 'Persistence and the causal perception of failure: modifying cognitive attributions', *Journal of Educational Psychology* 70: 154–66.

Baker, L. and Brown, A.L. (1984) 'Metacognitive skills and reading', in P.D. Pearson (ed.) *Handbook of Reading Research*, New York: Longman, pp. 353–94.

Bandura, A. (1982) 'Self-efficacy mechanism in human agency', *American Psychologist* 37: 122–47.

Bandura, A. (1986) *Social Foundations of Thought and Action: A Social Cognitive Theory*, Englewood Cliffs, NJ: Prentice-Hall.

Bandura A. and Cervone, D. (1983) 'Self-evaluative and self-efficacy mechanisms governing the motivational effects of goal systems', *Journal of Personality and Social Psychology* 45: 1017–28.

Bandura, A. and Schunk, D.H. (1981) 'Cultivating competence, self-efficacy, and intrinsic interest through proximal self-motivation', *Journal of Personality and Social Psychology* 41: 586–98.

Borkowski, J.G. and Cavanaugh, J.C. (1979) 'Maintenance and generalization of skills and strategies by the retarded', in N.R. Ellis (ed.) *Handbook of Mental Deficiency, Psychological Theory and Research*, 2nd edn, Hillsdale, NJ: Erlbaum, pp. 569–617.

Brown, A.L., Palincsar, A.S. and Armbruster, B.B. (1984) 'Instructing comprehension-fostering activities in interactive learning situations', in H. Mandl, N.L. Stein and T. Trabasso (eds) *Learning and Comprehension of Text*, Hillsdale, NJ: Erlbaum, pp. 255–86.

Cantor, N. and Kihlstrom, J.F. (1987) *Personality and Social Intelligence*, Englewood Cliffs, NJ: Prentice-Hall.

Collins, J. (1982) *Self-efficacy and Ability in Achievement Behavior*, paper presented at the meeting of the American Educational Research Association, New York, March.

Corno, L. and Mandinach, E.B. (1983) 'The role of cognitive engagement in classroom learning and motivation', *Educational Psychologist* 18: 88–108.

Corno, L. and Snow, R.E. (1986) 'Adapting teaching to individual differences among learners', in M.C. Wittrock (ed.) *Handbook of Research on Teaching*, 3rd edn, New York: Macmillan, pp. 605–29.

Covington, M.V. (1984) 'The self-worth theory of achievement motivation: findings and implications', *Elementary School Journal* 85: 5–20.

Cronbach, L.J. and Snow, R.E. (1977) *Aptitudes and Instructional Methods*, New York: Irvington.

Dweck, C.S. (1975) 'The role of expectations and attributions in the alleviation of learned helplessness', *Journal of Personality and Social Psychology* 31: 674–85.

Ellis, S. and Rogoff, B. (1982) 'The strategies and efficacy of child versus adult teachers', *Child Development* 53: 730–5.

Fabricius, W.V. and Hagen, J.W. (1984) 'Use of causal attributions about recall performance to assess metamemory and predict strategic memory behavior in young children', *Developmental Psychology* 20: 975–87.

Feldman, R.S., Devin-Sheehan, L. and Allen, V.L. (1976) 'Children tutoring children: a critical review of research', in V.L. Allen (ed.) *Children as Teachers: Theory and Research on Tutoring*, New York: Academic Press, pp. 235–52.

Festinger, L. (1954) 'A theory of social comparison processes', *Human Relations* 7: 117–40.

Frieze, I.H. (1980) 'Beliefs about success and failure in the classroom', in J.H. McMillan (ed.) *The Social Psychology of School Learning*, New York: Academic Press, pp. 39–78.

Fuson, K.C. (1979) 'The development of self-regulating aspects of speech: a review', in G. Zivin (ed.) *The Development of Self-regulation Through Private Speech*, New York: Wiley, pp. 135–217.

Gaa, J.P. (1973) 'Effects of individual goal-setting conferences on achievement, attitudes, and goal-setting behaviour', *Journal of Experimental Education* 42: 22–8.

Hallahan, D.P., Kneedler, R.D. and Lloyd, J.W. (1983) 'Cognitive behaviour modification techniques for learning disabled children: self-instruction and self-monitoring', in J.D. McKinney and L. Feagans (eds) *Current Topics in Learning Disabilities*, vol. 1, Norwood, NJ: Ablex, pp. 207–44.

Harari, O. and Covington, M.V. (1981) 'Reactions to achievement behavior from a teacher and student perspective: a developmental analysis', *American Educational Research Journal* 18: 15–28.

Harris, K.R. (1982) 'Cognitive-behavior modification: application with exceptional students' *Focus on Exceptional Children* 15: 1–16.

Higgins, E.T. (1981) 'Role taking and social judgment: alternative developmental perspectives and processes', in J.H. Flavell and L. Ross (eds) *Social Cognitive Development: Frontiers and Possible Futures*, Cambridge: Cambridge University Press, pp. 119–53.

Licht, B.G. and Kistner, J.A. (1986) 'Motivational problems of learning-disabled children: individual differences and their implications for treatment', in J.K. Torgesen and B.W.L. Wong (eds) *Psychological and Educational Perspectives on Learning Disabilities*, Orlando: Academic Press, pp. 225–55.

Locke, E.A., Shaw, K.N., Saari, L.M. and Latham, G.P. (1981) 'Goal setting and task performance: 1969–1980', *Psychological Bulletin* 90: 125–52.

Markus, H. and Nurius, P. (1986) 'Possible selves', *American Psychologist* 41: 954–69.

Markus, H. and Wurf, E. (1987) 'The dynamic self-concept: a social psychological perspective', *Annual Review of Psychology* 38: 299–337.

Marsh, H.W. and Shavelson, R. (1985) 'Self-concept: its multifaceted, hierarchical structure', *Educational Psychologist* 20: 107–23.

Mead, G.H. (1934) *Mind, Self and Society*, Chicago: University of Chicago Press.

Mize, J., Ladd, G.W. and Price, J.M. (1985) 'Promoting positive peer relations with young children: rationales and strategies', *Child Care Quarterly* 14: 211–37.

Montemayor, R. and Eisen, M. (1977) 'The development of self-conceptions from childhood to adolescence', *Development Psychology*, 13: 314–19.

Mosatche, H.S. and Bragonier, P. (1981) 'An observational study of social comparison in preschoolers', *Child Development* 52: 376–8.

Nicholls, J.G. (1978) 'The development of the concepts of effort and ability, perception of academic attainment, and the understanding that difficult tasks require more ability', *Child Development* 49: 800–14.

Nicholls, J.G. (1983) 'Conceptions of ability and achievement motivation: a theory and its implications for education', in S.G. Paris, G.M. Olson and H.W. Stevenson (eds) *Learning and Motivation in the Classroom*, Hillsdale, NJ: Erlbaum, pp. 211–37.

Paris, S.G., Cross, D.R. and Lipson, M.Y. (1984) 'Informed strategies for learning: a program to improve children's reading awareness and comprehension', *Journal of Educational Psychology* 76: 1239–52.

Pintrich, P.R., Cross, D.R., Kozma, R.B. and McKeachie, W.J. (1986) 'Instructional psychology', *Annual Review of Psychology* 37: 611–51.

Raphael, T.E. and McKinney, J. (1983) 'An examination of fifth- and eighth-grade children's question-answering behavior: an instructional study in metacognition', *Journal of Reading Behavior* 15: 67–86.

Rogers, C.G. (1990) 'Motivation in the primary years', this volume.

Rosenberg, M., and Kaplan, H.B. (1982) *Social Psychology of the Self-concept*, Arlington Heights, Ill.: Harlan Davidson.

Rosenthal, T.L. and Bandura, A. (1978) 'Psychological modeling: theory and practice', in S.L. Garfield and A.E. Bergin (eds) *Handbook of Psychotherapy and Behavior Change: An Empirical Analysis*, 2nd edn, New York: Wiley, pp. 621–58.

Ruble, D.N. (1983) 'The development of social-comparison processes and their role in achievement-related self- socialization', in E.T. Higgins, D.N. Ruble and W.W. Hartup (eds) *Social Cognition and Social Development*, New York: Cambridge University Press, pp. 134–57.

Ruble, D.N., Boggiano, A.K., Feldman, N.S. and Loebl, J.H. (1980) 'Developmental analysis of the role of social comparison in self-evaluation', *Developmental Psychology* 16: 105–15.

Ruble, D.N., Feldman, N.S. and Boggiano, A.K. (1976) 'Social comparison between young children in achievement situations', *Developmental Psychology* 12: 191–7.

Rumelhart, D.E. and Ortony, A. (1977) 'The representation of knowledge in memory', in R.C. Anderson, R.J. Spiro and W.E. Montague (eds) *Schooling and the Acquisition of Knowledge*, Hillsdale, NJ: Erlbaum, pp. 99–135.

Scheirer, M.A. and Kraut, R.E. (1979) 'Increasing educational achievement via self concept change', *Review of Educational Research* 49: 131–50.

Schunk, D.H. (1982) 'Effects of effort attributional feedback on children's perceived self-efficacy and achievement', *Journal of Educational Psychology* 74: 548–56.

Schunk, D.H. (1983a) 'Ability versus effort attributional feedback: differential effects on self-efficacy and achievement', *Journal of Educational Psychology* 75: 848–56.

Schunk, D.H. (1983b) 'Developming children's self-efficacy and skills: the roles of social comparative information and goal setting', *Contemporary*

Educational Psychology 8: 76–86.

Schunk, D.H. (1984)'Sequential attributional feedback and children's achievement behaviors', *Journal of Educational Psychology* 76: 1159–69.

Schunk, D.H. (1985a) 'Participation in goal setting: effects on self-efficacy and skills of learning disabled children', *Journal of Special Education* 19: 307–17.

Schunk, D.H. (1985b) 'Self-efficacy and classroom learning', *Psychology in the Schools* 22: 208–23.

Schunk, D.H. (1987) 'Peer models and children's behavioral change', *Review of Educational Research* 57: 149–74.

Schunk, D.H. (in press) 'Self-efficacy and cognitive skill learning', in C. Ames and R.E. Ames (eds) *Research on Motivation in Education*, vol. 3, San Diego: Academic Press.

Schunk, D.H. and Cox, P.D. (1986) 'Strategy training and attributional feedback with learning disabled students', *Journal of Educational Psychology* 78: 201–9.

Schunk, D.H. and Hanson, A.R. (1985) 'Peer models: influence on children's self-efficacy and achievement', *Journal of Educational Psychology* 77: 313–22.

Schunk, D.H., Hanson, A.R. and Cox, P.D. (1987) 'Peer model attributes and children's achievement behaviors', *Journal of Educational Psychology* 79: 54–61.

Schunk, D.H. and Rice, J.M. (1984) 'Strategy self-verbalization during remedial listening comprehension instruction', *Journal of Experimental Education* 53: 49–54.

Schunk, D.H. and Rice, J.M. (1985) 'Verbalization of comprehension strategies: effects on children's achievement outcomes', *Human Learning* 4: 1–10.

Schunk, D.H. and Rice, J.M. (1987) 'Enhancing comprehension skill and self-efficacy with strategy value information', *Journal of Reading Behavior* 19: 285–302.

Shavelson, R.J. and Bolus, R. (1982) 'Self-concept: the interplay of theory and methods', *Journal of Educational Psychology* 74: 3–17.

Strain, P.S., Kerr, M.M. and Ragland, E.U. (1981) 'The use of peer social initiations in the treatment of social withdrawal, in P.S. Strain (ed.) *The Utilization of Classroom Peers as Behavioral Change Agents*, New York: Plenum Press, pp. 101–28.

Veroff, J. (1969) 'Social comparison and the development of achievement motivation', in C.P. Smith (ed.) *Achievement-related Motives in Children*, New York: Russell Sage Foundation, pp. 46–101.

Weiner, B. (1985) 'An attributional theory of achievement motivation and emotion', *Psychological Review*, 92: 548–73.

Weiner, B., Graham, S., Taylor, S.E. and Meyer, W. (1983) 'Social cognition in the classroom', *Educational Psychologist* 18: 109–24.

Winne, P.H. (1985) 'Cognitive processing in the classroom', in T. Husen and T.N. Postlethwaite (eds) *The International Encyclopedia of Education*, vol. 2, Oxford, England: Pergamon Press, pp. 795–808.

Wylie, R.C. (1979) *The Self-Concept*, vol. 2 *Theory and Research on Selected Topics*, Lincoln, NE: University of Nebraska Press.

Chapter six

Motivation in the primary years

Colin Rogers

Editors' introduction

The following chapter offers a review of recent work on motivation and its development throughout the primary years. The last decade or so has seen a marked increase in interest among researchers in this topic, following from the development of a number of cognitive models. With their emphasis on the style of thinking characteristic of different individuals and the impact of the environment upon these styles, such theories lend themselves to further development within an educational context.

The work reviewed by Rogers in the following chapter draws attention to a number of key aspects of the individual child's experience of schooling by placing an emphasis on the qualitative aspects of the child's motivational responses. The articulation of the theories that are being developed can serve as a useful aid to teachers engaged in the complex task of developing their own responses to the pupil.

Some of the work discussed here also illustrates the ways in which motivational theory might be used to investigate some of the functions and modes of operation of the hidden curriculum, in this instance by investigating the child's acquisition of certain basic attitudes towards different parts of the school curriculum. It is important to note that Rogers's conclusion is that modes of presentation can have an effect on the development of these attitudes that is by no means unimportant when set beside the effects of the content of the curriculum area itself. Even with a totally prescribed curriculum, teacher action matters.

There are a number of links here that the reader ought to look out for. In particular the chapter by Schunk (Chapter 5) dealing with the self-concept will contain a number of close parallels. The reader might also like to consider some of the implications of the work reported here for the development of gender differences discussed by Croll and Moses (Chapter 11). The impact of various educational experiences might not always be immediately apparent, but remains instead, dependent upon the development of appropriate cognitive structures to set beside them.

Introduction

I suspect that for most primary school teachers a major perceived advantage of their work conditions, in comparison with their colleagues in the secondary sector, is that motivating their pupils is not seen to be a major problem. The typical primary school child is seen to be interested, lively and enthusiastic. As a primary teacher said to me recently:

> The great thing about kids at this age is that they *want* to learn. They do not have to be bullied or cajoled. They might not all succeed in learning as much as I would like them to, but the desire to try is there. I have always been put off of secondary work by the pupils. So many of them seem to have lost interest, they are detached, unco-operative. I don't know why that is, but it does seem to be a major difference.

Of course, it is clearly the case that there will exist considerable degrees of variation between pupils at the primary level in terms of their motivation. Some will be seen to be more strongly motivated than others, but the general style of the majority of pupils is seen to be a positive and desirable one. These impressions are substantially supported by research (Nicholls 1984; Stipeck 1984). There is a well-documented decline in motivation that seems to be related to the age of the child. Details of this will be examined later, but at this stage it is worth noting that some of the decline seems to stem from the child's increasing capacity to analyse the situation that he/she finds themselves to be in. However, it is also worth noting (Stipeck 1984) that the organization of schooling for children at different ages may in itself be partly responsible for these changes. However, before we can begin to examine the changes that may occur in motivation within a child over time, it is necessary to examine just what is meant by the term motivation itself.

Again it is useful to begin with some impressions of the ways in which teachers themselves might conceptualize motivation within their pupils. My own experience of talking to teachers about motivation leads to the conclusion that motivation in pupils is often assessed in quantitative terms and in terms of the degree to which a pupil matches up to the requirements of the school. Thus pupils are described as having a high level of motivation, or as lacking in motivation. The well-motivated pupil is described as being easy to work with, obedient, unlikely to be late or to miss periods of schooling. The poorly-motivated pupils are the ones who will be absent (in spirit if not in body), likely to be in and out of trouble on a regular basis and so on. Pen portraits of well-motivated pupils written by practising teachers could almost have been the result of a request to describe the ideal pupil from a teacher's point of view.

Recent developments in motivational theory go some way in challenging much, but not all, of the conceptions alluded to above (Ames 1984; Weiner 1986). These recent developments are varied in detail but share as a common reference point the view that the perceptions of the individual child are a key element in defining and determining the nature of the motivational process. Motivation becomes more than just a fixed disposition that some people are lucky to have more of than others and becomes instead an active and dynamic process. The outcomes of this process will have an effect upon the way in which the individual relates to the environment around him or her but will at the same time be affected by that environment. Indeed Ames (1987) has concluded from her work that any attempt to change the motivation of pupils must give prominence to the role played by the classroom environment. The implication is that motivation cannot simply be regarded as something that the pupils bring with them to school which, at best, the school might enhance and, at worst damage. Rather motivation is the result of interaction between pupil and school and all those elements that make up the child's environment. Motivation is created by the child's experience of school.

A qualitative approach to motivation

In the development of my own thinking about the nature of motivation during the primary years, the work of Atkinson (Atkinson 1964; Atkinson and Raynor 1978; Weiner 1980) has been influential. Atkinson and his colleagues have been concerned to develop a model of the motivation process that would ultimately allow precise predictions to be made about the type of behaviour that an individual might engage in, and how that behaviour results from changing motivational states. In many respects, the theory that has been produced is of greater relevance to the psychological laboratory than it is to the school classroom, and for this, and other reasons, it is not likely to be have a major, direct bearing upon classroom practice. However, Atkinson's work is important for the way in which it draws attention to the complexities inherent in motivational processes.

One particular aspect of Atkinson's work is relevant here. Atkinson has claimed that the motivational forces that direct behaviour in any particular situation are a combination of elements of that person's personality and elements of the situation. Thus we would expect to find fairly consistent differences between individuals across a range of situations, to the degree that those people have differing personalities. However, we would also expect to find variation in the responses of one person as he or she moved from one context to the next. Some people are generally well motivated, but even they will still appear to be less motivated in some situations than others.

More specifically, Atkinson argued that the relevant personality structure was itself complex and needed to be thought of in terms of a number of related components. For Atkinson, each individual is influenced by one aspect of personality concerned with their need to achieve success. The stronger this personality trait, the more eager a person will be to experience the fruits of success. The individual also brings a second personality trait, however, one that is concerned with failure, and the anxiety that this produces. The stronger this 'fear of failure', the less likely the person will be to engage in tasks where success, and therefore failure, is possible. The most certain way to avoid failure is never to attempt to achieve anything. While nothing being ventured leads to nothing being gained, it also ensures that we have no reason to fear not reaching our targets.

Any situation in which success or failure are possible, that is, any situation where one's performance may be measured (by oneself or others) against some standard of excellence, will thus give rise to conflict. To the degree that our behaviour is governed by the need to achieve success, we will wish to engage in the task in order to enhance the prospect of being successful. To the degree that our behaviour is governed by fear of failure we will wish to avoid the task in order to diminish the prospect of failure. Atkinson's work goes on to specify in detail how this conflict may be resolved and how the nature of the resolution will vary from person to person, and from situation to situation. There is not the space here to discuss these details, but the following should be noted. First, Atkinson is primarily concerned here with the workings of intrinsic motivation. He is concerned with the fear of failure and the desire to succeed in their own right. The failure may be a completely private one that no-one else will be interested in, but the fear of failure can still be invoked. The experience of failure can still provide a threat to our self-esteem and sense of competence. In many situations success and failure will also give rise to concerns with aspects that are extrinsic to the task itself. If we are successful others may reward us, others may hold us in higher esteem. If we are unsuccessful we may be punished or lose out on some of the material benefits of success. These concerns will also have an effect upon our behaviour, and there will be other elements of personality structure that will be relevant to these.

Second, Atkinson emphasizes the importance of attempting to understand the perspective of the individual whose behaviour is of interest to us. In order to avoid the worst consequences of failure, a pupil may chose to persist at tasks that are clearly far too difficult. Persistently undertaking and failing very difficult tasks is not educationally adaptive, but Atkinson draws our attention to the possibility that such behaviour may well be adaptive for the individual in that the very difficulty of the task provides the pupil with some protection against the personal consequences of failure. If the task is so difficult that failure has to be reasonably expected, then it cannot be too threatening. How much more threatening it would be to risk failure at a task that one ought to be able to succeed at. Avoiding challenging tasks by sticking at those that are very difficult, or very easy, may make little educational sense, but if one's concern is with avoiding failure, rather than with gaining success, it might appear to be a very sensible strategy to adopt. In short, it would be wrong to assume that the pupil whose behaviour does not seem to lend itself very readily to the requirements of the educational system is not motivated. Atkinson's work suggests that such a pupil may be very strongly motivated, but that their style of motivation is not one that the school system will find congenial.

Perceptions of success and failure

While Atkinson's work has drawn attention to the importance of analysing situations from the perspectives of the individuals within them, his theory does not really succeed in making available the means by which this might be readily done within the classroom context. To this extent the work of Bernard Weiner (1979, 1984, 1985, 1986) has already proved to be significant and is likely to continue to influence research into motivational processes within the classroom in the years to come. Weiner has developed a view of the nature of the dynamics of achievement motivation that is based upon one of the major theories within social psychology – attribution theory. As this perspective provides the basis for the research to be reported here later it will be attended to in some detail.

Attribution theory is generally regarded as having its origins in the work of Heider (1958) and in developments provided by people such as Kelley (1983) and Jones and Davis (1965). The basic concerns of the theory are to explore what has been referred to as 'naïve psychology', that is, the everyday rules of thumb that people use in order to make sense of the world around them and the people within it with whom they have to deal. The sense that we make of the world around us, and of our own role within it, will, according to attribution theorists, play a large part in determining our own behaviour.

The major assumption made by attribution theorists is that a central part of this process of making sense of the world involves causal attributions. A trivial example can readily illustrate the point. If, in a busy shopping street, someone steps on my foot, I will, of course, experience some degree of pain. But what else might I expect or do? If

I assume the action to have been unintended, caused merely by the crowded condition of the pavement, my reaction will be different than if I conclude that the passer-by had stepped on my foot with the deliberate intention of causing me harm. My own action (doing nothing in the first instance, running away before the other person gets really nasty in the second) will owe more to the attribution that I make about the cause of the other person's behaviour than it will to the action itself.

Weiner's analysis of achievement motivation has been based on very similar assumptions. In this case the event to be understood, in terms of making attributions for its causes, will be an instance of success and failure. As with the example above, the assumption is made that while the success or failure in itself will produce given reactions often of an emotional nature (Weiner 1985, 1986), it will be our understanding of the cause of that success or failure that will determine many other aspects of our response.

Clearly there are a number of causes to which a success or failure event could be attributed. A large number of causes have been identified by researchers (see, for example, Weiner 1985; Little 1985, and the research of the present author to be discussed below). Even allowing for the fact that two causes, ability and effort, generally emerge as the most frequently cited ones, at least among adult, western samples, the number of individual causes employed is large enough to make analysis of the effects of different types of attributions difficult without some attempt at categorization. Several such categorizations have been suggested and the reader who is interested in observing the development of these is advised to study the reviews published by Weiner himself (Weiner, *et al.* 1972; Weiner 1979, 1983, 1984 and 1985).

For present purposes it is sufficient to dwell on two causal dimensions that have been most frequently and most reliably identified, those of stability and locus. Stability refers to the degree to which the cause assumed to be responsible for an event is judged to have a consistent and repeatable effect over time. Ability and effort, the two most commonly-used individual causes, are judged to lie towards opposite ends of this dimension. Ability is a stable cause of success or failure. To the adult at least, one's ability is seen to be stable and enduring. If I perceive myself to lack a certain ability now, then I am likely to believe that I will lack that ability on later occasions. It is important to be clear as to the difference between ability and performance. As a possible cause of performance differences, ability is seen as something that underlies one's performance level. If one's performance level rises as the result of practice, this will be due to one's now being able to make greater use of the ability that one possesses. The underlying ability itself has not changed, just the degree that one is able to make use of it.

It follows from this that performances are seen to have been primarily the result of ability are performances that will themselves be expected to be repeated. On the other hand, performances that are seen to be the result of a less stable cause, such as effort, are believed to be less certain to be repeated as the cause itself is liable to fluctuation. This has been summarized by Weiner (1985: 559) as the expectancy principle.

Atkinson's work, briefly discussed above, indicated the importance of the expectations that an individual has for success and failure. An individual's response to a success or failure situation would be determined by their personality structure and the degree to which success was expected. For Weiner, expectations are also important and are seen to be directly related to the pattern of attributions that an individual makes. Take the individual who, for whatever reason, is likely to make attributions for success outcomes to the presence of high ability, and for failure outcomes to low effort. What might be the main consequences of this? Under these circumstances Weiner's theory would predict that each success would lead to higher expectations for further success as success is being attributed to a stable cause. Each instance of failure, however, has a less marked effect on expectations as these are attributed to unstable causes. Thus the overall trend is for increasing expectations of success. The individual becomes increasingly confident that engagement in achievement-related tasks will lead to success outcomes. Conversely, the individual who attributes success to high effort and failure to low ability will increasingly come to expect failure. For it is now each instance of failure that leads to increased expectations of the same, as these are the outcomes that are now assumed to have been caused by stable factors. Successes do not do much to alter the gloomy prognosis as they are seen to have been caused by an unstable factor, effort. Such an individual is therefore likely to come increasingly to expect to fail, and therefore to become less motivated to engage in achievement-related tasks.

While effort and ability differ in terms of their degree of stability, they are alike in that they are both seen to reside within the individual. In terms of the second major dimension they are both said to have an internal locus. Causes with an external locus are seen to reside outside of the individual concerned. One might believe that one has failed at a task because one lacks ability (an internally-located cause) or one might believe that the task set was too difficult (an externally-located cause). In many respects these two statements may appear very similar (they both seem to imply that the level of ability that one has was insufficient to perform a task of a given order of difficulty) but Weiner has claimed that there is an important psychological difference between them. The nature of this psychological difference has shown some development and change as the theory itself has developed, but is currently held to concern the degree to which one's feelings of self-esteem will be involved. Outcomes that are attributed to internally-located causes are more likely to affect one's feelings of self-esteem (positively for success and negatively for failure) than are outcomes attributed to externally-located causes. A failure due to task difficulty might be seen as one that is really somebody else's fault (the teacher should have known that I would not be able to perform this task and therefore should never have set it) while one that is internally attributed implies that the task was legitimate and that one's own inadequacies led to the failure.

There are other dimensions that have been examined and these too will have their effects. The dimensions of stability and locus are, however, the most important. As was again the case with Atkinson earlier, it is possible to identify styles that are more or less adaptive from the educational point of view. The individual who typically attributes success outcomes to stable and internal causes will both come to expect more success with greater confidence and to reap greater gains in terms of enhanced self-esteem from those successes. If they also attribute failures to unstable and external causes they can reduce the expectation of failure and minimize the negative impact that failure is always likely to have upon their self-esteem. The opposite pattern, attributing success to unstable and external causes, and failure to stable and internal ones will have the opposite effect. Here, one would come increasingly to expect failure and to suffer the more serious consequences for self-esteem.

The antecedents

Clearly if we were all able to choose our attributional patterns, in the light of the above argument, we would all choose to attribute our successes rather than our failures to stable and internal causes. This does not always happen. Attributions are made in accordance with a series of constraints that effectively determine the nature of the process. Again it is not the present intention to give anything like a full review of the research work that has been done here (for further details see Ames and Ames 1984; Ames and Ames 1985; Weiner 1986).

One obvious consideration is the past history of the individual. There is a clear connection between the degree to which an event is expected and the degree to which it is likely to be attributed to stable causes (Weiner 1986). Highly-expected events are more likely to be attributed to a stable cause than ones that were unexpected. Thus the pupil who expects success, through having had plenty of it in the past, is more likely to attribute that success to a stable cause. We have already seen that such an attribution is likely itself to have an effect on the further expectations that the individual has. Expecting success promotes attributions to stable causes, attributions to stable causes lead to increased expectations of success. Conversely, low expectations for success are likely to lead to attributions to unstable causes and these in turn further promote low expectations. In both cases cyclic processes are established which are set to become more deeply entrenched each time they operate, in the first case beneficently, in the second viciously.

Of more interest to the classroom teacher, however, is the idea that the pattern of attributions that a child makes, and the pattern of motivational behaviour that follows from this, can be influenced by the activities that take place within the school setting. One prime candidate for generating any such effects is likely to the classroom teacher.

A useful introduction to the idea that the teacher can influence the attributions made by the pupil is to be found in Bar-Tal (1982) and further information and ideas can be obtained in Dusek (1985). Bar-Tal's summary of the research shows that teachers can influence the attributions made by pupils via a number of different processes. The five major categories into which these processes can be classified are given by Bar-Tal as verbal appeals, instructions, reinforcements, verbal feedback and direct references to causality. Some of these are explored further below.

The impact of direct references to causality has been best demonstrated by a number of studies (Andrews and Debus 1978; Dweck 1985; Maehr and Kleiber 1987) that have sought to assess the effectiveness of attributional retraining. In these studies individual children are selected on the grounds that they have some motivational problem. The problem is then attended to by endeavouring to get the child to attribute their failures to a lack of effort rather than to a lack of ability. To the extent that a child can be persuaded to view a lack of effort rather than ability as the causes of their failure, motivational improvements are likely to take place. However, it is not yet entirely clear just how important the direct attempt at changing the attributions actually is. What does seem to be important is that the child comes to accept that increased effort can produce increased performance outcomes. Under some circumstances different experiences of success and failure might in themselves be sufficient to bring about this change in the child's perception.

Dweck is cited by Bar-Tal in support of his claim that the verbal appeals made by teachers can influence the attributions made by pupils. In this study (Dweck, *et al.* 1978) the interactions that took place between teacher and pupil were observed and these observations then related to the attributions that pupils made. In short, Dweck's claim was that in cases where the teacher relatively frequently criticized a pupil for non-academic aspects of their work (attendance, classroom behaviour, neatness, grooming, and so on), the pupils were in turn less likely to see ability as a prime cause for their failures. Dweck's argument has a compelling ring to it. Pupils who receive relatively little criticism for the non-academic aspects of their work are less likely to be able to find plausible reasons for their failures other than their lack of ability. What made many people attend to Dweck's study was the fact that she claimed that the patterns of teacher–pupil interactions she had observed to be related to attributions, were also related to the gender of the pupil. Girls were held to be less likely to receive criticism for the non-academic aspects of their work and therefore more likely to come to conclude that their relative lack of ability was responsible for any lack of success they experienced.

In spite of the compelling ring that Dweck's argument has, there is other evidence available that suggests that events may not always be as she suggests. Eccles and Wigfield (1985) draw attention to a number of studies that have failed to support aspects of the claim made by Dweck, often referring to the sex-linked nature of the process but also challenging the more basic link between teachers' actions and pupils' attributions. In their own review Eccles and Wigfield point to the possibility that more general aspects of classroom life may have an effect on the attributions made by pupils. Included in their considerations is the work of Cooper (Cooper and Good 1983; Cooper 1983, 1985). Cooper's interest in attributions arose from a concern with the teacher expectancy effect (Rogers 1982; Dusek 1985). Since the publication of *Pygmalion in the Classroom* by Rosenthal and Jacobson (1968), considerable interest has been shown by educationalists in the idea that teachers may, quite unwittingly, influence pupil performance, perhaps unfairly, by virtue of the expectations that the teachers hold for them. Cooper's concern was to attempt to identify some of the processes involved in the translation of expectations into pupil performance. Essentially Cooper has claimed that teachers are likely to want to exercise greater control over the interactions that they have with pupils considered to be of relatively low ability in order to be able to give greater assistance to those pupils. However, an unintended consequence of this apparently sensible policy decision is that the pupils concerned find it very difficult to initiate any meaningful interactions with the teachers and to exercise any substantial control over the work that they themselves do. This in turn can give rise to the pupils' coming to see themselves as lacking efficacy and therefore coming to make attributions that match this. They are increasingly more likely to take the view that their own efforts count for little and that it is their lack of ability, about which they can do virtually nothing, that causes their lack of progress. An important implication of Cooper's work, and one that requires further enquiry, is that a useful focus for the researchers' interests will be upon the conditions that are most likely to lead to teachers believing that they ought to exercise such control over certain of their pupils.

A developmental perspective

From the primary teacher's perspective, the role of attributions in motivation needs to be understood against a background of developmental change. Nicholls has been an important researcher in this respect (Nicholls 1984) and before going on to report details of some of my own primary based work I wish briefly to examine some of his claims.

It will be recalled that the causes of ability and effort are given a prominent role by Weiner and his colleagues in their consideration of the way in which attributions for success and failure might affect the behaviour of individuals. Ability and effort are held to have different effects from each other as they lie on different parts of the stability dimension. Ability is seen to be a relatively stable cause of success and failure while effort is relatively unstable. It is primarily for this reason that attributions of failure to lack of ability are likely to have more harmful effects than attributions to lack of effort. A lack of ability will be seen to be an enduring characteristic of oneself and will therefore continue to depress performance in the future. Effort levels can be increased, however, so present low attainment levels might also rise.

One of Nicholls' major claims is that young children do not necessarily share this view of the nature of ability. Nicholls has claimed that the child's conceptions of ability will progress though a number of stages from an initial starting point at which the relationship between cause and effect was not really understood at all. The child sees ability and effort as being essentially similar in that both are liable to change. By trying harder one can become cleverer. Effort is clearly seen as the major cause of success and failure. At this stage, as some of my own research shows, young children will assume that if everybody tries equally hard then everybody will do equally well. It is only later, sometimes not until the secondary years of schooling, that children come to acquire the adult view of ability as a fixed and enduring entity that acts to set an upper limit on what we can achieve. From this point onwards, attributions to ability for failure begin to carry with them the implication that future failure has to be expected. Prior to this point attributions to ability carry no particular threat.

For this and other reasons (see the collection edited by Nicholls 1984 for a much fuller discussion, and Rogers, 1989) the primary years are likely to be extremely important. It is during this period that a child's general motivational style will be developing. Ames (1986) draws attention to a distinction between children who are ego- or task-involved. Ego-involved children are more concerned with the consequences of success and failure for their own self-esteem (and are therefore likely to experience anxiety when confronted by difficulty), while task-involved children concentrate on the completion of the task itself. Dweck and her colleagues (Diener and Dweck 1978; Dweck and Wortman 1982) have made a similar distinction between children who are mastery oriented and those who experience helplessness. When experiencing difficulty with a task the former group are likely to assume that they are adopting an ineffective strategy, and will therefore begin to look for ways to improve it, while the latter, helpless children, assume that they lack the required ability and therefore begin to give up.

It is likely that these patterns of response, while general in nature, will not be completely uniform with respect to different types of tasks. Due to the beliefs that children have about the nature of certain tasks, a task or mastery-oriented approach may be more likely under some circumstances than others. Work of the present author to be reported below explores aspects of children's understanding of the nature of task requirements related to the curriculum area from which the task was drawn and the way in which it was presented.

Children's understanding of success and failure for different types of work

Children from the top infant and second and fourth year junior classes from two primary schools took part in the study. Each child was asked to nominate one classmate that they considered to perform at a higher level than themselves at each of three types of work and then one that performed at a lower level. Having done this each child was then asked to explain, in their own words, why these higher or lower performances were obtained. The children's responses were recorded and then later categorized.

The three types of work that the children were asked to think about were chosen so as to juxtapose curriculum area with style of presentation. Two curriculum areas were chosen, mathematics and reading. The two styles of presentation selected were tests based on classwork, and schemes in which each child would make his or her way through a series of graded activities at their own pace. Reading was represented only in the schemes version while mathematics was represented by both forms. Children therefore made their judgements in respect to three sets of work, (1) tests – mathematics tests taken by the whole class based on work done on a whole class basis, (2) mathematics schemes, (3) reading schemes. These recorded responses were categorized into a coding system that was based upon work reported by Little (1985). The final coding system contained twenty-one categories and these are summarized in the following Table.

Table 6.1 Brief definitions of categories used in the analysis of children's responses

Category	Brief definition
Performance ability	Description of observable outcomes: 'He's finished more books'.
Specific competence ability	A dispositional term like 'can' combined with a particular outcome: 'He's good at sums'.
General competence ability	An unspecified attribution to ability: 'She's brainy'.
Previous achievement	An explicit reference to earlier achievements: 'She did good work last year'.
Effort and interest	A conscious involvement in the work which is inferred from observed behaviour: 'He tries harder'.
Motivation	A statement of a future goal that explains the present event: 'He wants to be a computer programmer'.
Involuntary time spent	Differences in time spent on an activity that are beyond the individual's own control: 'She did more maths than me at her last school'.
Voluntary time spent	An observation of greater task involvement but without the inference of a psychological response as in the effort and interest category: 'He does more sums at home'.
Other persons	The effects of others' behaviour or attitudes: 'Her Mum's a teacher and helps her at home'.
Task difficulty	Performance variation is attributed to characteristics of the task not the person: 'He has easy problems to solve'.
Behaviour	Teacher-sanctioned behaviour: 'She copies'.
Age	Age differences explain success and failure: 'He's older than me'.
Facilities	Instruments and facilities available: 'He has a ruler'.
Mood and physical state	Temporary individual characteristics: 'She's happy'.
Domestic situation	Home circumstances: 'He comes from a happy home'.
Speed of working	Speed of working but lacking an attribution of ability: 'She is a fast worker'.
Sex stereotype	References to what boys and girls are supposed to be able to do: 'Boys can do maths'.
Personality	References to the other's personality characteristics: 'She's a nice girl'.
Chance	Random, probabilistic events: 'He just guessed right'.
Other's attributions	References to others' explanations for success/failure. No explicit reference is made as to how these might influence the behaviour of either party: 'Her Dad thinks that she is clever'.
Don't know/no reply	After more than one chance the child is unable to offer any account.

Note All examples can be considered to be responses to the question 'Why does he/she do better than you in maths?'

Children within this age range make use of a wide range of different types of explanations. It is not intended to make reference here to all of the points that could be made about the findings summarized in the Table, but rather to concentrate upon some of the more notable ones.

As children grow older they are more likely to make use of ability as an explanation of better or worse performance. In particular, the oldest children in the sample were relatively more likely to make use of references to abilities that relate to a specific skill ('He's got a mathematical brain') as well as to more general ability ('He's just very clever'). Both of the junior years were more likely to refer to effort as a cause of relative success and failure, while the second year juniors were particularly more likely to make reference to behaviour (in the sense of the other displaying or not displaying teacher-sanctioned behaviour, being well behaved being an explanation of success and poor behaviour an explanation for failure). The sex of the pupil made very little difference to the use of the different categories, which is generally in keeping with other findings (Covington and Omelich 1979) which suggest that sex differences in attributions may be relatively rare when the data has been collected in natural classroom settings. Perhaps surprisingly, the clearest tendency towards a difference between the sexes was found with the youngest children. This might suggest that as children have longer experience of the school system the effects of gender on attributions begin to decline.

The effects of school experience are certainly implicated in the findings related to the different curriculum areas and forms of work organization. Reading seemed to be understood as making different demands on the child than either version of mathematics. In particular, Voluntary Time Spent on the Task was seen as being implicated in both success and failure in reading. Children who did well at reading did so because they spent more time at it, and this was the time which they could have devoted to other activities ('In the evening she reads instead of playing out'). In addition to Voluntary Time Spent, a lack of a Specific Ability was also frequently used to explain a lack of success in reading. It is worth noting here that explanations for failure were generally not just the opposite of the explanations given for success.

While reading success was clearly seen to be related to the amount of practice that the children were judged to be getting, success in mathematics was more likely to be explained by reference to ability, provided the mathematics in question involved the use of tests. Children were particularly likely to use references to General Ability, together with references to Effort and Behaviour, to explain success in mathematics tests. Failure at these tests was seen as being particularly related to a lack of effort. When mathematics was approached via a scheme, however, the pattern of attributions seems to be quite different.

There was no apparent pattern of use for General Ability here when the children were attempting to explain relative success, while references to Specific Ability were conspicuous by their absence. Failure at work within a mathematics scheme was seen to be particularly associated with behaviour, specifically the presence of aspects of behaviour that would not be sanctioned by the teacher.

Conclusion

More extensive research along the lines of that described above needs to be carried out before any firm conclusions can be drawn. However, having given the usual caveat, it is worth briefly commentating on the implications that might be said to exist. The results of this research clearly seem to indicate that the developing attributions of primary school children are related to both the curriculum area that they are concerned with and the way in which that work is presented. As well as learning their mathematics and developing their skills as readers, children are also developing their understanding as to what it is that one needs to be in order to be able to perform well at these, and other, subjects. The way in which these attitudes develop is likely to be crucial in determining the pupil's later motivation for that subject. If mathematics comes to be seen as a subject that can only be succeeded at if one has a high level of general ability, it is likely to pose a bigger threat to self-esteem in the later years (see, for example, the work of Covington (1984) and his colleagues) and therefore more likely to be avoided. The results of the work reported above suggest that a child is more likely to develop such an attitude if his or her early experiences with mathematics involve frequent class-based tests than if they do not.

It would be clearly imprudent to advise teachers not to carry out such tests in the light of these few results, but the strategy involved in this research is one that could be sensibly taken up on a larger scale. Attribution theory provides a framework within which it is possible to analyse the motivational style of individual pupils. It is already clear that there are possibilities for remedial work on this basis (Maehr and Kleiber 1987). It is now also apparent that attribution theory can provide a means by which the effects of different classroom practices and the means by which classroom material is presented to children can also be assessed. Work has already been done on the effects of co-operative versus competitive learning (Ames 1984). Such systematic analysis may provide us with some further insights into the decline of motivation throughout the school years, and hopefully some suggestions as to how it might be arrested. More importantly, it also provides a means by which teachers are able to begin to analyse some of the effects of their own decisions regarding the ways in which classrooms are to function.

References

Ames, C. (1984) 'Competitive, cooperative and individualistic goal structures: a cognitive-motivational analysis', in R.E. Ames and C. Ames (eds) *Research on Motivation in Education*, vol. 1, *Student Motivation*, London: Academic Press.

Ames, C. (1986) 'Effective motivation: the contribution of the learning environment', in R.S. Feldman (1986) *The Social Psychology of Education: Current Research and Theory*, Cambridge: Cambridge University Press.

Ames C. (1987) 'The enhancement of student motivation', in M.L. Maehr and D.A. Kleiber (eds) *Advances in Motivation and Achievement*, vol. 5, *Enhancing Motivation*, Greenwich Conn.: JAI Press.

Ames, R.E. and Ames, C. (eds) (1984) *Research on Motivation in Education*, vol. 1, *Student Motivation*, London: Academic Press.

Ames, C. and Ames, R. (eds) (1985) *Research on Motivation in Education*, vol. 2, *The Classroom Milieu*, London: Academic Press.

Andrews, G.R. and Debus, R.L. (1978) 'Persistence and the causal perception of failure: modifying cognitive attributions', *Journal of Educational Psychology* 70: 154–66.

Atkinson, J. (1964) *An Introduction to Motivation*, Princeton, NJ: von Nostrand.

Atkinson, J. and Raynor, J. (1978) *Personality, Motivation and Achievement*, Washington, DC: Hemisphere.

Bar-Tal, D. (1982) 'The effect of teachers' behaviour on pupils' attributions: a review', in C. Antaki and C. Brewin (eds) *Attributions and Psychological Change*, London: Academic Press.

Cooper, H.M. (1983) 'Teacher expectation effects', in Bickman L. (ed.) *Applied Social Psychology Annual*, vol. 4, London: Sage, pp. 247–75.

Cooper, H.M. (1985) 'Models of teacher expectation communication', in J.B. Dusek, (ed.) *Teacher Expectancies*, London: Lawrence Erlbaum Associates.

Cooper, H.M. and Good, T. (1983) *Pygmalion Grows Up: Studies in the Expectation Communication Process*, New York: Longman.

Covington, M.V. (1984) 'The motive for self-worth', in R.E. Ames and C. Ames (eds) *Research on Motivation in Education*, vol. 1, *Student Motivation*, London: Academic Press.

Covington, M.V. and Omelich, C.L. (1979) 'Are causal attributions causal? A path analysis of the cognitive model of achievement motivation', *Journal of Personality and Social Psychology* 37: 1487–1504.

Diener, C. and Dweck, C. (1978) 'An analysis of learned helplessness: continuous changes in performance, strategy and achievement cognitions following failure', *Journal of Personality and Social Psychology* 36: 451–62.

Dusek, J.B. (ed.) (1985) *Teacher Expectancies*, London: Lawrence Erlbaum Associates.

Dweck, C. (1985) 'Intrinsic motivation, perceived control and self-evaluation maintenance: an achievement goal analysis', in C. Ames and R. Ames (eds) *Research on Motivation in Education*, vol. 2, *The Classroom Milieu*, London: Academic Press.

Dweck, C.S., Davidson, W., Nelson, S. and Enna, B. (1978) 'Sex differences in learned-helplessness'; II, The contingencies of evaluative feedback in the classroom'; III, 'An experimental analysis', *Developmental Psychology* 14: 268–76.

Dweck, C.S. and Wortman, C.B. (1982) 'Learned helplessness, anxiety and achievement motivation', in H.W. Krohne and L. Laux (eds) *Achievement, Stress and Anxiety*, London: Hemisphere Publishing Corporation.

Eccles, L. and Wigfield, A. (1985) 'Teacher expectations and student motivation', in J.B. Dusek (ed.) *Teacher Expectancies*, London: Lawrence Erlbaum Associates.

Heider, F. (1958) *The Psychology of Interpersonal Relations*, New York: Wiley.

Jones, E.E. and Davis, K.E. (1965) 'From acts to dispositions: the attribution process in person perception', in L. Berkowitz (ed.) *Advances in Experimental Social Psychology*, vol. 2, New York: Academic Press, pp. 219–66.

Kelley, H.H. (1983) 'Perceived causal structures', in J. Jaspars, F. Fincham and M. Hewstone *Attribution Theory and Research: Conceptual, Developmental and Social Dimensions*, London: Academic Press.

Little, A. (1985) 'The child's understanding of the causes of academic success and failure: a case study of British schoolchildren', *British Journal of Educational Psychology* 55: 11–23.

Maehr, M.L. and Kleiber, D.A. (eds) (1987) *Advances in Motivation and Achievement*, vol. 5, *Enhancing Motivation*, Greenwich, Conn.: JAI Press.

Nicholls, J. (ed.) (1984) *Advances in Motivation and Achievement*, vol. 3, *The Development of Achievement Motivation*, London: JAI Press.

Peterson, P.L., Wilkinson, L.C. and Halliman M.T. (1985) *The Social Context of Instruction: Group Organisation and Group Processes*, New York: Academic Press.

Rogers, C.G. (1982) *A Social Psychology of Schooling*, London: Routledge & Kegan Paul.

Rogers, C.G. (1989) 'Early admission. Early labelling', *British Journal of Educational Psychology*, Special Monograph Series, no. 4, *Early Childhood Education*.

Rosenthal, R. and Jacobson, L. (1968) *Pygmalion in the Classroom*, New York: Holt, Rinehart & Winston.

Stipek, D.J. (1984) 'Young children's performance expectations: logical analysis or wishful thinking', in J. Nicholls (ed.) *Advances in Motivation and Achievement*, vol. 3, *The Development of Achievement Motivation*. London: JAI Press.

Weiner, B. (1979) 'A theory of motivation for some classroom experiences', *Journal of Educational Psychology* 71: 3–25.

Weiner, B. (1980) *Human Motivation*, New York: Holt, Rinehart & Winston.

Weiner, B. (1983) 'Speculations regarding the role of affect in achievement-change programmes guided by attributional principles', in J.M. Levine and M.C. Wang, (eds) *Teacher and student perceptions: Implications for learning*, Hillsdale, NJ: Lawrence Erlbaum Associates.

Weiner, B. (1984) 'Principles for a theory of student motivation and their application within an attributional framework', in R.E. Ames and C. Ames (eds) *Research on Motivation in Education*, vol. 1, *Student Motivation*, London: Academic Press.

Weiner, B. (1985) 'An attributional theory of achievement motivation and emotion', *Psychological Review* 92: 548–73.

Weiner, B. (1986) *An Attributional Theory of Motivation and Emotion*, New York: Springer-Verlag.

Weiner, B., Frieze, I., Kukla, A., Reed, L., Rest, S. and Rosenbaum, R.M. (1972) 'Perceiving the causes of success and failure', in E.E. Jones, D.E. Kanouse, H.H. Kelley, R.E. Nisbett, S. Valins and B. Weiner (eds) *Attribution: Perceiving the Causes of Success and Failure*, New York: General Learning Press.

Chapter seven

Social development of the child and the promotion of autonomy in the classroom

Peter Kutnick

Editors' introduction

'Social development of the child and the promotion of autonomy in the classroom' combines two separate issues and opens various scenarios through which teachers may more effectively structure the learning context of their classrooms. The issues are not separate from one another. Theories of social development describe the potential and experiences for the behaviour and understanding displayed by children. Autonomy describes various expectations of the 'classroom performance' of the primary pupil and ways in which these expectations may be met.

This chapter explores the relational context of the classroom and the effects (on relationships) of various teaching strategies. This chapter intends to dispel as myth that autonomy is a simple or easily achievable classroom product. If autonomy is described as self-directed pupilhood, how is that self-direction achieved? It cannot arise from purely individualized instruction, for studies show that this is most likely to lead to pupil dependence on the teacher. Rather the self is seen as a social product, developed through diverse relationships with adults and peers. The actual relationships may vary in quantity and quality. The focus here is on quality, and it is the closeness engendered in relationships with teachers and classroom peers that encourage the possibility of autonomy.

In reviewing a number of classroom and experimental studies, this chapter identifies various uses of autonomy and the particular types of relationships that they are based upon. All of the studies show that the teacher is in a central role in structuring the experiences that are offered to pupils. Structuring of experience includes the traditional academic presentation of learning materials and the learning groups in which children participate. Based on earlier chapters in this volume, present discussions further explore classroom groups, social interaction and the developing child. The chapter leads into specific consideration (in chapters of Wright (Chapter 8) and Slavin (Chapter 13) of the roles and relationships that can be structured between teacher and pupils and provides a rationale for the integrated use of co-operative learning techniques.

Introduction

This chapter considers the potential of the child from a social developmental perspective and questions how this development may be encouraged in the primary school classroom. Most readers will have considered overt stages of cognitive development (in their various guises of Piagetian, Brunerian and other schemes) which provides a broad backdrop for this discussion. This chapter will review major features in the child's social development and definitions of autonomy will be described. Observational and experimental research into the real world of classrooms will then be drawn upon to question whether and how classroom context promotes social development and autonomy. The discussion concludes by reviewing a number of ways in which the classroom can be structured for autonomy. The heart of the argument considers the teacher's role in a tightly-constrained educational system; whether a child-centred approach is self-contradictory, and if innovations such as co-operative learning should be integrated into the classroom.

Autonomy: movement away from simple models

For many years it has been acknowledged that the role of primary education should include (see DES 1985) cognitive, social and emotional aspects. In providing such an education for children, primary schools must encourage the psychological realities of autonomy and competence coincidently with the development of knowledge and understanding in their pupils. These realities may be identified simply as promoting the child's realization that they are each separate and individual units (a relative autonomy from others), and that they are able to master tool, object, word usage and conceptualization of knowledge. In a simplistic sense, teachers and psychologists would agree that autonomy and primary education are intertwined and their duty towards children is to find (and use) a concept of motivation which will allow the development of cognitive, social and emotional skills while encouraging the child to undertake these skills as an individual and self-guided unit.

There is always a 'but' to add to simple definition agreements; and this is where the role of social psychology of primary schools becomes more fully explained. Within this world of primary education and development of autonomy we acknowledge that the relationships engendered in schools and the social context of the classroom define how development will take place. On one hand, we can name a number of theories and exhort that teachers naively adhere to them if autonomy is to be successfully promoted. On the other hand teachers and classroom researchers find autonomy development hindered by pupil dependence, ineffective social relationships in groups and a central focus on practical aspects of the core curriculum in primary classrooms. Even in the post-Plowden years with the design of numerous curricula to promote individual autonomy, the likelihood of autonomy actually taking place is limited by the context and structure of intellectual and social relations in the classroom (see Simon 1981).

Any consideration of autonomy in primary schools must ask what is actually meant by autonomy and how this definition may be put into practice. Theories and approaches to autonomy are based on various ideas of the developing child. The simple expectation that children will become autonomous by adhering to any (developmentally-oriented) curriculum is quickly dispelled when we look at the various definitions of autonomy in the literature; especially those generated in psychology and sociology.

Psychological theories include consideration of 'learning' and 'cognitive development'. Autonomy, as explained in 'learning' theory, identifies children's understanding as the result of a system of positive or negative sanctions (or rewards) that are administered in co-ordination with some event undertaken by the child. Both teachers and peers are sources of rewards and serve as models for children. Autonomy can be said to take place when the child has undergone a succession of positive rewards (designed to progressively encourage the individual) so that children may provide their own reward for learning. Learning theorists find it difficult to explain how the necessary movement from an 'external' reward (provided by the teacher) to an autonomous state whereby the child can undertake and regulate an 'internal' system for rewards can be encouraged. Principles of reinforcement are evident in a number of classroom-based teaching approaches (see Deci, Nezlek and Sheinman 1981), where teachers reward information-oriented and self-controlled behaviours by pupils; and there are successful results within the strict experimental parameters of these studies. An alternative conceptualization of autonomy is based upon an understanding of 'cognitive development' derived from theorists such as Piaget (see Piaget 1971). This approach identifies a series of stages through which the child's intellect may progress (and may appear to assume children to be autonomous if the stage of formal operations is achieved). The stage approach has been used in many curricula and individualized teaching techniques currently used in science, mathematics and other areas in primary schools. This understanding of autonomy as intellectual development has been under much criticism lately, a criticism which forces the realization that cognitive development takes place in a social relationship context, and learning and autonomy are embedded in the experiences offered to the child (see Kutnick 1988). A cognitive developmental view of autonomy would encourage the child into a position of sufficient intellectual and social relational skills where the motivation to learn and understand would come from within the individual and would be unconstrained by lack of immediate information and personnel around the child (the child is not purely dependent on the teacher for support and knowledge). A rough approximation of the progression towards autonomy identified by psychologists is present in Table 7.1.

Table 7.1 Development of social relationships, with logical-mathematical, moral and social perspective (developmental) parallels

Social relationships	Logical-mathematical	Moral	Social perspective
0. Reflex behaviour/neonatal capacities	Sensori-motor	Autistic	
1. Sensori-motor-affective schemes			Egocentric
2. Development of dependent relationship	Pre-operational	Heteronomous	
3. Early rule/authority application, reflective egocentric understanding			
4. Concrete and rational rule/ authority application; self-reflective questioning	Concrete operational	Co-operative	
5. Involvement with peers, reflective mutual social development			Socio-centric
6. Reflective ability to balance and apply constraining and/or co-operative principles	Formal operational	Autonomous	

Source Kutnick, 1988: 53.

Children's initial development moves socially and intellectually away from dependence on people and objects. Development progresses to include relations with other adults (teachers) and peers which facilitate a more critical appreciation of events around the child, thus encouraging autonomous as opposed to dependence learning.

Apart from the psychological theories, a range of social approaches to autonomy and development is evident. Social approaches include functional behaviours and the description of interactional processes leading to autonomy (or its inhibition). Functional approaches identify an end-product (as fitting into society) and establish patterns of action within the school to produce that end-product. On the surface, functional approaches are closely aligned to learning theories and may disguise serious flaws in promoting autonomy. In identifying an end-product, functional approaches demand a conformity to social standards set by school authority. These standards may not include 'self-direction' by the pupil if it conflicts with teacher and school requirements. Phenomenological approaches observe actual happenings in the classroom; the establishment of rules, rituals and negotiations that take place between interactors in the classroom. Information is provided concerning abilities of children, teachers and variations in the way individuals act. Interactional approaches include the understanding that: intellectual as well as social developments take place in a social environment, interactors bring particular qualities to the environment, and that interactions and context can be so structured as to promote particular variations in the development of autonomy.

Both psychological and social approaches present a range of autonomy models; conformity to a set standard (by teacher or school system) or an active involvement in the learning context. Any simple assumption that unplanned participation in the classroom will lead to autonomy should be quickly quashed. Current psychological theories have shown that the child is more than an 'empty jug' or 'tabula rasa'. The development of competence leading to autonomy must take place in a planned context (by the teacher) and should not be left to chance. Teachers' desire for effective learning may be combined with the functional need to operate in an overcrowded classroom and an individualized conceptualization of learning, although a developmental/ interactional view of autonomy occurring through processes of the classroom is at odds with a functional approach. Autonomy is neither simple nor easy to implement.

Social developments in childhood, a background for autonomy

Children are born into a number of social relationships and demonstrate many competencies with objects and people that surround them. The amount and type of experience that they are offered structures children's understanding of the world and creates the possibility for further development. It should be accepted, as an understatement, that all early development of the child takes place in or near the presence of other people (usually parents or caregivers in development terminology). It is a misconception to assume that a child's development can take place in isolation or that development is so purely 'cognitive' that it is not affected by the presence of others and the quality of cultural experiences offered at home or in society.

Social development is concerned with the stimulating and expanding world around the child through social interactions. Initially, some qualifications should be identified. It is only common sense to acknowledge that differences may exist between the potential for interaction and understanding, and the reality of that interaction and understanding taking place (which is affected by the amount, type and quality of experience offered to the child). Many social relationships within which the child interacts are 'close' relationships of love and affection; providing security to participate in the trial and error process of development without having to 'do it right'. Close relationships are, thus, different from general social relationships of acquaintance or loose friendship. What the child derives from close interactions is most basic to both intellectual (cognitive) and social development – movement away from an egocentrically dominated world (see Furth 1980). Realization that others may have a different point of view from oneself and the ability to adjust to this moves the child into a 'social-centric' world. Thus, knowledge is seen as a social process (as observed and described by Edwards and Mercer 1987) resulting from actions with others; development is not just simple discovery by the child, it is a discourse between the child and others. Others, with whom the child interacts and develops close relationships, are usually archetypically termed as adult and peer. Each of the archetypes has a particular quality of relationship with the child; yet the child needs to develop quality relationships with both types to provide a background for autonomy (see Youniss 1980). Shantz (1982) states that the child's main social responsibility in development is to construct a workable social theory that will allow her/him to participate in the actual social environment.

The world of adults

The child's relationship with adults is obviously the first relationship to develop and the most long-lasting. This relationship lays the background for future 'sociability' and establishes the basis for acceptance of and reaction to authority (facilitating relationships with teachers, social conventions and early moral development). Classically, adults have been seen as the vital and only link between the child and society, although this view seriously belittles the potential relationship with peers (according to Youniss 1980). In their position as adults, parents have been shown to structure the child's social, emotional and cognitive experiences. Within this relationship the child is socialized into an expected social conformity.

Probably the best example of the experience offered by parents is 'attachment'. Attachment is 'an affectional tie that one person forms between himself and another specific one – a tie that binds together in space and endures over time', according to Ainsworth *et al.* (1974). The child's realization of attachment usually occurs between 9 and 12 months of age. The child, who previously was quite settled in the presence and care of many others, begins to show a distinct preference for one or very few individuals. This tie to particular others has been preceded by a quality relationship of care and stimulation between the child and caregiver (usually parent or very near relative). While occurring early in life, the existence of attachment will affect the child's later cognitive and social development. Ainsworth has found that children with the most secure attachment relationships (measured by the amount of acceptance, sensitivity and co-operation as opposed to rejection, insensitivity and interference between child and caregiver) are more likely to explore unfamiliar surroundings and objects than children with poor attachment. Exploration and curiosity lead to cognitive stimulation and development of understanding. Upon achieving school age, children with good attachment are more competent at exploring their new environments and more effective in their interactions with teachers and peers (see Waters and Srouf 1983). Affection in attachment also takes place with an adult who is bigger than the child and who controls resources (food, comfort and stimulation). Children's understanding is parentally dominated by regularities such as 'knowing' what is right and wrong, when to get up and go to bed, and assertion of gender roles within the home. Attachment is thus a relationship of hierarchical authority and love. The regularities of behaviour leading to attachment co-occur with authority and rule interactions. Piaget (1932a) describes this social regularity as introducing a 'morality of constraint' to the child; the basis for further experiences with rules and others which should, eventually, lead to autonomy.

In their way, parents (or caregivers) provide the social experience upon which children are able to form their understanding of rules, conventions, morality, and ways to interact with others. Obviously variations in the way that parents interact with their children will affect future behaviours displayed by the child. Research by Baumrind (1971) has shown that the authority style adopted by the parent will affect the child's ability to control their own behaviour and ability to initiate and follow through activities in the nursery school (for example, parents who set, explained and negotiated rules tended to have children best adapted to starting school). And children, for their part, will show variations in the way that they interact with the authority situation. One type of interaction is known as dependence/independence proneness – whereby children may demonstrate greater or lesser need for teacher direction, approval and feedback. Children's affiliation to adults (as opposed to peers) may also be determined by birth order, with first-born and only children having a stronger tie to adults than later born children.

Parents or caregivers play a major role in the stimulation of thought and understanding for the nursery-aged child according to Tizard and Hughes (1984). Home-based relationships allow the child to be interacted with as an individual and to participate in quality conversations about sequences of household events, mathematical and logic skills. Dissimilarly, children in nursery schools are often conversed with (by teachers) in the presence of other children. Teacher participation is often limited to initiating conversations and giving signs of approval or disapproval before being drawn into other conversations. Parents stimulate the child's activity by providing intensive discourse with their children concerning 'embedded' concepts (that are real and meaningful rather than abstract).

Underlying the world of adults is the constant presentation of a hierarchical relationship, whether in power-subordination, expert–novice, knower–seeker. The relationship with adults is an obvious model for the child's entry into primary school, in which the teacher is focused upon as a source of security and attachment while structuring the classroom environment, rules and knowledge for the child. This hierarchical relationship explains only part of the child's social development and only one step towards autonomy.

The world of peers

Relationships with peers have been noted for encouraging co-operation and close relationships of intimacy and mutuality. Peers also have been described as providing models to be copied, social reinforcement of approved behaviour and educational tutors for one another (according to Field 1981). Older-aged peers have been found to teach 'socialized' behaviour of manners, norms and dominance hierarchies to younger children (see Hartup 1978). Studies of early infancy have found that children will prefer to look at and interact with one another (as opposed to adults) from as young as two months. If allowed opportunities to consistently interact with a particular peer, evidence of friendship has been found as early as 12 months (see Vandell and Mueller 1980). Peers can help overcome fear of strangers. There have been cases in which peers form attachments with one another in preference to adults (see Freud and Dann 1951).

The world of peers presents two distinct features:

1. They engage in preparation for adult life. Children practise classic patterns of dominance and subordination (leader and follower games) and sex-role differences (around Wendy houses and play

hospitals). They replicate adult behaviour in play; a non-threatening interaction where children do not have to be absolutely correct and will often switch roles between themselves. They participate in these activities with some intensity but invariably with a smile on their faces (see work on rough-and-tumble play by Blurton-Jones 1976).

2. Peer activity is distinctive from adult behaviour. Children, especially young children, are able to compare themselves with one another and find similarity of size, strength and experience. Youniss (1980) notes that sharing goods and pleasurable activities amongst peers can lead to a sharing of private thoughts and feelings, and development of a sense of mutual consideration. This ability to be 'the same as' is the basis for Piaget's (1932a) assertion that only peers can develop the 'morality of co-operation'; an ability to consider other children's points of view and come to joint decisions. The morality of co-operation necessitates movement beyond an egocentric world to one of 'sociocentrism' (rules can be adapted and changed to maintain play). Children as young as 4 and 5 can resolve social conflicts and help one another if they are in a stable social group according to Strayer (1980). Pullantz and Gottman (1981) found that antisocial children can learn how to become accepted by their peers by observing and adopting appropriate strategies used by other peers. Recent research in the UK has found that children with pre-school experience are more socially and cognitively advanced than children without preschool experience, as measured at the end of primary schooling (see Osborne and Millbank 1985).

The potential for various relationships (with social and intellectual outcomes) does not necessarily mean that enhanced social awareness and cognitive development will come to fruition simply by being placed in the presence of peers. Readers with experience of young children may not find (the ideal of) co-operative activity occurring frequently. Conflicts of possession and current friendship are more likely to occur in the intensity of peer interactions. Conflicts can cause disruption in relationships between peers and tend to spill over into classroom disruption. Conflicts have two divergent results:

1. Antagonism between children may lead to constant changes of friends, the possibility of fights and general disruption.
2. On the other hand, conflicting perspectives between peers lead to argumentation or discourse, the resolve of which enhances social and intellectual understanding (see Edwards and Mercer 1987).

Piaget (1932b) states:

If we watch the child when he is not with adults...we will see him develop a social life with other children, and we will notice that while he is developing socially he is also intellectually acquiring the power of thought and criticism.

Recent cognitive experiments (see Bearison *et al.* 1986) have paired non-conserving peers and assigned them a conservation task. The result was much discussion leading to intellectual movement originally beyond the capability of either of the peers.

Interaction between peers potentially lays the background for cognitive development. But not all relationships between peers will promote cognitive development or even friendship. There will be variation between childrens' ability to get on with one another. Peer relations such as friendship may be inhibited by classic social psychological constraints of proximity (availability of children to interact with each other), similarity (such as sex, race, ability and age distinctiveness), and quality of play objects (single child toys will encourage competition while two child toys encourage co-operation). The actual occurrence and role that peers can play will be sharply defined by the society and structured interactions in which they are allowed to participate (see Kutnick 1988, for further discussion).

Bringing together the social developmental worlds of adults and peers two final points can be made. First, the reader is reminded that human thought and understanding are based in social relations and communication, and that knowledge is constructed through joint activity and discourse (from Edwards and Mercer 1987). Adults and peers each have unique and overlapping contributions to make to this development. A second point demonstrates the unique contributions from adult and peer, and provides a diagrammatic display of the development of autonomy. Figure 7.1 displays the social authority characteristics and interpersonal relations generated in relationships with adults and peers. The figure is an adaptation of Piaget's research concerning moral development. It represents the contributions of constraint and co-operation applied to relations with adults and peers, and how the combined aspects of authority and relationships are essential bases for the development of autonomy. In this diagram the importance of adults in generating an understanding of 'constraint' and peers in 'co-operation' is stressed as well as the balance between co-operation and constraint. The balance is fundamental for autonomy, where the child has the initiative and freedom to interact fully with adults and peers without being dominated by either.

Figure 7.1 Reinterpretation of Piaget's stages of moral development as a stair-like matrix

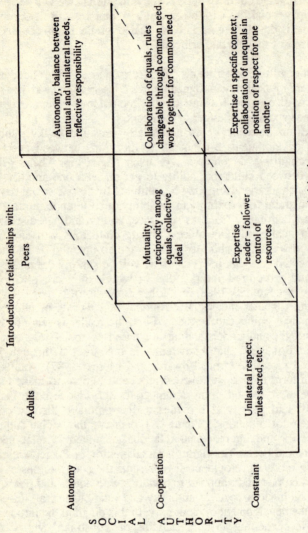

Introduction of relationships with:

	Adults	Peers	
Autonomy			Autonomy, balance between mutual and unilateral needs, reflective responsibility
Co-operation		Mutuality, reciprocity among equals, collective ideal	Collaboration of equals, rules changeable through common need, work together for common need
Constraint	Unilateral respect, rules sacred, etc.	Expertise leader – follower control of resources	Expertise in specific context, collaboration of unequals in position of respect for one another

SOCIAL AUTHORITY

Social and logical-mathematical development

Source Kutnick, 1988: 85.

Social developmental potential: points concerning action and structure

The social worlds provided by adults and peers describe the potential for development and question what is necessary to bring that potential about. The potential for social development is often at odds with actual occurrence in the child's social world. Previously it was found that peers working together (co-operatively) are able to promote conservation skills in advance of individual skill levels (see Perret-Clermont 1980; Bearison *et al.* 1986; and others). It would be ideal if children's groupings in primary schools supported this development. Instead of cognitive potential being enhanced, pupil groups often show children working only for themselves or competing with one another for limited resources or toys. While there may be potential for co-operation amongst children, they do not usually take advantage of it (in western societies). Obviously other societies whose life practices are dependent on co-operation will use it with greater frequency (as the kibbutz in Israel, and less-developed, and agrarian societies, according to Shapira and Madsen 1969 and Whiting and Whiting, 1975).

A distinction between general social and close relationships is vital for the consideration of co-operation, learning and autonomy. While children generally need social interaction, their most meaningful learning and development takes place in close relationships. Closeness is associated with affectional ties, mutuality, sensitivity and security between the child and specific others. This closeness is generally characteristic of the attachment relationship with parents and transfers to teachers in the early stages of primary school. Closeness amongst peers is not generally found until the child is able to achieve mutuality and intimacy with a 'best friend' (which may not take place until adolescence, according to Youniss 1980) unless teachers make an active effort to promote closeness by structuring co-operative learning actions (see Slavin in this volume) or some form of trust exercises (see Kutnick and Brees 1982). If the developmental route to autonomy found in Figure 7.2 is to be followed, children must be allowed to experience closeness with peers as well as adults. This experience of closeness should take place as early as possible in their school careers.

In promoting autonomy we must consider that the development of thought and the actions in which children participate are intimately related. Piaget has described this relationship as the 'law of conscious realization'. Children entering the primary school (pre-operatively) need to involve themselves in activities and repeat this involvement over and again before they come to realize that their knowledge and behaviour is changing. There are many examples of the constant activity of water play (leading to conservation of liquid) and social play (leading to shared understanding of rules and co-operation) that can be cited; the child must be fully involved in these activities. Children who are more able to use their reflexive (concrete) thought are able to come to an immediate understanding of that activity – but they still need to participate in action before coming to understanding. As children 'learn' from the actions in which they participate, teachers much consider that the structuring of these actions is an essential practice. It is primarily the experience of particular activities and with whom/how they are undertaken that are the bases for the child's learning and development. Jerome Bruner (1986), citing research by Vygotsky (1978), speaks of 'scaffolding' intellectual and social experience for children by the teacher. Scaffolding may appear a complex term, but it graphically represents the need to structure activities in the classroom for types of participation (whether discourses between child and teacher or between peers). On the social developmental side, we find that children involved in enjoyable activities tend to form friendships with their co-participants (promixity leading to similarity). Any grouping established for children's participation in events should be considered critically. Children will become attached to groups (especially classroom ability-based groups established by teacher) in which they act and tend to disassociate themselves from other groups who are perceived as 'different' from themselves (see Tajfel 1978). Action and structure are key elements in bringing about social and cognitive development.

To what extent is social development catered for in the classroom?

Recommendations from the Plowden Report (1967) have been cited as providing legitimacy for a more child-centred primary education with emphasis on social development, individualized curricula and mixed ability classroom groups. However, recent research on classroom activity finds that child-centred, social development is rare. To explain the rarity of the social developmental classroom (with implications for autonomy) let us question to what extent social development has occurred in the classroom and how it may be creatively integrated. Reviewing social development and autonomy-inducing aspects of educational research is a complex task. There are two distinct types of study that can be cited, with little or no overlap between them. The studies may be termed 'naturalistic' and 'experimental'. These studies attempt to describe the educational experiences of a number of classrooms or set out to prove a particular point respectively.

Naturalistic

Naturalistic studies of the classroom provide a holistic picture of inter-actions and educational outcomes that characterize the behaviour of teachers and pupils. (These studies are mainly labelled as 'process – product' in that they do not fully account for the backgrounds of teacher and pupils or the broad context of the school.) In focusing on classroom interactions and their outcomes, some studies have considered whether child-centred or progressive teaching methods promote better outcomes than traditional methods. Other studies simply provide a general picture of the classroom and explain certain outcomes by the classroom regime. In both types of study classroom organization is a central concern, and better organized classrooms correlate with higher outcome for the pupil. Regarding social development, we can ask three questions: Does child centredness make a difference? Do teacher actions actually promote a progressive education? And do children actually display behaviour that will promote their social and autonomous development? Insights into these questions are provided by the following:

1. Bennett (1976) published results purporting that traditional classrooms produced better academic results than informal and mixed-style classrooms (although the highest scoring classroom happened to be the most progressive). Bennett's results caused much controversy, leading to one clear conclu-sion – 'the central factor emerging from this study is that a degree of teacher direction is necessary, and that this direc-tion needs to be carefully planned, and that the learning experiences provided need to be clearly sequenced and structured' (Bennett 1976: 162).

2. The ORACLE team (see Galton, *et al.* 1980) challenged Bennett's assertion that a formal teaching style produced better results than an informal style. They observed teacher and pupil behaviour in junior school classrooms. None of the teaching styles that they observed could be labelled child centred. In the main, pupils were taught traditional subjects by traditional (didactic control) methods. Pupils, for their part, undertook their 'learning' as an individualized activity – even though they were placed in groups; pupils did not co-operative with peers.

3. A similar lack of social cohesion and co-operation was described in infant classrooms by Bennett (Bennett *et al.* 1984). In these classrooms teachers mainly adopted an indiv-idualized approach to learning and relied on individualized

curricula to encourage development. They found that the pupils responded to the curricula, although when a problem arose children had to rely on the teacher for support, direction, and remedial attention. Large queues build up around the teachers' desk. Teachers took on a functional and controlling role to get through the number of questions and maintain order in the classroom. Guidance and diagnosis by the teacher became subverted by pupil dependence and the need to organize the classroom.

4. Interactions in the classroom do provide the structure for relationships and what comes to be known by pupils. Kutnick (1983) observed teacher and pupil behaviour in infant and junior schools and questioned children about teachers and classrooms. Evidence of the 'law of conscious realization' was a main finding; with infants interacting with their teachers and slowly coming to describe teachers by the learning and caring activities that they participated in. In addition to expected learning activities of the classroom, juniors showed increased interaction with peers. They were warned by teachers that 'learning' was not taking place while they 'chatted' to peers. Correspondingly, juniors described their teachers as having both learning and control responsibilities in the classroom.

5. A final study shows that children may not naturally display co-operation in the classroom, but they are very aware of social processes. Amongst many results cited, Pollard (1985) found that pupils often worked in groups in class and developed group-based friendships. The groups, whether teacher appointed or child preferred, tended to be based on ability, with children quickly discovering a classroom hierarchy of ability and choosing friend/groups on a basis of perceived similarity to one's own ability.

Where does naturalistic research lead? It informs us that many primary school teachers tend to use traditional control methods, focusing on children's behaviour rather than stimulating cognitive aspects of pupil development. Children learn from what is actually done in the classroom. While they may be placed in groups in an informal setting, they take little responsibility or control over their own learning. In classroom learning, children tend to approach problems as individuals; they do not make use of peers or co-operation. They depend on the teacher to resolve intellectual and social problems.

Experimental

Experimental studies ask that a class be taught by a specific method (usually to enhance child autonomy), and compare performance to a parallel class that has been taught by traditional methods. The most frequently cited studies have been undertaken in the United States, and assume that children who demonstrate independence in the classroom will learn more (conceptually) and achieve better academic results. In these studies independence is equated to autonomy and autonomy is achieved through the (behaviourist) reinforcement of some learning behaviours in preference to other behaviours. In studies undertaken in elementary schools, results tend to confirm the development of autonomy and neglect to account for academic achievement. Examples of this research include:

1. Deci, *et al.* (1981) instructed experimental teachers to use more autonomy-oriented behaviour (use of rewards to promote an information-oriented classroom rather than a control orientation). They found pupils increased on measures of personal responsibility and self-control in these classrooms.

2. Ryan and Grolnick (1986) studied children's self-perception of control, and found those who felt responsible for their own behaviour (as opposed to those who felt their behaviour) was controlled by teachers) were more likely to have positive concepts of self-worth and an ability to demonstrate cognitive competence than other pupils.

3. Grolnick and Ryan (1987) withdrew children from their classrooms, provided them with one of three types of teaching sessions (traditional, structured/child-centred and unstructured), and tested the children for rote learning, conceptual learning and interest. Results showed more rote learning took place with traditional methods. More interest, conceptual learning and longevity of learning took place in the structured and unstructured sessions.

These studies conclude that the greater control pupils feel they have over their own learning (greater 'autonomy') the greater are their feelings of self-worth and conceptual learning. The studies do not question the extent to which conceptual learning should dominate the classroom nor do they provide any but the simplest behavioural definitions of autonomy.

As a result of the above studies, two divergent recommendations for a socially-structured classroom can be made:

1. The traditional classroom may be the most effective situation for promoting 'learning'. Croll and Moses' (1988) observations of junior classrooms found that whole class instruction provided the greatest amount of control for the teacher, and teachers were able to use this for effective questioning. Pupils, correspondingly, spent more 'time on task' (which correlates to classroom learning).

2. An alternative recommendation comes from Ingram and Worrell (1987), who experimentally introduced negotiation and pupil self-determination (an individualized form of autonomy) into a primary classroom. They found that pupils were capable of sharing responsibility and providing effective intellectual opportunity/challenge for learning without autonomy being reduced to teacher dependence.

The divergent recommendations are each supported by different areas of classroom and psychological literature: the traditional, well-ordered classroom calls for a 'functionally' well-behaved pupil with a conformist definition of autonomy; the negotiating classroom allows for discussion, argumentation and cognitive conflict supported in a cognitive definition of autonomy. One's definition of learning outcome and autonomy must be carefully considered before choosing classroom structure.

Promoting social development and autonomy in the classroom

The traditional view

From the previous discussion we find that the well-ordered, traditional classroom is able to support academic and creative learning, at least to a similar extent of progressive classrooms. Traditional classrooms, for the most part, are happy places where children listen to and work with the teacher. Teacher control may be didactic, but this disguises a range of authority types. Teacher authority may span authoritarian, authoritative and permissive types (similar to parental authority types found by Baumrind 1971), and children tend to respond most positively to the authoritative style (where they can negotiate and assume some responsibility). This authority style is mirrored in children's preference for teachers who are 'firm, but fair' and 'serious, but human' (see (Nash 1973; Pollard 1985). Children appear to feel secure and able to learn in the traditional but caring classroom. Pupil preference for a particular style of teacher will be based on a range of experiences that they have been offered in their schooling, and few pupils will have actually experienced the progressive alternative. We are unable to say what pupils think of progressive teachers or whether this style is preferred. It should be noted that within the traditional classroom there are a number of practices which may inhibit social development. Inhibition of social and autonomous development may be a result of individualization in learning (cutting the child off from the cognitive enhancing potential of peer interaction), ineffective groupwork (with dependence on the teacher for direction and support), generation of classroom hierarchies and cliques (differentiating pupils from one another), and the perception that the responsibility for learning is solely controlled by the teacher. Dependence-based learning has been 'effective' in the past and still works today; especially in areas of rote learning. In these circumstances, teachers who care, communicate well, establish organized and sequential practice, and set good examples, will be most effective with their pupils.

Alternative views

Moving away from the traditional classroom, we note that the sharing of planning and decision-making by teacher and pupil will increase feelings of involvement by pupils. One view of classroom-based autonomy calls for greater pupil involvement. Greater amounts of negotiation provide grounds for consensus between teacher and pupil (see Pollard and Tann 1987) and lead to a non-traditional understanding of learning and behavioural obligations, shifting responsibility from teacher to include the pupil. Research undertaken by Ryan and colleagues has found that pupil responsibility leads to enhanced feelings of self-control and self-worth, and pupil learning is seen as intrinsically motivating. 'Autonomy' identified by Ryan and colleagues is based upon individual encouragement by the teacher. Positive results for this individualized presentation of autonomy have been found in experimental settings but remain to be verified in the classroom over time.

This review of social development also leads to a more dynamic approach to autonomy. A dynamic approach requires that pupils develop effective interaction with teachers and peers as necessary bases for autonomy. With effective peer interaction, the child will have a viable alternative to weigh against teacher dependence and control. Effective interaction with peers has not generally been found in primary classrooms (where pupils are most likely to co-act rather than co-operate). A number of studies have shown that work with peers can be effective in co-operative learning (see Slavin in this volume). Co-operative learning is not a simple exercise and requires active planning/ structuring by the teacher and the development of a group reward system. Results from co-operative learning studies in classrooms show that cognitive and social development is enhanced and pupils are less disruptive. Pupils working effectively with one another (and developing a 'close' relationship) may help to ease teacher dependence and add a co-operative dimension to their actions (see Figure 7.2), providing firm bases for autonomy.

In both the traditional and alternative views of autonomy, teachers play a central role. They must be aware of the social and developmental potential of children as well as understanding how this potential can be brought into the classroom context. Teachers must plan and structure the action and activities of the classroom for pupil participation. Planning and structuring is not synonymous with control. To provide for autonomy the teacher must focus on the individual or the group and generate a viable alternative to teacher dependence. Without this devolution of control, classrooms will remain as effective as they traditionally have been – and dependence, differentiation, limited cognitive enhancement and effective control will remain as problems of schooling. The autonomous classroom (which incorporates social development into its structure) is able to draw upon effective relationships with teacher and peers to promote security amongst pupils, more effective cognitive development (through discourse with peers) and co-operation.

References

Ainsworth, M., Bell, S. and Stayton, D. (1974) 'Infant-mother attachment and social development: "socialization" as a product of reciprocal responses to signals', in M.P. Richards (ed.) *Integration of a Child into a Social world*, London: Cambridge University Press.

Baumrind, D. (1971) 'Current patterns of parental authority', *Developmental Psychology Monographs* 4: 1–103.

Bearison, D., Magzaman, S. and Filardo, E. (1986) 'Socio-cognitive and cognitive growth in young children', *Merrill-Palmer Quarterly* 32: 51–72.

Bennett, S.N. (1976) *Teaching Style and Pupil Progress*, London: Open Books.

Bennett, S.N., Desforges, C., Cockburn, A. and Wilkinson, B. (1984) *The Quality of Pupil Learning Experiences*, London: Lawrence Erlbaum Associates.

Blurton-Jones, N. (1976) 'Rough-and-tumble play among nursery school children', in J. Bruner, K. Sylva and A. Jolly (eds) *Play*, London: Penguin.

Bruner, J. (1986) *Actual Minds, Possible Worlds*, London: Harvard University Press.

Croll, P. and Moses, (1988) 'Teaching methods and time on task in junior schools', *Educational Research* 30: 90–7.

Deci, E., Nezlek, J. and Sheinman, L. (1981) 'Characteristics of the rewarder and intrinsic motivation of the rewardee', *Journal of Personality and Social Psychology*, 40: 1–10.

Department of Education and Science (DES) (1985) *The Curriculum from 5–16*, Curriculum Matters no. 2, London: HMSO.

Edwards, D. and Mercer, N. (1987) *Common Knowledge: The Development of Understanding in the Classroom*, London: Methuen.

Field, T. (1981) 'Early peer relations', in P.S. Strain (ed.) *The Utilization of Classroom Peers as Behavioral Change Agents*, New York: Plenum Press.

Freud, A. and Dann, S. (1951) 'An experiment in group upbringing', *Psychoanalytic Study of the Child* 6: 127–68.

Furth, H. (1980) *The World of Grown-ups*, New York: Elsevier Press.

Galton, M., Simon, B. and Croll, P. (1980) *Inside the Primary Classroom*, London: Routledge & Kegan Paul.

Grolnick, W.S. and Ryan, R.M. (1987) 'Autonomy support in education: Creating the facilitating environment', in N. Hastings and J. Schwieso (eds) *New Directions in Educational Psychology*, Lewes: Falmer Press.

Hartup, W. (1978) 'Children and their friends', in H. McGurk (ed.) *Issues in Childhood Social Development*, London: Methuen.

Ingram, J. and Worrell, N. (1987) 'The negotiating classroom: child self-determination in British primary schools', *Early Child Development and Care* 28: 401–15.

Kutnick, P. (1983) *Relating to Learning*, London: Allen & Unwin.

Kutnick, P. (1988) *Relationships in the Primary School Classroom*, London: Chapman.

Kutnick, P. and Brees, P. (1982) 'The development of cooperation: explorations in cognitive and moral competence and social authority', *British Journal of Educational Psychology* 52: 361–5.

Nash, R. (1973) *Classrooms Observed*, London: Routledge & Kegan Paul

Osborne, A.F. and Millbank, J.E. (1985) 'Long-term effects of pre-school education', paper given at Preschool Education Conference at the University of London, Institute of Education.

Perret-Clermont, A.N. (1980) *Social Interaction and Cognitive Development in Children*, London: Academic Press.

Piaget, J. (1932a) *The Moral Judgement of the Child*, New York: Free Press.

Piaget, J. (1932b) as cited in A.N. Perret-Clermont (1980) *Social Interaction and Cognitive Development in Children*, London: Academic Press.

Piaget, J. (1971) *The Science of Education and the Psychology of the Child*, London: Longman.

Plowden Report (1967) *Children and Their Primary Schools*, 2 vols, Report of the Central Advisory Council for Education in England, London: HMSO.

Pollard, A. (1985) *The Social World of the Primary School*, London: Holt, Rinehart & Winston.

Pollard, A. and Tann, S. (1987) *Reflective Teaching in the Primary School*, London: Cassell.

Pullantz, M. and Gottman, J.M. (1981) 'Social skills and group acceptance', in S.R. Asher and J.M. Gottman (eds) *The Development of Children's Friendships*, London: Cambridge University Press.

Ryan, R.M. and Grolnick, W.S. (1986) 'Origins and pawns in the classroom: Self-report and projective assessment of individual differences in children's perceptions', *Journal of Personality and Social Psychology* 50: 550–8.

Shantz, C. (1982) 'Children's understanding of social rules and the social context', in F.C. Serafica (ed.) *Social-cognitive Development in Context*, New York: Guildford Press.

Shapira, A. and Madsen, W. (1969) 'Cooperative and competitive behaviour of kibbutz and urban children in Israel', *Child Development* 40: 609–17.

Simon, B. (1981) 'The primary school revolution, myth or reality?', in B. Simon and J. Willcocks (eds) *Research and Practice in the Primary School*, London: Routledge & Kegan Paul.

Strayer, F. (1980) 'Childhood ecology and the study of pre-school social relations', in H.C. Foot, A.J. Chapman and J.R. Smith (eds) *Friendship and Social Relations in Children*, Chichester: Wiley.

Tajfel, H. (1978) *Differentiation between Social Groups: Studies in the Social Psychology of Intergroup Relations*, London: Academic Press.

Tizard, B. and Hughes, M. (1984) *Young Children Learning*, London: Fontana.

Vandell, D.L. and Mueller, E.C. (1980) 'Peer play and friendship during the first two years', in H.C. Foot, A.J. Chapman and J.R. Smith (eds) *Friendship and Social Relations in Childhood*, Chichester: Wiley.

Vygotsky, L. (1978) *Mind in Society: The Development of Higher Psychological Processes*, London: Harvard University Press.

Waters, E. and Srouf, F. (1983) 'Social competence as a developmental construct', *Developmental Review* 3: 79–97.

Whiting, B. and Whiting, J.M.W. (1975) *Children of Six Cultures*, Cambridge, Mass.: Harvard University Press.

Youniss, J. (1980) *Parents and Peers in Social Development*, Chicago: University of Chicago Press.

Chapter eight

Towards an adequate conception of early moral development

Derek Wright

Editors' introduction

Initiating the focused section, Derek Wright combines a theoretical background with commonsense realities to stimulate consideration of the teacher's role in encouraging moral development in pupils. The chapter is written distinctively from a teacher's point of view. It stresses the importance and quality of relationships that can be engendered in the classroom. The chapter opens an important issue in consideration of moral development.

Wright has worked with teachers and others in the field of moral development over many years. His concerns about relationships should be familiar with many teachers. His discussion moves away from criticism of the overpresence of didactic teaching methods in the primary classroom. He introduces the possibility that teachers may engage in two distinctly different types of relationship with pupils, that of constraint and that of collaboration. He points out that teachers have been successful in the past for engendering the development of morality in their charges. What he does not say is that the teacher's role is even more important in today's society as school and teacher may provide the only consistent experience of moral values that the child encounters; especially if we accept that past incarnations of moral experience (of the church, extended and nuclear family) are declining in importance.

This chapter also links the quality of relationship between teacher and child with particular conceptions of moral development. The didactic teacher does promote a certain moral understanding of rules and children's obligation of acceptance. Rule knowledge and the generation of moral habits are important for young children but they also have implications for the child's 'personhood'. The collaborative or co-operative relationship that can develop between teacher and pupil provides a 'richer' sense of morality, and is seen at the root of discourse and fairness. Thus Wright encourages teachers to consider the relationships in which they interact with pupils and effects on the child's moral and personal development. These working and classroom relationships are particularly important when considering children with special needs (Galloway, Chapter 12) and the need for the teacher to structure actions for themselves and the pupils (further amplified in the context of play in Chapter 9 by Smith).

Introduction

The focus of this chapter is upon how we, as teachers and parents, can best conceive of the nature of moral development in children. No attempt will be made to review the relevant psychological theories and research findings, though the writer's knowledge of this work lies behind the discussion, and two theoretical perspectives, those of Freud and Piaget, will be briefly outlined. Not only would it be impossible to do justice to this theory and research in a short chapter, but the interested reader can find such accounts elsewhere (for example, Wright 1971; Sapp 1986). More important, the present aim is to explore our *conception* of moral development, by which I mean our overall idea of how it occurs, or, more accurately, to contrast two basic ideas which have strong echoes in commonsense. Particular psychological theories are always partial, limited in scope, and focused upon certain aspects of the process, and empirical findings are always piecemeal and designed to test particular predictions.

As adult moral agents we already have some conception of how moral development occurs, and this conception shapes the way we treat children within our living relationships with them. Moreover, we cannot be so far off target, because overwhelmingly children grow up to be moral agents themselves in greater or lesser degree – as we have. However, it is my experience, both of myself and of the many teachers I have worked with, that our conceptions of moral development are largely implicit and unexamined, and that therefore we may be less effective in promoting moral growth in the young than we might be. The hope behind the chapter is that it will edge the reader towards greater clarity and understanding of the process, and therefore of how to promote it.

In my own efforts towards clarity I shall be drawing on certain ideas developed in detail by Freud, and in much less detail by Piaget, in order to contrast the two fundamental conceptions of how moral agency evolves in children. I have chosen these two theorists, partly because of their enormous influence, but mainly because their ideas resonate strongly with commonsense and with our ordinary experience of the moral life. It is this aspect of their work I want to stress.

The teacher's experience

It must surely be the experience of all teachers that they find themselves at different times relating to children in one of two different ways or modes. For convenience I will call them the control mode and the equality mode. Though they may alternate frequently in the course of a single lesson, it is difficult to see how they might occur at the same time.

Because of their extensive responsibilities and the complex network of their accountabilities, teachers have no choice but to spend a lot of time controlling, directing, and even dominating their pupils. Without such control and direction the ordinary business of school learning could not take place. Children themselves need, and indeed want, to be controlled by teachers. It creates for them a sense of security and safety and relieves them of the stress of responsibilities they are not ready for. Of course, the ways in which such control is exercised can vary widely, from the crudely aggressive at one end to the subtle and sensitive at the other.

Teachers are not just concerned with the professional business of teaching and learning, however, As moral agents themselves they inevitably feel that children should not steal, lie, bully or cheat, and should be helpful to each other, work hard, be truthful, and so on. In the control mode of relating, the moral sense of the teacher finds its expression in prescribing how children should behave, in reprimanding and perhaps punishing for wrong behaviour, and in some way rewarding the right behaviour. In other words the teacher asserts control in order to ensure as much as possible that children behave in ways she or he judges they ought to behave. The children experience morality as, so to speak, imposed from outside through the teacher's assertion of authority and power though, of course, they can experience it as more or less aggressively and compellingly imposed.

It is when teachers feel able to relax out of the controlling mode that the equality mode of relating becomes possible. It is this aspect of their work with children which many teachers find the most richly rewarding. It includes moments of shared sadness or laughter, occasions of democratic decision-making, times when there is real and authentic exchange of thoughts between teacher and child in which each listens seriously to the other, and that kind of co-operative activity in which the teacher is equally a participant. In short it means those times in the classroom when teacher and child experience each other as ordinary persons on a more or less equal footing.

In regard to moral issues, the equality mode is present when there is genuine reciprocity between teacher and child. Children feel as free as teachers to give expression to their own moral voice in relation to their own behaviour and that of the teacher, and in relation to the rules and organization of the school. Teachers themselves are able to acknowledge their own unfairnesses and mistakes, and are seen to try to put things right. Moral issues arising in the life of the school or outside it are open to free discussion between teacher and pupils with the goal of reaching agreement.

Piaget's terms (Piaget 1932) for these two forms of relatedness that have been briefly outlined are unilateral respect and constraint on the one hand, and mutual respect, co-operation and reciprocity on the other. From the point of view of the teacher, each carries an underlying and implicit conception of how moral development is fostered in the child, and each has implications for how we understand the moral life. Since it may be assumed that all teachers experience both kinds of relatedness with children in some degree, both conceptions are present in the teachers themselves. In what follows the attempt will be made to bring both conceptions out into the light of day so that we can ask to what extent they are compatible (Piaget is emphatic that they are not), and which of the two takes us to the heart of the matter (Piaget argues that it is the second). It must be stressed, though, that we shall be concerned with conceptions of relationship, moral development and morality, and not with descriptions of the actual relationships teachers have with their children, for these will always be unique to particular teachers and the children they teach. The goal is to help teachers, in their efforts to nurture moral growth in children, to be a little clearer about what they are doing and why.

The control conception of moral development

The main features of this conception are very familiar. It is what many people seem to mean by 'teaching children to be moral'. Children are initiated into, and sustained within, the moral world when adult caretakers exercise their natural power and authority in a firm and kindly way by telling them how they ought and ought not to behave and why, rewarding them with approval and affection when they comply, and expressing disapproval and perhaps punishing when they do not conform. The underlying message from the adult is 'I know how you ought to behave and I am going to do my best to ensure that you do behave in that way'. From the children's point of view, morality is experienced as external to themselves, as deriving from adults, and as having the authority of adults behind it. Their function is to respect and obey what adults tell them to do.

It is probably inevitable, and possibly necessary, that to some extent children should experience morality in this way. However, the more the relationship between children and adults is characterized by unilateral respect, that is, the more strongly and rigidly adults assert their controlling power in morally constraining and directing children, the more their obedience will be conditioned by fear and anxiety, and the more they will experience frustration and conflict. When such moral training is taken to extremes, we may well agree with Piaget that 'one realizes most keenly how immoral it can be to believe too much in morality, and how much more precious is a little humanity than all the rules in the world' (Piaget 1932: 189).

Implicit in this idea of how morality develops in children is a conception of morality as itself derived from some external authority, either that of society, or of God, or of a church or religious culture, or of a sacred scripture. The assumption is that morality consists of a number of rules of conduct which have behind them an authority external to all individual human beings and to which the individual is obliged to submit. The function of adults in relation to children is to transmit these rules and convey the sense of authority behind them by asserting their own authority over the children. We might label this understanding of morality as vertical or hierarchical since it implies that morality is imposed on the individual from 'on high'.

It is also implicit in this concept of moral development that without the controlling authority of adults children would not become moral beings. Moral agency is not intrinsic to being human but a set of attitudes and beliefs which have to be somehow engrafted on to the child. The problem in this view has been expressed by Piaget when he asserts that 'the adult's command, in spite of the nimbus which surrounds it, will always remain external, "stuck on" as it were, to a mind whose structure is of a different order' (Piaget 1932: 163).

However, it does appear to be the case, as Freud has argued, that, given the child's dependence on adults, and given that the unilateral respect relationship is softened to some extent by reciprocal affection, the child will 'identify' with adults and 'internalize' their prescriptions, and thus form a conscience or super-ego. In Freud's account the aggression provoked in the child by the adult's controlling power is turned inwards upon the self, and makes possible the familiar experience of self-blame and guilt, and also the tendency to blame others who break the rules. As Freud put it, 'the external restrictions are introjected, so that the super-ego takes the place of the parental function, and thenceforward observes, guides and threatens the ego in just the same way as the parents acted to the child before' (Freud 1933: 85).

Whether or not we go along with Freud's psychodynamic explanation (and there is an alternative, behaviouristic account of essentially the same process), it seems clear that within relationships of unilateral respect which are moderated by a degree of reciprocal caring and attachment, the rules imposed by adults can become more or less permanently lodged within the child's mind. Young children can become very scrupulous about observing the rules of adults in their absence, can obviously experience guilt when they do not, and may be quite strict in their insistence that younger children conform to them. Indeed, the moral voice of authoritarian adults can become so embedded in the child's mind that it can become more demanding than the adults themselves were. Some children can be too conscientious for their own good.

This very brief account of the control conception of moral development will, I hope, be sufficient, for it is likely to be very familiar to the reader. It appears to be the dominating conception in the minds of many people and probably deserves the label 'traditional'. Most of us have some experience of its effectiveness, for it relates directly to our experience of conflict between an inner moral demand and wishes, desires and wants. At the very least, children learn how adults expect them to behave, and up to a point useful habits or regularities of behaviour may be developed. It can be argued that the moral domain is far too important and complex for children to be left to work it out for themselves.

However, there are important questions to be asked. Is moral development simply the internalizing of adult rules and prescriptions? Is the concept of morality implicit in this approach an adequate one? Though it appears to work with many children, it manifestly does not with others. Certainly teachers are all too familiar with the fact that it has little effect with some. Before turning to an exploration of what I have called the equality approach, it is worth looking more critically at the conception I have outlined.

A critique of the control conception

First of all, since I have drawn on Freud's ideas to support the claim that the control conception can be effective in certain ways, it is worth exploring his thinking a little further in order to bring out some of the limitations he saw in the development of a conscience or super-ego morality. For it is fundamental to his account that the process of identification with, and introjection of, the powerful parental moral voice involves for the child the repression, or denial, in greater or lesser degree, of 'immoral' desires and motives. Thus, on this theory, the more the child internalizes the 'high moral standards' prescribed by adults so that they become a semi-autonomous agency within the child's personality, the more the child will live with a state of inner conflict and tension. Add to this that the more or less compulsively internalized rules may be far from rationally justifiable, and the scene is set for personal problems in living later on.

It is worth mentioning another phenomenon to which Freud has drawn attention, which is perhaps especially relevant for teachers, namely, what he calls 'identification with the super-ego'. The state of being identified with the super-ego is one in which the individual's conscience is, for the moment, turned outwards onto others who have clearly done something of which that conscience strongly disapproves. This creates a momentary resolution of the inner state of tension and conflict, for ego and super-ego are one, and the condemnatory and repressive aggression usually turned inwards as an autonomous braking mechanism for wrongdoing is turned outwards on someone else. When this happens it is, for the moment, virtually impossible for the individual to feel that 'there but for the grace of God go I', or, perhaps more important, 'there despite the grace of God went I'. Compassion is swept away by 'righteous' anger, which can easily issue in unjustly punitive action when the individual has power over another.

Though Freud clearly thought that some degree of super-ego development was essential if the child is to become a civilized adult, his therapeutic experience made him acutely aware of how destructive to full and creative living a severe conscience could be. Indeed, it could be said that in his account of the therapeutic experience he has given us the germ of an alternative theory of moral development which finds fuller description in Piaget. For our purposes the relevant aspect of the therapeutic process is the progressive transformation of the super-ego, or compulsive parental morality, into an ego morality; a morality consciously chosen by the self through the reflective experience of understanding the self in relation to others. As Freud put it in his last, unfinished publication, 'The analytic physician and the patient's weakened ego, basing themselves on the real external world, have to band together into a party against the enemies, the instinctual demands of the Id and the conscientious demands of the super-ego' (Freud, 1986: 406). The striking feature of the psychotherapeutic process is that the therapist goes to the very opposite extreme from the moralizing adult of the child's experience, and is as completely nonjudgemental, in both the moral and nonmoral sense, as it is possible to be, whatever the patient may report having done or not done. In the presence of someone who refuses to pass moral judgements, the patient is able to find her or his own moral voice, and separate from the introjected moral voice of parents.

Freud thus presents us with two conceptions of moral development, a super-ego conception which he developed in great detail, and an ego conception which remains embryonic in his writing. The former has the implication of a relatively split-off and compulsive conscience which represents internally the moral voice of adult authorities, and the latter a more or less rational and integrated moral sense which represents the individual's own, unique moral voice. They correspond more or less to the control and equality conceptions as described here.

Clearly, within relationships of unilateral respect, adult moral prescriptions may ring true to the child's own undeveloped and precarious moral voice. When this happens, the child's own moral voice is strengthened and supported, and given clear verbal structure. But the two can easily be in conflict. Bonhoeffer (1965: 367) gives a brief illustration. A teacher asks a boy in front of the class whether his father came home drunk last night. The boy denies it, though in fact his father did come home drunk. As Bonhoeffer points out, the boy has lied, but in doing so is bearing witness to a deeper truth, namely that it is none of the teacher's business. The boy's own intuitive moral sense in conflict with the teacher's demand leads him to break a moral 'rule'. An important question to ask of any school is the extent to which the assertion of control by teachers compromises the nascent moral integrity of pupils.

This simple example raises a much more fundamental limitation of the control conception. It is that morality itself is altogether too rich and complex a phenomenon to be reduced to a set of rules and prescriptions that can be communicated by adults. Central moral notions like truthfulness and fairness cannot be spelled out in any final set of rules to be obeyed. The way such notions influence behaviour in relation to others must always be a matter of individual intuitive and reflective judgement.

As a final point, consider the following imaginary dialogue between a teacher and Bertrand Russell, aged seven. It is intended to illustrate a simple point of logic, or moral mathematics as some philosophers have called it. I have chosen Russell aged seven because it is likely he would have responded this way, and if his moral mathematics is valid for him, it must also be valid for other children aged seven, whether or not they can realize or understand it.

Teacher: Russell, you should always tell the truth.
Russell: Sir, you must know as well as I do, that *I* cannot possibly conclude from what you have just said that *I* should always tell the truth unless I assert a second premiss, namely that I should do what you tell me to do. I cannot deduce that second premiss from anything you might say. If I am to assert it, I must have a reason. There is only one good reason I could have. That is that I too think I should always tell the truth.

This logical point is given a more psycho-logical slant by Piaget when he says:

For conduct to be characterised as moral there must be something more than outward agreement between its content and that of commonly accepted rules: it is also requisite that the mind should tend towards morality as an autonomous good and should itself be capable of appreciating the value of the rules that are proposed to it.

(Piaget 1932: 409)

Let us for a moment imagine the exchange continuing. The teacher would seem to have two options. The first is to enter into a rational dialogue with Russell as between two equals, sharing reasons and reflections in order to reach agreement. The second is to switch into controlling power assertion and say, in effect, 'I know what is right and you will do as I say'. When adults adopt the second response to children, there are two possible outcomes. The children may submit with an inner sense of protest, or they may suppress their own moral voice, at least for the time being, and, in Freud's phrase, identify with the aggressor.

The equality conception of moral development

This conception can be easily summarized. Its goal is the nurturing and strengthening of the child's own moral voice, or her or his 'ego morality'. Behind this is the assumption that having a moral voice is as intrinsic and emergent a feature of being human as consciousness or thinking or loving. There are two conditions which encourage its development. The first is as much experience of relationships of mutual respect, co-operation, and reciprocity, founded on reciprocal sympathy, with both peers and adults, as possible. The second is the stimulation to consciously realize and generalize the morality implicit in such relationships. The child's understanding of morality will then not be dependent upon adult authority, but will have about it a self-evidence authenticated by the child's own experience. The function of the adult is to respect and support the child's own moral realizations.

There are at least three basic assumptions about morality and the moral life which underlie this conception. As with all assumptions they are to be questioned and explored, though that cannot be done here. The first is that though persons are factually unequal in an indefinite number of ways, as moral agents (originators of judgements of what should and should not be done) they are on an equal footing, and it is morality itself which asserts this. Persons, as persons, are to be valued equally, and moral agency is central to being a person. Second, morality is between persons in the sense that it represents the ideal way in which relationships between persons should be regulated. Third, the irreducible heart of morality is to be found in a limited number of core moral ideas, not in a set of rules of behaviour. Rules are frequently in conflict and it is usually possible to think of situations in which they ought to be broken.

It is for the reader to explore what these core moral ideas might be. But there are surely certain central ones. These are: respect for persons as persons; fairness and justice; truthfulness; and that keeping of promises and contracts which is essential to all community life and co-operative activity. These ideas are rich and complex. To illustrate, in numerous workshops with teachers and pupils in which they have been asked to unpack what they understand by respecting another person as a person, the writer has always found the following emerging: listening to others with that kind of attention which accords the same status to their thought as to one's own, though of course not necessarily agreeing; not intruding upon their body space, personal possessions and private life without their agreement; being sensitively supportive of their self esteem; and so on.

In discussing relationships of mutual respect it must again be stressed that I am speaking of a conception of how relationships might be, rather than giving a description of how they ever are. Piaget is sceptical whether they ever exist in pure form: 'It can even be maintained that mutual respect and cooperation are never completely realized. They are not only limiting terms, but ideals of equilibrium' (Piaget 1932: 90).

This relates to another feature of the equality conception of morality, namely, that failure is intrinsic to it. If morality is understood in the impoverished sense as a set of relatively simple rules imposed by external or internal authority, then it is at least possible that an individual might obey them without fault. When morality is understood in the richer sense, as the embodiment of core moral ideas like fairness and truthfulness in human relationships, then it becomes the idea towards which we struggle rather than a state that we achieve. It is sometimes said that parents and teachers should 'set an example' of moral rectitude for the young. If adults do try to 'set an example', then inevitably they are creating a false image of themselves which in time children will come to realize. In the equality conception of moral development, the important example that adults need to be is that of people who cope creatively and constructively with their own moral failure in relating to others.

However, in so far as children experience such relationships with their peers, and are drawn into and sustained within such relationships with adults, to that extent the optimum conditions for the flowering of their personalities and self-confidence exist. It is for them, says Piaget, 'a necessary condition of autonomy under its double aspect, intellectual and moral', and 'from the moral point of view, it replaces the norms of authority by that norm immanent in action and in consciousness themselves, the norm of reciprocity and sympathy' (Piaget 1932: 103).

The critical point here is that core moral ideas of the kind mentioned are, in Piaget's term, 'constitutive' of relationships of mutual respect and co-operation. That is to say, such relationships cannot be sustained, unlike relationships of constraint and unilateral respect, unless such ideas are at least to some extent implicitly shaping them. For children, living with such relationships is living the moral life whether they know it or not. Each party to such relationship exercises a degree of moral autonomy, and therefore each is answerable to the other for the moral judgements they originate and express. The inevitable controlling influence that adults must at times assert over children needs to be understood by both child and adult; it is not the imposition of rules by those who know what is right, but a necessary consequence of the contractual and co-operative relationship between them which results from the considerable factual inequalities between them, and their reciprocal and complementary responsibilities.

It is worth looking briefly at how fairness and justice issues might be dealt with within mutual respect relationships between teachers and children. It may well be that responsibility for a particular decision rests with the teacher, say, in regard to assessment of work or a sanction for misbehaviour, and teachers want to be fair. The equality conception of morality asserts that we can only have confidence that a decision is fair when all parties to it, in this case the children, also see it as fair. Within the mutual respect relatedness, if the children see it as unfair, they would be supported in saying so. Not only would they be listened to, but the issue would be explored together in detail, and if necessary and possible, the decision modified in order that they see it as fair. The point is that within such relationships both parties actively participate in making fairness. Children's understanding of fairness and justice, and their confidence in it, can only really come about through their experience of trying to make it.

This brings us to the other major aspect of the equality conception of moral development, namely the stimulation of their conscious realization of their own intuitive moral sense, and its progressive structuring in conscious thought. This happens through discussion with others, in which the child tries to articulate her or his own thoughts, listens to others and learns that they think differently, and tries through reflection to rethink and reach some kind of agreement with others. The issues can be immediate and living moral issues within relationships, or more artificially constructed tasks initiated by the teacher. The teacher's role is through sensitive questioning and the putting of considerations that have not been mentioned in order to extend the children's thinking. The process of consciously realizing and making rational our own moral institutions is a lifelong task. But it is an essential task if we are to be able to give meaning and structure to our own moral voice. If the reader is interested, Kohlberg has given us a preliminary account of how the child's moral reasoning develops and a full account of his work can be found in Kohlberg 1981 and 1984.

Experienced teachers who have read thus far are likely to be impatiently aware as a reality of their daily life that some children are disruptive, antisocial, violent and hostile to peers and teachers alike. It is this experience which is most likely to trigger the control conception, and indeed be held to justify it. Since we are human, this may at times be inevitable, and in the short term be expedient. But it is also likely to be part of the teacher's experience that in the long term the more or less aggressive assertion of the teacher's disciplinary control is ineffective in producing a real change in such children. The reason is, of course, that for such children the conditions are not propitious for the internalization of the teacher's prescriptions, though they may learn as a matter of prudence to modify their behaviour.

However difficult and slow it may be, the equality conception invites us to set up situations in which we can offer our own respect for such children as persons because they are persons. This means listening with sympathy, and sensitively questioning them in order for them to give full voice to their own confused feelings and thoughts – probably the first time an adult has done that. And if the teacher listens carefully, she or he is likely to hear as a kind of base line to what is being said, a muddled and inarticulate sense of having been treated unfairly all along the line. Indeed, much antisocial behaviour can be construed as at least partly an inarticulate protest against being treated unfairly, though of course it is due to much more than that. The equality conception would suggest that the teacher try to get such children to articulate what they see as unfair in their school experience, explore with them what would make things more fair, and do something positive to bring that about. This small step would at least create the beginnings of a relationship of mutual respect that might subsequently be built upon. But I have no illusions about the difficulty in doing this, especially under the stressful conditions in which teachers work, and especially when the childs' antisocial stance has hardened. The equality conception would claim, however, that something of the kind must happen if that stance is not to become permanent.

Concluding remarks

The emphasis of this chapter has been upon teachers rather than children. The reason is that the experience children have within school depends so much upon how teachers conceive their task. The aim has been to help teachers a little towards clarifying their own conceptions of moral development, and therefore how they relate to children in that respect.

Two contrasting conceptions of moral development have been outlined. Neither will be new, since both, it is hoped, have a clear resonance with commonsense and teachers' experience with children. The bias of the writer is clear enough. It is not claimed that the control conception is wholly invalid. It has its own echo in our experience and is related to a certain conception of the nature of morality itself. But it is my view that the equality conception takes us close to the heart of the process of moral development, and implies a more adequate conception of morality. There is, of course, a great deal more to be said. If this chapter stimulates the reader to pursue these matters further for herself or himself, it will have achieved its task.

References

Bonhoeffer, D. (1965) *Ethics*; London: Macmillan paperback edition.

Freud, S. (1933) *New Introductory Lectures*, London: Hogarth Press.

Freud, S. (1986) 'An outline of psychoanalysis', in vol. 15, *Historical and Expository Works on Psychoanalysis*, London: Penguin Books.

Kohlberg, L. (1981) *Essays on Moral Development*, vol. I, New York: Harper and Row.

Kohlberg, L. (1984) *Essays on Moral Development*, vol. II, New York: Harper & Row.

Piaget, J. (1932) *The Moral Judgment of the Child*, London: Routledge & Kegan Paul.

Sapp, G.L. (ed.) (1986) *Handbook of Moral Development*, Birmingham, Alabama: Religious Education Press.

Wright, D. (1971) *The Psychology of Moral Development*, London: Penguin Books.

Chapter nine

The role of play in the nursery and primary school curriculum

Peter K. Smith

Editors' introduction

The role of play is accorded a central place in the activities of children generally, and especially those attending pre-school and primary schools. Peter Smith provides an extensive overview and analysis of definitions, processes and effects of play on early schooling. In the overview he also stresses the importance of relationships between children and their teachers, and that a considered and structured approach is necessary for children to receive the range of benefits made possible through play.

This chapter organizes criteria and categories of play. More usefully, the diagrammatic presentation of teachers' and childrens' roles in structuring play provides an insightful means to quantify benefits which may occur in various schemes of play. We are reminded that play is not a simple or singular occurrence. Effects of play are gradually built up by the child but are dependent upon the actions in which the child participates and whether the interpersonal focus of play is on the teacher or peers. Results from and means of studying play are thoroughly reviewed. We are made aware that constructive aspects of play are related to intellectual growth and development. Teachers can tutor children to use various types of play. Children invariably enjoy themselves when playing. And, there are advantages in mixing various types of play for children.

Pertaining centrally to the themes of this volume, we are made aware that social relationships are necessary for a number of types of play to take place, and that there are various social benefits of play due to the type and quality of relationships that children gain with adults and peers. Thus, while it is important that teachers structure play (either as initiators or respondents), they must also be aware that outcomes of these activities may lead to short-term cognitive gains, conformity, social relational skills and longer-term intellectual development. It is interesting that the types of benefit derived from play relate to adult and peer relations respectively. The chapter coincides with themes of the type and quality of relationships introduced in earlier chapters, and the role and structure brought to play by the teacher. Themes from play will be taken up in the next chapter on friendship (Chapter 10) and seen later in gender roles (Chapter 11) that may be generated in the classroom.

Introduction

The aim of this chapter is to examine the role of play in the education of the young child. Some of the relevant research is from the UK; some is from the USA where schooling commences at 6 years. I have incorporated material on older pre-school children, as well as primary school age children, in this review.

What is play? Types of play seen in young children

It is not really satisfactory to attempt to give a definition, one definitive statement, of what is or is not 'play'. For too many behaviours, it is contentious whether they constitute play, or not. We might perhaps all agree that children 'pretending' to act out roles such as 'mother' and 'baby' are playing; but what about a child painting a picture, or making a copy of a model with wooden bricks? We might not agree so well about whether these behaviours are 'play'.

Two main ways have been used to cope with this problem. One is to use 'play criteria'. The other is to use 'play categories'.

Some psychologists have suggested that we use certain signs, or *criteria* to decide whether behaviour is playful or not. The more such criteria are present, the more likely it is that we would decide 'this is play'. The criteria usually suggested (Krasnor and Pepler 1980; Rubin, *et al.* 1983) are that play:

(i) is intrinsically motivated – done for its own sake and not brought about by basic bodily needs, or by external rules or social demands;
(ii) shows attention to means rather than ends – the child is more interested in the performance of the behaviour itself than in the results or outcome of the behaviour;
(iii) is characterized by pretence – is not serious but has an 'as if' or make-believe quality;
(iv) has positive affect – is pleasurable and enjoyable to the child;
(v) shows flexibility – some variation in form or context.

Some other suggested criteria are that play is distinct from exploratory behaviour, distinct from organized games, and is characterized by active engagement.

In one empirical study (Smith and Vollstedt 1985) it was found that

145

the criteria (ii), (iii), (iv) and (v) above were all used by observers making judgements about whether behaviour in children in a nursery school was 'play', or not. Criterion (i), intrinsic motivation, was not used. However, this study was made in a context where a lot of free play was allowed. Certainly, activities initiated and strongly structured by teachers would not be considered play, by criterion (i), and would not be so considered by most observers.

A somewhat different approach is to categorize different types of play; each category should be defined, or at least illustrated by clear examples of 'paradigm cases'. Thus Piaget (1951) distinguished between 'practice play', 'symbolic play' and 'games with rules'. Practice play included the sensorimotor and exploratory play of the young infant – especially 6 months to 2 years; symbolic play, the pretend, fantasy and socio- dramatic play of the child, from about 2 or 3 to 6 years; while games with roles characterized the activities of children from 6 or 7 years onwards.

Much of the play of the primary school child will be *symbolic* in Piaget's scheme. Children pretend that some action or object has some meaning other than it's usual, real-life meaning; for example if a child rotates his arms, goes 'poop-poop', and gives out pieces of paper, he is pretending to turn a steering-wheel, sound a horn and give out bus tickets. When – as in this example – these actions are sufficiently well integrated, then we can say that the child is in 'role-play', in this case, pretending to be a bus driver. If two or more children are engaged in role play together, this is 'socio-dramatic play'. Empirical research suggests that such forms of play increase with age then decline, through the 3 to 7 year age period (Cole and LaVoie 1985; Peisach and Hardeman 1986).

Smilansky (1968) changed Piaget's scheme by including also a category of 'constructive play', in which objects are manipulated to construe or create something. This accords with the fact that many teachers regard such activities as play. It departs from the analysis of Piaget, who stated that 'constructive games ... occupy ... a position halfway between play and intelligent work, or between play and imitation'. The goal-directed nature of constructive activities meant that Piaget saw it a more 'accommodative' (the child adapting its behaviour to fit reality), whereas symbolic play was more 'assimilative' (adapting reality to fit the child's own wishes).

Certain kinds of play do not fit well into the schemes of either Piaget or Smilansky. In particular, physical activity play (running, climbing, sliding, swinging and other gross muscular play) and rough-and-tumble play (playful fighting, wrestling and chasing) are neither constructive nor necessarily symbolic. Even though these forms of play are very characteristic of the behaviour of children during break-time at school, they have been rather neglected by psychologists and educationists.

Generally, it is constructive play and symbolic play which have had most interest for discussions of primary school curricula.

Play in relation to the aims of the primary school curriculum

Educators in the kindergarten and primary school period have pointed to a number of aims in early childhood education (for example, Taylor, Exon and Holley 1972). These aims include:

(a) Social – to help each child make warm, stable relationships with other children and adults, encourage responsibility and consideration for others, and to help build self-confidence, independence, and self-control, so that he or she has every chance of leading a full and happy life.

(b) Intellectual – to encourage each child to use his or her intellectual powers to the full, by fostering the use of language, stimulating natural curiosity, and developing the ability to learn and form concepts.

(c) Home/school – to help parents to a fuller understanding of the needs of young children and of making the child's educational life smoother and happier, and easing the transition of the child to formal schooling.

(d) Aesthetic/creative – to provide opportunities for the child to experiment with a variety of materials in the fields of art and music, to encourage creativity and expressiveness, and a growing awareness and appreciation of beauty.

(e) Physical – to help the child develop motor and manipulatory co-ordination and skills, and to meet physical needs through the provision of fresh air, space to play and sleep, good food, training in personal hygiene, and regular medical inspection.

How does the encouragement of play rate, in relation to these aims? It can be argued to be relevant to most if not all of them, depending in part on the forms of play considered:

(a) Much play is social. Socio-dramatic play and rough-and-tumble play necessarily involve co-ordination of activities with one or more play partners. Such forms of play can form a primary mode of social interaction in this age range. This is less true of constructive play, which can, but need not be, social. Most forms of play occur naturally between like-aged children, but play can also foster child-adult relationships if the adult engages in a play activity with the child.

(b) Many theorists claim that play has intellectual benefits. Socio-dramatic play may foster language and role-taking skills, while constructive play may encourage cognitive development and concept formation. Such aspects of cognitive development may overlap with, though are not identical to, school-based criteria of academic achievement. Rough-and-tumble play is not usually claimed to have intellectual benefits.

(c) Play experience is probably least relevant to the aim of home/school transition. If later schooling is to be more formal or structured in nature, then play experience may not provide direct matching for the sort of demands to be made on the child at the later time. On the other hand, play opportunities can be a useful point of contact between school staff and parents.

(d) Because play is often defined as internally motivated, and flexible, many theorists believe that it is the optimal way of enhancing creativity and imagination. Children have the freedom to try out new ideas in play and can express themselves in their own way, especially in socio-dramatic and fantasy play.

(e) Much play is physically active. Constructive play may practise fine motor skills, while gross physical play and rough- and-tumble play can provide whole-body exercise and motor co-ordination.

Thus, a case can be made that playful activities can further many or most of the likely aims of early child education. However, many other activities, such as more structured or didactic activities, organized games, physical exercises, story-telling, and real-life tasks such as preparing food, and tidying the classroom, can also further such aims. Therefore, any benefits of play must be considered against any benefits of non-playful activities. This issue is further complicated, not only by the different kinds of play, but also by the different ways in which play can be used in the early school curriculum.

Ways in which constructive play and fantasy/socio- dramatic play are (or are not) used in the education of the young child

Depending on the theoretical perspective of staff, and the needs they perceive in the children, constructive and dramatic play may or may not have an important role in the curriculum. (I will defer consideration of physical activity and rough-and-tumble play until a later section.) One way of conceptualizing this is to use a four-fold classification, as shown in Figure 9.1:

Teacher initiating/child responding

The teacher structures activities according to perceived needs of the child, for example, arranging organized activities often in a group format; the child primarily follows the instructions of the teacher, or imitates others. This very 'formal' or 'structured' curriculum would have little if any place for spontaneous play. Rather, adults impart or instruct children in certain skills.

Teacher initiating/child initiating

The teacher structures activities, but takes account of the kinds of needs or preferences which the child expresses. Thus, some forms of playful activity, as well a non-play activities, may be used as the basis for the teacher to encourage the development of skills such as language, co-operation, concept development, and the planning of sequenced activities towards a goal. Both constructive and dramatic play might be structured in this way by adult intervention. The skill of the teacher lies in diverting the play to challenging ends without sacrificing too much of the child's spontaneity and enjoyment of play.

Teacher responding/child initiating

The teacher does not structure activities, but does respond to the child's own needs and activities. Thus, the teacher will encourage the play of the child by providing suitable play materials, and will often take the opportunity to comment on the play, make suggestions, and so on. However, the initiative is left clearly with the child. Here, great value is placed on play and the spontaneous nature of playful activity.

Teacher responding/child responding

The teacher does not structure activities and only responds to the child in respect of physical needs, such as avoiding danger, toilet training, meal times, and conforming to institutional demands. The adult has a custodial role rather than an educative one. Much of the child's activity may be play, but the encouragement or enhancement of play is not seen as of great importance.

As an example of these four kinds of approaches, consider the aim of fostering language development:

(i) In an A-type curriculum, children might be led in singing in a group; or a teacher might engage in language drill exercises with children individually or in small groups.

(ii) In a B-type curriculum, a teacher might ask a child to talk about something which happened to them recently, or about what they may have just made in play or construction; or to make up a song or story; or might take part in a pretend play episode and try to extend

149

the child's language while directing or structuring the play.

(iii) In a C-type curriculum, a teacher could see language skills as being fostered by spontaneous play; enhancing such play would be a primary means of enhancing language skills, although the teacher might also comment on or encourage a child to talk about their play.

(iv) In a D-type curriculum, no effort would be made to foster language development beyond allowing the normal process of social communication between children themselves, in a safe and healthy environment.

Figure 9.1 A four-fold scheme for conceptualizing teacher attitudes to play.

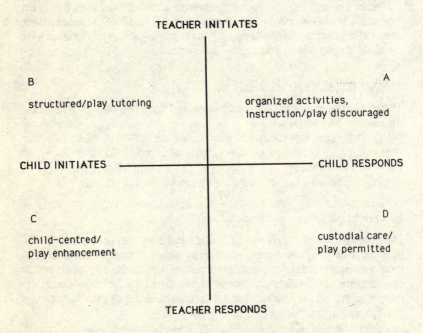

The influence of beliefs and theories about play

Historically, play was not seen as educationally valuable in Western Europe when nursery and infant schools began to be introduced in the eighteenth and nineteenth centuries. In the main, children were seen as in need of instruction and, in the case of religious doctrines, redemption from sinful behaviour. The beginnings of an emphasis on the value of the child's own spontaneous growth, the image of the child was more noticeably 'good' and hence of spontaneous play as more valuable, stems from the Czech writer Comenius, the Swiss writer Rousseau, and early social reformers and educators such as Owen (UK), Pestalozzi (Switzerland), Froebel (Germany) and Montessori (Italy). Such writers and educators generally saw the value of active teacher involvement, while wishing also to respect the child's own natural growth.

They would thus tend to be in quadrant B in Figure 9.1, though with considerable variation in the kinds of activities recommended. Montessori, for example, favoured constructive play activities using specifically designed materials, but did *not* encourage fantasy or socio-dramatic play.

However, a more positive attitudes to the value of spontaneous play and dramatic play came about in much of Western Europe in the twentieth century, especially in the period 1930 to 1970. This play 'ethos' has regarded spontaneous play as an important if not essential component of the child's social and intellectual development, and of creative and personal growth. It is epitomized in the phrase 'play indeed is the child's work, and the means whereby he or she grows and develops' (Isaacs 1929: 9.) It is re-echoed in, for example, the Plowden Report:

> we now know that play – in the sense of 'messing about' either with material objects or with other children, and of creating fantasies – is vital to children's learning and therefore vital in school. Adults who criticize teachers for allowing children to play are unaware that play is the principal means of learning in early childhood.
>
> (Plowden Report 1967: 193).

In part, this play ethos seems to have come about from theoretical perspectives such as evolutionary biology (suggesting the value of play throughout mammalian species) and psychoanalysis (suggesting the role of play in expressing emotions and working through personal conflicts). In part, it seems to have been influenced by broader socio-economic changes (such as smaller families, reduced child mortality, the separation of work from home life, and the growth of the toy industry) which led to greater concentration on children as in a separate world with separate needs from adults. For whatever reasons, the play ethos has been a powerful force in the curriculum for nursery and primary school. Play has been seen as worthwhile in its own right, and argued to have great cognitive or social benefits. A number of theorists, such as Singer, Bruner and Smilansky have argued along these lines, and the work of other theorists such as Piaget have to some extent been reinterpreted in this way. Such views would tend to favour curricula in quadrant C in Figure 9.1. The emphasis is more on respecting the child's spontaneous play, the initiative the child makes, than on the teacher structuring or directing this activity.

Little firm evidence was available to support this very positive view of spontaneous play through the period in which these views became prominent. The evidence from recent decades, to be discussed next, is mixed. Views about the importance of play are divided amongst educators and child psychologists. The play 'ethos' remains influential, but there has been some shift back to more structured curricula activities (quadrants B and A in Figure 9.1). The Schools Council Project in Structuring Play in the Early Years at School (Manning and Sharp 1977) reflects a belief that play, while motivationally valuable, can be made more so by some degree of adult involvement, encouragement and structuring. The work provides some valuable ideas for helping children, though the effectiveness of the programme has not been evaluated empirically.

Empirical evidence concerning the role of play in development and its use in early child education

Does it matter whether we incorporate time for play in the early school curriculum, and how we do so? The answers will vary depending on the aims of school provision or education. However some empirical studies may help in making such decisions. Evidence about the role of play in development, primarily constructive and dramatic forms of play, will be considered first; followed by a review of studies comparing school and pre-school curricula, which do, or do not, incorporate much free play, or structured play. Some of these studies are *correlational* in nature; others are more *experimental*.

In the *correlational* studies, observations and measurements are made on a number of children. It is possible to see then whether those children who naturally play the most, or in more complex ways, are also more advanced in skills such as language or intelligence. These studies are usually more based on real-life situations, but permit multiple interpretations of the findings. For example, if children who play more are found to also have more expressive language, this could be because (i) play helps language development, *or* (ii) language ability facilitates play, *or* (iii) some other factor, such as high intelligence, or secure home background, facilitates both language development and play.

In *experimental* studies, some children are selected to have a different kind of experience (for example, enriched play, or stimulation of play) compared to other, similar children who do not have this. Measurements are made of skills such as language or intelligence. These studies usually allow more definite conclusions, since if the children with more play experience score higher this should be due to the different experiences, such as the enriched play. However, these studies may be more artificial in their design. How natural is the play produced by the interventions, for example? Both kinds of study – correlational and experimental – have their own advantages and drawbacks.

Correlational studies of the role of play in development

Quite a large number of investigations have compared children who naturally engage in a lot of play behaviour, with those who engage in rather little. Do such children differ in other ways?

(i) In one study of English 3 and 4-years-old (Davie, *et al.* 1984) records were made of the behaviour of 165 children in the home environment. About 12 per cent of their waking time was spent in some form of fantasy play, though only about 3 per cent was role-play (the remaining 9 per cent was representational object play, that is, pushing a toy car along making motor noises). The investigators also assessed the intellectual level of each child using an intelligence test. There were no significant correlations (either positive or negative) between the time spent in any type of fantasy play, and intelligence test score. This might suggest that such forms of play are neither beneficial nor harmful to intellectual development at that age.

(ii) A study in the USA of children aged 4 to 7 years (Peisach and Hardeman 1986) found the children who engaged in more imaginative play (as assessed by observation, and interview) scored less highly on measures of cognitive ability (multiplication of classes, class inclusion, spatial viewpoint of others), especially at 5 years, but more highly on measures of social perspective taking, especially at 5 and 6 years.

(iii) In another study of children in the USA aged 3 to 5 years (Connolly and Doyle 1984), the amount and complexity of social fantasy in children was correlated with intelligence scores, and also with measures of social competence. There was again a zero correlation between fantasy play, and intelligence, but a positive correlation with the amount of social activity of the child, and a measure of role-taking skill. In a further study of 2- to 6-year-olds, however, (Cole and LaVoie 1985), the positive correlation of fantasy, and socio-dramatic play to role-taking skill was not confirmed.

(iv) Another study of 4-year-olds in the USA (Johnson *et al.* 1982) distinguished between socio-dramatic and constructive play. Again, dramatic play showed no correlation with intelligence scores, but the amount of time spent in constructive play correlated positively with intelligence, and negatively with the amount of time spent unoccupied.

Summary:

The results of these and similar studies are not conclusive. The value of a correlation can be due to some third factor (such as gender, personality) and need not reflect an actual causal relationship between play and, for example, intelligence or role-making skills. In so far as we do take this evidence as important, it tends to suggest that the amount of time spent in play is neither strongly beneficial nor strongly harmful to other aspects of development. Possibly, constructive play seems more useful for intellectual skills than dramatic play.

Experimental studies of the role of play in development

(i) Some investigators have tried to show the benefits of play experience using small-scale experimental studies. In such studies, carried out with children aged 3 to 6 years, children are taken individually to a small room. They are first given either a 'play' condition – allowed free play with objects – a 'training' condition (for example, being asked to compare the objects, by an adult) – or a 'control' condition (for example, colouring in a drawing). Then, the child is given some form of task or problem to solve. For example, the child might be asked to think of unusual uses for the objects they have just had; or to use the objects to construct a tool to retrieve a distant object. The typical design of such studies is shown in Figure 9.2 (obviously, the details have varied from one study to another).

At first these studies seemed to show that children who had free play with objects would do better on the problem tasks. However, subsequent studies suggest that this may not be so. Some of the earlier results seem to have been due to 'experimenter effects' – that is, the experimenter expected the children in the 'play' conditions to do better, and, probably unknowingly, gave them some extra help (perhaps encouraging them more by head nods or smiles as they made the right steps towards solving the problem). When the experimental studies are carried out with proper precautions, rather few differences between the 'play', 'training' and 'control' conditions seem to be found (Simon and Smith 1985). Probably this is because of the artificial nature of these studies, and their short duration (usually about 10 to 20 minutes). Although these studies now seem to fail to show any benefits of play experience, the sorts of play experience may be so different from those that children have in school or kindergarten, that the results are not very relevant to those situations (Smith 1988).

Figure 9.2 Typical design of experimental studies of the effects of play experience on problem solving

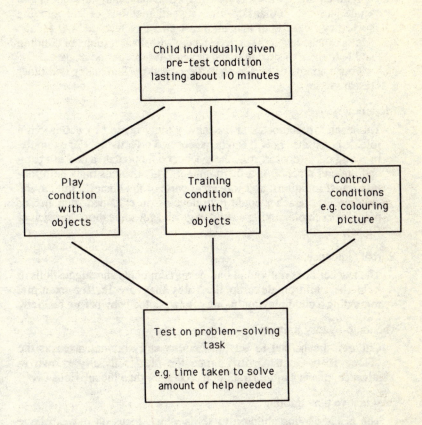

(ii) Another series of studies have been on a larger scale. These are the so-called 'play tutoring' studies, which attempt to increase the amount of fantasy or socio-dramatic play in classrooms. These studies usually last two or three months, and approach in scope the experimental studies of curricula, to be discussed in the next section.

The idea of 'play tutoring' was introduced by Smilansky (1968). She argued that socio-dramatic play was very important for the development of social, cognitive and language skills in young children. She thought there was value in both fantasy (make-believe transformations) and in role-playing. She therefore gave a high priority to increasing the amount and complexity of socio-dramatic play in children who seldom engaged in such play in schools and kindergartens. Smilansky tried several methods of encouraging such play, and found that the most effective method was for the adults or teachers to initiate role-play with small groups of children and help them to sustain it and develop it for a period of time.

Four variants of this method were used by Smilansky and other researchers:

Modelling.

The teacher participates in the play, joining in, and by acting out a role demonstrates how it can be performed effectively. For example, in acting out a 'doctor' role, the teacher could pretend a doll is a baby and pretend a pencil is a thermometer. This demonstrates both fantasy transformations, and some real parts of the doctor's role, to the children. The teacher could help develop an extended sequence of play, for example, asking a child to go and get some more 'medicine' for her.

Verbal Guidance.

The teacher does not join in but makes comments and suggestions to help the children develop the roles they are in, for example, reminding a child playing 'mother' to wash the baby before bedtime.

Thematic-fantasy training.

Children are helped to act out familiar story-dramas, such as the 'Three Billy-Goats Gruff'. Since the plot is usually known in advance, this is a more structured procedure than the previous two.

Imaginative play training.

The teacher trains children in skills which focus on make-believe activ- ities. For example, they are trained to use finger puppets, or practising using facial expressions to represent different emotions. Or, children might sit under a large sheet of grey paper and pretend to be outside on a rainy day. This kind of training focuses on fantasy and does not usually involve role-playing.

Smilansky and most other researchers have found that such forms of adult encouragement and training *do* increase the amount and complexity of fantasy and socio-dramatic play in young children, especially if they do not show much of this play initially. Furthermore, some increase is maintained even if the play training is stopped. But how successful is such play training? Do the children benefit from it? Many researchers have used a design like that shown in Figure 9.3. After pre- assessment, some children experience fantasy play training, others a control condition in which an adult is also present. This is followed by a post-assessment. These studies suggested that there are strong benefits to fantasy and socio-dramatic play. Children who had had play training improved on social, cognitive and intellectual skills more than the children in control groups.

Figure 9.3 Typical design of a study investigating the effects of fantasy play training

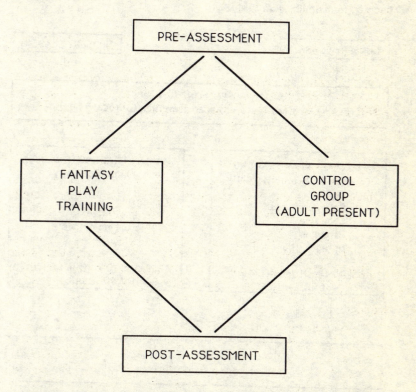

Unfortunately, these studies are not convincing experiments because of the inadequate nature of the control groups. In these control groups, an adult was usually present but only in a fairly passive way. The children in the fantasy play training groups received a lot of extra adult conversation and encouragement. Thus, the greater gain they made could be due *either* to the increase in fantasy or socio-dramatic play, *or* to the extra adult involvement. To choose between these alternatives, a better control condition is needed. I, and some other investigators, have compared fantasy play training with skills training. Skills training involves an equal amount of adult involvement, but *not* in a fantasy context. Rather, children might be encouraged in shape and colour matching, jigsaws, picture dominoes, and so on. The play of such a research study (Smith, *et al.* 1981) is shown in Figure 9.4. It is an expansion of the design shown in Figure 9.3; it includes an additional follow-up assessment.

Figure 9.4 Plan of a study comparing the effects of play tutoring and skills tutoring (from Smith, *et al.* 1981)

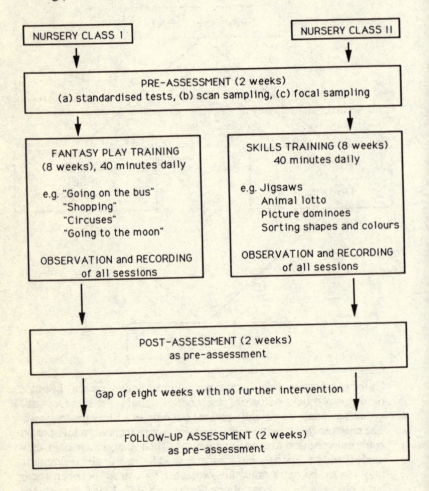

The results of this and similar studies (Christie 1983; Christie and Johnsen 1985) show that the fantasy play training and the skills training conditions are about equally effective. So far as the cognitive and language skills are concerned, children in either condition made gains, irrespective of which condition they experienced. This suggests that it is adult involvement which is the crucial factor, not the encouragement of fantasy. The children in fantasy play training have sometimes been found to be more sociable with other children, and more physically active, after the training is over. This may relate to the kinds of activities encouraged in the fantasy play and skills conditions in these particular studies (for example, the skills training activities were often sedentary), but which need not necessarily be the case.

Summary:

Fantasy and socio-dramatic play training is usually found to be enjoyable for children and teachers. It is one way of promoting active adult-child involvement. It may assist many aspects of children's development, but probably no more so than other kinds of involvement which do not involve fantasy or socio-dramatic play. It is, however, a useful way of increasing adult-child involvement without detracting from child-child interactions, and it may indeed enhance the latter.

Correlational studies of early childhood curricula varying in their use of spontaneous or structured play

These studies have looked at different schools or nurseries, and correlated the kinds of ways in which they do or do not use the opportunity for play (as, for example, in Figure 9.1) with the behaviour of the children and assessments of their development:

(i) In one study (Prescott 1973) 112 children aged 2 to 5 years were observed in fourteen day-care institutions in the USA. Each child was watched for about three hours. Of the fourteen pre-schools, seven were broadly type A in Figure 9.1, and seven were broadly type C. The children in type C centres were more physically active and exploratory, but less often challenged in cognitive ways. The children in type A centres directed more attention to adults, and received more adult guidance. They were observed to meet teacher's expectations more, but to be more often rejected or frustrated in their attempts to communicate or interact with teachers or peers.

(ii) In another study, 141 children aged 2 to 5 years were observed in five different pre-school institutions in the USA (Huston-Stein *et al.*

1977). These institutions varied in the extent of adult-directed activities (that is, types A,B versus C,D in Figure 9.1). There was more fantasy play in those institutions with less adult direction. Children in these institutions tended to be both more helpful, and more aggressive, to other children. Children in the institutions with more adult direction showed a higher level of conformity to adult expectations. They waited more patiently during delays, were more attentive during group activities, and took more responsibility for tidying up toys at the end of play sessions.

(iii) In another study of nineteen pre-school institutions in Oxfordshire for 3- to 4-year-olds (some nursery schools, some parent-organized playgroups) a distinction was made between 'structured programmes' and 'free programmes' (Sylva *et al.* 1980). All the institutions allowed some free play but in the 'structured programmes' there were also some compulsory, group-led activities. Children in the free programmes spent more time in fantasy play, but less time with structured activities. The observers felt that the children were presented with more cognitive challenges in the structured programmes. Children who experienced some structured sessions, also played in a more mature and challenging way when free play was allowed. The conclusion of this study was that some structured sessions which involved an adult with one or a few children were beneficial, but that too much structure (for example, largely or entirely adult-led activities) led to a decline again in cognitive challenge. There was an optimal amount of time spent in structured activities, preferably in small group work.

(iv) In a further study by the same investigators (Jowett and Sylva 1986), ninety children were observed when they were just starting primary school, at 5 years of age. Forty-five had previously attended nursery schools, usually characterized by more adult-structured activities (usually types A and B in Figure 9.1), while forty-five had attended play-groups (usually types C or D in Figure 9.1). The children were matched for age, sex and family structure.

It was found that the children who had attended nursery schools showed a higher level of cognitive challenge in their free play activities. They also spent more time on self-initiated writing and use of work cards, and were more persistent in the face of difficulties. In general, the children who had attended nursery school seemed more ready for primary school and more task oriented. Again, it should be emphasized that the nursery school curricula studied here were not structured all the time, and some considerable amount of free play and directed play would still have occurred.

(v) A study in London (Gardner 1942) examined the achievements of children in ten infant school classes. In five of these classes considerable time was given over to spontaneous play activities, and reading, writing and arithmetic were introduced largely through play or self-initiated activity (for example, writing through helping a child label a drawing; numbers through playing at shops). Thus, much of the curriculum would be of type C or type B in Figure 9.1. In the other five classes, matched for social composition, there was most emphasis on formal instruction (type A in Figure 9.1). The children were tested after about one and a half years in the classes. The children in the play-centred classes scored higher on measures of creativity and artistic achievement, such as assembling materials into pictures, and expressing ideas through drawing. They tended to stay at an activity for longer periods, and to score higher on physical training and some aspects of language development. They were more friendly with other children and adults.

There were no differences between the classes with respect to neatness, memory, vocabulary or reading skills. The children from the classes with formal instruction were clearly better at writing skills, and tended to be better at mathematical skills.

(vi) In a study of Canadian 5- to 7-year-olds (Evans 1979), observations were made in twenty school classrooms. In ten of these, the curriculum was described as 'play-based' or 'child-centred' (types C or B in Figure 9.1). The other ten comparison classes were less child-centred (type A in Figure 9.1). The children in the play-based classrooms showed more fantasy and role play, and more exploratory play. They engaged in more social interaction with other children, and more independent work which they initiated. In the comparison classes, children spent more time in teacher-led group experiences such as reading, word analysis and phonics and printing.

At the end of the school year, the children in the twenty classrooms were tested on a number of measures. There was little or no difference between the 'play-based' and comparison classes in language development, perceptual memory, role-taking skills, understanding of classification, or non-verbal intelligence. However, the children in the comparison classes did significantly better in two areas: reading and mathematics. They scored higher on tests of reading ability, reading comprehension, and understanding and testing mathematical concepts.

Summary:

These correlational studies, although they vary in detail, suggest that children in more 'play-directed' pre-school programmes engage in more playful and exploratory activities, and may interact more with other children. However, their play may be less cognitively complex, or challenging, than children who experience at least some degree or amount of adult-structured activities. More adult structure leads to greater conformity to institutional demands, and, at 5 to 7 years, to better achievement in reading and mathematics.

The conclusions of these studies are limited for two main methodological reasons. First, children were not assigned randomly to different pre-school curricula. Thus, differences in curricula may be partly due to differences in the children as they entered the pre-schools. Second, the curricula may have varied in a number of ways, not just whether they were play-based or not. For example, they may have varied in staff teaching, staff-child ratio, availability of space and equipment. These other factors may confound some of the results reported.

A survey by Osborne and Millbank (1987) of the progress of nearly 7,000 children who had experienced different kinds of pre-school provision (or none) has revealed the complexity of such relationships. The children were assessed on cognitive and behavioural measures at both 5 and 10 years of age. The effects of a large number of child background variables were taken account of statistically, such as social disadvantage, family size and composition. The main finding (having allowed for these factors) was that, compared to having no pre-school experience, attendance at pre-school *did* seem to help cognitive and educational development, the effect still being present at ten years. Some differences were found in the long-term effects of different types of pre-school, though these were not directly related to curricula effects or the kind of model shown in Figure 9.1. However, these differences were small, and the authors state that 'our findings persistently show that despite the many and considerable differences we have found between LEA nursery schools, playgroups, day nurseries, etc., their apparent effect on children's educational progress was remarkably similar' (Osborne and Millbank 1987: 241).

Experimental studies of early childhood curricula varying in their use of spontaneous or structured play

These studies have randomly assigned children to different curricula. The curricula have planned contents, and vary in the use made of spontaneous or structured play:

(i) In one study (Thompson 1944) nineteen 4-year-old children were randomly assigned, eleven to a free play pre-school programme (type D in Figure 9.1) and eight to a more adult-directed programme (probably like type B in Figure 9.1). After an eight- month period, it was found that the children who had the more adult-directed programme were more constructive when faced with possible failure, and showed more leadership, sociability and social competence with other children. There were no differences on intelligence test scores.

(ii) In another study (Smith and Connolly 1980), forty-four children were randomly assigned, twenty-two to a free play pre-school programme (type D) and twenty-two to a more adult-directed programme (mixed type, A, B). This experiment also lasted for an eight-month period. The children in the free-play programme engaged in more fantasy play, more physically active play, and generally interacted more with other children. They seemed to learn to control their social relationships and especially conflicts with other children, rather better than the children in the other programme. The children in the adult-directed programme engaged in more quiet activities, such as table work, and had more conversations and contacts with the adults in the pre-school. At times the adult-led activities did not fully gain children's attention, so they were more often observed as being 'uninvolved in any activity'. However, the adult-directed activities did seem to improve the children's concentration and attention span at activities. This progressively improved over the eight-month period. At the end of the period both groups of children experienced a modified free play curriculum for a few weeks, and during this time the children who had had adult-directed activities maintained their greater span of attention. No difference was found between the two groups of children on tests of cognitive ability, or language skills;

(iii) In another study (Miller and Dyer 1975), over 200 4-year old children were randomly assigned to fourteen pre-school classes. Eight of these were highly adult-directed (type A in Figure 9.1), while six were more child-centred (types B or C in Figure 9.1). The children were tested after eight weeks and again after six months. It was found that the children in the structured, adult-centred classes tended to do better in tests of cognitive and academic ability. The children in the more child-centred classes showed more inventiveness and curiosity and greater social participation with other children. A follow-up was made of the children four years later, at primary school. The differences found in areas of cognitive and academic ability at age four were not found at this later time point, though some differences in the non-cognitive areas were more stable.

(iv) In a further study (Schweinhart *et al.* 1986), sixty-eight children aged about 4 years were assigned to either a very adult-structured programme (type A in Figure 9.1), a programme which involved adults helping children plan activities (type B in Figure 9.1), and a more child-centred programme (type C in Figure 9.1). The children were assessed while at pre-school, and also through their years of school experience. The children experiencing the adult-structured (type A) programme showed at first the greatest gains in intellectual ability, but by the age of 10 years there was no remaining difference between the groups on this measure. On a subsequent assessment, when the children were 15 years of age, it was reported that the children who had experienced the other two programmes (types B and C) scored higher on good relationships with family participation in sports, and positive social adjustment.

Summary:

These experimental studies suggest that adult structuring of activities is beneficial for children's immediate concentration and attention span. Highly formal (type A) programmes may lead to the most rapid cognitive gains, but these may not be long lasting. If some degree of child choice is allowed, this stimulates curiosity and sociality with other children, and one study has found that such effects may be more long lasting than any cognitive effects of pre-school.

Physical activity and rough-and-tumble play

Almost all of the research on children's play has concentrated on constructive and dramatic or fantasy play, and it is these forms of play that teachers have sometimes encouraged or structured in the pre-school and infant school. However, young children can also spend quite a lot of time in physical activity play (such as running, climbing, sliding, swinging) either freely or with large apparatus such as climbing frames, and in rough-and-tumble play, where they chase and grapple with each other in an apparently friendly way. These kinds of play are more likely when plenty of space is provided, and in outdoor play. Rough-and-tumble play is more likely on soft surfaces. Young children confined for a while into a fairly restricted indoor space, are likely to engage in markedly increased physically active play when more space is available.

Young children are naturally active and need physical exercise for healthy physical growth and muscle development. Free outdoor play can provide this, though physical exercise can also be obtained from organized physical activities such as gymnastics and dance routines.

Rough-and-tumble play can involve large groups of children and may have some benefits in the social domain. Children generally choose to rough-and-tumble with friends, and possibly the activity helps to maintain friendship bonds. Also, in rough-and-tumble children need specific skills to distinguish play from aggressive intent, and they exercise reciprocal turn-taking skills such as chasing, then fleeing. This has led Pellegrini (1987) to hypothesize that rough-and-tumble play can facilitate social skills in children. It is not usually thought to have educational benefits in the cognitive sense. Some teachers discourage it or do not allow it because it can be noisy and disruptive. Other teachers allow it as a natural social behaviour which is very enjoyable for some children. Rough-and-tumble play seems to be clearly distinct from real fighting, so far as young children are concerned. For older children (approaching adolescence) it has been suggested that the distinction cannot be made so clearly. For a review see Humphreys and Smith (1984) or Smith (in press).

Conclusions

1. Spontaneous fantasy and socio-dramatic play is enjoyable for most young children. Some theorists believe it has intrinsic value for cognitive growth, but the empirical evidence tends to support the view that a child's fantasy play reflects its level of cognitive development rather than actively encouraging it. Such play may also be valuable for emotional development, but firm evidence is lacking.

2. Fantasy and socio-dramatic play can be readily encouraged and developed in younger children by school staff. This provides one way of facilitating adult–child interaction within the framework of an approach which allows scope for the child's own initiative. There may be benefits for the child's cognitive and social development, though probably no more than could be obtained from other forms of structured activities not involving fantasy.

3. In general, both correlational and experimental studies show that pre-school and infant school curricula which encourage the child to use some initiative in the choice of activities (types B and C in Figure 9.1), enhance children's curiosity and exploratory activity, and the quality of social relationships between children.

4. In general, both correlational and experimental studies show that pre-school and infant school curricula in which the staff play an active role in initiating and structuring activities (types A and B in Figure 9.1), enhance children's concentration span and persistence, the amount of cognitive challenge with which they are presented, their level of cognitive development and reading, writing and mathematical skills. Also, children conform better to immediate adult expectations and institutional requirements.

5. There is some evidence that the effects of early school experience on the child's cognitive development are less long lasting than the effects on personality and social relationships.

6. There may be advantages in an approach (such as type B in Figure 9.1) which tries to combine the cognitive advantages of adult structuring with the social advantages of allowing child choice. This

can be done, for example, by adults helping children to plan their own activities, support them, and review their progress. Such approaches may or may not use 'playful' modes of operation; the 'play-tutoring' approach uses socio-dramatic play in this way, but other, less playful, activities can also be used.

7. There may be advantages in mixing different ways of using play. Some periods of free play allow child choice and (with outdoor play) physical exercise and free exploration. There is some evidence that having periods of more adult-structured activities raises the level of maturity which children then show in free play periods.

8. Ultimately, any choice must relate sensibly to the needs of the children and of their society. Decisions about the role of play in the infant school curriculum must allow for many considerations, including (a) the previous experience and expectations with which children come to school; (b) the different types of play shown by young children; (c) the different ways in which play can be made use of in school; and (d) the aims and objectives of school institutions, within the society as a whole.

References

Bruner, J. (1972) 'The nature and uses of immaturity', *American Psychologist* 27: 687–708.

Christie, J. F. (1983) 'The effects of play tutoring on young children's cognitive performance', *Journal of Educational Research* 76: 326–30.

Christie, J.F. and Johnsen, E.P. (1985) 'Questioning the results of play training research', *Educational Psychologist* 20: 7–11.

Cole, D. and LaVoie, J.C. (1985) 'Fantasy play and related cognitive developments in 2- to 6-year olds', *Developmental Psychology* 21: 233–40.

Connolly, J.A. and Doyle, A.B. (1984) 'Relation of social fantasy play to social competence in preschoolers', *Developmental Psychology* 20: 797–806.

Davie, C.E., Hutt, S.J., Vincent, E. and Mason, M. (1984) *The Young Child at Home*, Windsor: NFER-Nelson.

Evans, M.A. (1979) 'A comparative study of young children's classroom activities and learning outcomes', *British Journal of Educational Psychology* 49: 15–26.

Gardner, D. (1942) *Testing Results in the Infant School*, London: Methuen.

Humphreys, A.P. and Smith, P.K. (1984) 'Rough-and-tumble in preschool and playground', in P.K. Smith (ed.), *Play in Animals and Humans*, Oxford: Basil Blackwell.

Huston-Stein, A., Freidrich-Cofer, L. and Susman, E.J. (1977) 'The relation of classroom structure to social behaviour, imaginative play, and self-regulation of economically disadvantaged children', *Child Development* 48: 908–16.

Isaacs, S. (1929) *The Nursery Years*, London: Routledge & Kegan Paul.

Johnson, J.E., Ershler, J. and Lawton, J.T. (1982) 'Intellective correlates of preschoolers' spontaneous play', *Journal of Genetic Psychology* 106: 115–22.

Jowett, S. and Sylva, K. (1986) 'Does kind of pre-school matter?', *Educational Research* 28: 21–31.

Krasnor, L.R. and Pepler, D.J. (1980) 'The study of children's play: some suggested future directions', in K. Rubin (ed.) *Children's Play*, San Francisco: Jossey-Bass.

Manning, K. and Sharp, A. (1977) *Structuring Play in the Early Years at School*, London: Ward Lock Educational.

Miller, L.B. and Dyer, J.L. (1975) 'Four preschool programs: their dimensions and effects', *Monographs of the Society for Research in Child Development* 40(162).

Osborne, A.F. and Millbank, J.E. (1987) *The Effects of Early Education*, Oxford: Oxford University Press.

Peisach, E. and Hardeman, M. (1986) 'Imaginative play and logical thinking in young children', *Journal of Genetic Psychology* 146: 233–49.

Pellegrini, A.D. (1987) 'Rough-and-tumble play: developmental and educational significance', *Educational Psychologist* 22: 23–43.

Piaget, J. (1951) *Play, Dreams and Imitation in Childhood*, London: Routledge & Kegan Paul.

Plowden Report (1967) *Children and Their Primary Schools*, 2 vols, Report of the Central Advisory Council for Education in England, London: HMSO.

Prescott, E. (1973) 'A comparison of three types of day care and nursery school/home care', paper presented at Biennial Meeting of Society for Research in Child Development, Philadelphia.

Rubin, K.H., Fein, G.G. and Vandenberg, B. (1983) 'Play', in P.H. Mussen and E.M. Hetherington (eds.) *Handbook of Child Psychology* (4th edn) vol. 4, Basel: S. Karger.

Schweinhart, L.J., Weikart, D.P. and Larner, M.N. (1986) 'Consequences of three preschool curriculum models through age 15', *Early Childhood Research Quarterly* 1: 15–45.

Simon, T. and Smith, P.K. (1985) 'Play and problem solving: a paradigm questioned', *Merrill-Palmer Quarterly* 31: 265–77.

Singer, J.L. (1973) *The Child's World of Make-believe*, New York: Academic Press.

Smilansky, S. (1968) *The Effects of Sociodramatic Play on Disadvantaged Preschool Children*, New York: Wiley.

Smith, P.K. (1988) 'Children's play and its role in early development: a re-evaluation of the "play ethos"', in A.D. Pellegrini (ed.), *Psychological Bases for Early Education*, Chichester: Wiley.

Smith, P.K., (in press) 'The role of rough-and-tumble play in the development of social competence: theoretical perspectives and empirical evidence', in B. Schneider, G. Attili, J. Nadel and R. Weissberg (eds) *Social Competence in Developmental Perspective*, Dordrecht, Holland: Kluwer.

Smith, P.K. and Connolly, K.J. (1980) *The Ecology of Preschool Behaviour*, Cambridge: Cambridge University Press.

Smith, P.K., Dalgleish, M. and Herzmark, G. (1981) 'A comparison of the effects of fantasy play tutoring and skills tutoring in nursery classes', *International Journal of Behavioural Development* 4: 421–41.

Smith, P.K. and Vollstedt, R. (1985) 'On defining play: an empirical study of the relationship between play, and various play criteria', *Child Development*, 56: 1042–50.

Sylva, K., Roy, C. and Painter, M. (1980) *Childwatching at Playgroup and Nursery School*, London: Grant McIntyre.

Taylor, P.H., Exon, G. and Holley, B. (1972) *A Study of Nursery Education*, London: Evans/Methuen Educational.

Thompson, G.G. (1944) 'The social and emotional development of preschool children under two types of educational programs', *Psychological Monographs* 56(5).

Chapter ten

The nature of friendship in the primary school

William Maxwell

Editors' introduction

William Maxwell's chapter on friendship combines a number of personal academic and practical perspectives. The chapter provides a thorough overview of the development of children's friendships, drawing upon earlier arguments in this volume concerning the roles of adults and peers. It poses that there is no simple interpretation or convention through which we can understand friendships in the classroom. And, while we can describe the roles and benefits of friendships for children, the existence of friendship is based on 'structured' access to other children and the social climate within which friendship activities take place. Maxwell also provides grounds for key classroom questions to be asked – especially the role and responsibility assigned to friendship groups for learning. Maxwell provides this information from the practised eyes of an educational psychologist.

Within the review the reader is made aware of the benefits, methodologies of studies, and developmental/structural aspects of friendship. Each section has educational implications, which are stated in relation to the area of study. The reviews raise many questions for the teacher and educational researcher: from first acknowledging that friendship has a vital role in the child's social (and learning) development; that not all friendships are the same, and there is evidence that 'close' friendship (as with other relationships) is the most meaningful for development; that the occurrence of friendship is strongly affected by the context within which it develops; and that friendship is not an all-at-once phenomenon but develops over time.

The review leads to a number of fundamental questions to be asked by the teacher. A key question is whether teachers should rely on children's self-provided friendship choices for learning groups. Teachers may find this strategy useful to initiate an informal atmosphere in the classroom, but the informality may co-occur with discriminatory choices of gender, ability and racial preferences. Group work can provide a very effective learning strategy, but its co-operative occurrence in friendship-orientated classrooms is questioned by Galton (Chapter 2) and its effective implementation (Slavin, Chapter 13) negates existing friendships in preference for those established in heterogeneous groups. The reader is referred back to considerations in this chapter of the dynamics of group and friendship formation and to question whether teachers may more effectively structure activities and groupings to facilitate learning-orientated friendships. In this consideration the role of personal/social education plays a major role in the classroom process and will lead to more effective curricular learning as called for in the national curriculum.

Introduction

Interaction with peers has long been acknowledged as playing a crucial role in child development. Damon (1983), like many authors before him, distinguishes between two social worlds in which children operate, the world of peer relations in which children seek each other out for companionship, affection and common amusement, and the world of adult–child relations based upon protection, care and instruction.

The fundamental characteristic of peer interaction which determines its distinctive developmental potential is the characteristic of equality. Peers, defined as children at similar stages of cognitive, social and emotional maturity, are at least potentially, equals. In contrast to interactions involving non-peers, there are no in-built differentials in terms of authority, knowledge or cognitive ability imposing a qualitatively different structure on interactions before they even begin. Whilst the growth of social groupings and hierarchies within any consistent peer grouping undoubtedly creates structure amongst the individuals involved, it is negotiated within the group, not imposed from the start. To use a term from Hartup (1978), peers are social co-equals.

Of course, peer interaction, from an early age, tends to occur within the context of regular groupings and within these social groups social networks of friendships develop. These networks of relationships act to constrain the nature and extent of interaction available to the members of the group. To enjoy satisfactory peer interactions children need to be able to integrate themselves into the pertaining social structure through developing relationships with their peers, making, keeping and breaking friendships in an appropriate manner. To a large extent children's friendships dominate their activity in the world of peers and their study is correspondingly a topic of central concern to students of peer interaction and the social development of children.

In the research literature a wide range of specific developmental functions have been proposed for interaction between peers and, particularly, between friends.

Some writers (for example, Hartup 1978) have stressed a socialization function, especially with regard to the child learning to control aggressive and sexual impulses in socially acceptable ways. This is said to be achieved primarily through the negotiation of relations with peers where the child directly experiences conflict resulting from unacceptable behaviour. If an ongoing friendship has existed between two peers in conflict with each other, then clearly the motivation to learn or apply skills which might resolve the situation is that much greater than if no such relationship has existed.

Other writers (for example, Rubin 1980) have stressed the role of peer relationships in the child's personal identity formation (for example, Mead 1934; Erikson 1968). Children construct images of themselves to a large extent through the eyes of those others with whom they most closely identify, that is, their peer group and, in particular, their friends. In the course of developing a self-image the child relies on feedback from others and on direct comparison with the attributes and characteristics of others. The peer group has a primary role in providing the child with this information on which his view of himself will be based.

Beyond simply providing information about him/herself to the child, the peer group also plays a crucial role in providing the set of values within which this information will be interpreted. The value of each child's particular set of friends will tend to determine which personal characteristics are valued positively and which negatively and to what extent they are accorded salience or importance. In this way, the extent to which children view their own self-image in positive or negative terms (self-esteem) is very much a product of the particular social group of which they are a member.

The acquisition of higher level social skills through interaction with peers has also been highlighted by some researchers (for example, Asher and Renshaw 1981). The peer group provides arguably the most efficient and highly motivating context for the learning and development of the social skills which will ultimately enable children to live effectively as a member of adult society. These are the skills of developing and regulating appropriate relationships with others at various levels, from professional or workplace acquaintanceships to close personal friendships.

Further, a crucial role for peer interaction in the process of cognitive development has been proposed. Piaget (1932) saw the conflict produced by interacting with similarly 'egocentric' peers as providing a crucial impetus in the process of decentration, a process which itself, according to Piaget, determines the structure of cognitive development in all spheres. More specifically, however, researchers in the recently-burgeoning field of social cognition have ascribed a central role for peer interaction in the development of cognitive constructs about others (Brooks-Gunn and Lewis 1978), about moral behaviour (Damon 1981), about the nature of human relationships (Selman 1981) and about the workings of society (Furth 1978). Thus, peer interaction is seen as playing a central role in specifically social areas of cognition as well as in promoting cognitive development generally.

Given the wide acknowledgement of the importance of children's friendships and peer relationships in the research literature, it is perhaps surprising that more account has not been taken of them as a factor in educational planning. To be sure, some of the more radical theorists in education, such as Montessori, Froebel and Steiner, were emphasizing the importance of children's social and personal development through experience with peers many decades ago, and the contemporary 'trend setting' national reports in the UK have also emphasized the need for more child-centred teaching methods with a greater emphasis on personal and social development and greater use of autonomous pupil groups (Scottish Education Department 1965; Plowden Report 1967). Yet over twenty years on from these reports, which were expected to revolutionize primary teaching, the radical shift towards pupil autonomy and group work does not appear to have taken a widespread hold (Kutnick 1988).

One of the factors underlying the failure to adopt the methods recommended by Plowden may be a lack of understanding of the social world of peer relationships and the role it plays in children's development. In many respects it is a closed world to adults, but research is gradually revealing its structure and functions. Through greater understanding it is to be hoped that teachers can more efficiently harness the powers of the peer group, both directly to encourage the fuller social and emotional development of pupils and to manage more effectively group-based methods of learning in the classroom. The aim of this chapter is to review the literature on children's friendships and peer relations with a view to promoting such understanding and identifying some practical implications for classroom practice. For convenience of organization, the review has grouped studies into the following: sociometric models of development, behaviour with friends, and individual differences.

Sociometric studies

One of the most prolific and enduring research traditions in the study of children's friendships and peer relations has been that based on the sociometric method.

First introduced by Moreno (1934), the sociometric method was soon widely adopted as a convenient way of exploring children's peer relationships. It has been in evidence consistently since then, adapted to tackle various different research questions. In its basic form the sociometric method involves asking all the members of a social group to nominate with which other members of the group they would most like to carry out a task, go to a social event, or simply be friends. This provides the researcher with a network of choices between members of the group, data which can be put to a number of uses.

Hallinan (1981), reviewing the body of sociometric research on children, identified three different lines of research within it: first, studies of factors correlating with popularity or sociometric status; second, studies of the determinants of individual friendship choice; and, third, studies of how contextual variables affect the structure of relationships within a group.

Popularity studies identify characteristics of children which determine whether or not they find it easy or difficult to make friends. Researchers used sociometric data to rank groups of children on the basis of the number of nominations they received from their fellows. A measure of peer acceptance was thus produced (for example, Potashin 1946). Later studies also asked children who they disliked amongst their peers (for example, Moore and Updegraff 1964) and categories of children grouped by sociometric status were produced. Thus Peery (1979) discriminated between 'popular' children (in receipt of many nominations, predominantly positive), 'amiable' children (few nominations, predominantly positive), 'isolated' children (few nominations, predominantly negative) and 'rejected' children (many nominations, but predominantly negative). The main aim of this line of research was to identify distinctive characteristics in popular children in the hope that knowledge of the bases of popularity would help teachers devise ways of helping unpopular children become better accepted. A number of characteristics of popular children have been consistently identified in this way. Hallinan (1981) lists the following in her review of the research: physical attractiveness, high intelligence, academic achievement, athletic ability, and high social class. Even the possession of a common Christian name has been associated with popularity (McDavid and Harari 1966). Some studies with a more explicit theoretical basis also appeared on the scene. Thus Marshall and McCandless (1957) found that dependence on adults was associated with poor sociometric status, and Hartup, *et al.* (1967) found that more popular children tended to dispense positive or 'friendly' acts to their peers with greater frequency, although popularity was unrelated to the frequency with which they dispensed negative or hostile acts.

It becomes apparent, however, that much of this research produced little that could help friendless children establish better social relationships. Most of the characteristics identified were either very broad and general, or were unalterable, and the correlations between them and sociometric status were, in any case, often weak. An easy way to boost the sociometric status of isolated and rejected children was not found.

The only line of research which has produced a substantial body of intervention work has been based on social learning theory (Bandura 1977). Evidence that children of poor sociometric status tend to display less confidence in general social skills than their more popular age mates (for example, Gottman, *et al.* 1975) was interpreted as indicating that isolated or rejected children were suffering the consequences of inadequate learning of social skills in their upbringing. It was therefore concluded that programmes of social-skill training which would teach these children basic social skills would enable them to then transform their social status and become popular. A variety of training techniques were tried. Initial studies using shaping and modelling techniques (O'Connor 1969, 1972) produced only short-term gains which were not replicated by later studies (Pullantz and Gottman 1981). More intensive coaching techniques yielded more promise on average (Gottman, *et al.* 1976; Oden and Asher 1977; Ladd 1981), but still some replication studies failed to get results (Hymel and Asher 1977). Some of the skills which were being taught in these studies were, for example, the skills of introducing oneself to new friends, maintaining a conversation with a partner, gaining entry to a group, developing co-operative play or managing conflict through compromise.

It may be that some of the problems encountered in creating consistently successful social-skill-coaching programmes may be caused by a lack of knowledge about the most effective skills to focus on (Asher, *et al.* 1979). It also seems likely, however, that it is over-simplistic to think of children's friendship patterns as simply reflecting their ability to perform a repertoire of key social skills. The aims and goals which children seek to fulfil through participating in peer relationships will have a major role to play in determining how they interact with their peers (Renshaw and Asher 1983). Thus, a child who may show himself to be capable of displaying appropriate social skills in certain situations may regularly behave in a manner which inhibits friendship development through the pursuance of maladaptive social aims (such as that of repeatedly demonstrating dominance over others or that of repeatedly eliciting evidence of liking from others). In these circumstances, therefore, the child's aims and goals have to be addressed as well as their skills.

Disillusionment with the quest for global determinants of sociometric status was responsible for the development of Hallinan's second research tradition. This was characterized by a search for the factors which influence individuals' decisions about whom they want to become friends with, regardless of their degree of overall popularity. As children of all levels of popularity do form friendships, it was reasoned that a better understanding of the basis on which individuals' compatibility as friends is determined would be potentially more helpful than a general indication of the characteristics of those at the extremes of the sociometric range. Generally speaking, friendship choices have been found to become more stable through the primary school years (Horrocks and Thompson 1946), and so the basis on which they are made presumably becomes more and more salient.

One individual characteristic which has been shown to have a very strong influence on friendship choice is gender (Tuma and Hallinan 1979). Children tend largely to choose friends of their own sex. Similarity of race has also been shown to have a strong effect on friendship (St John and Lewis 1975, Singleton and Asher 1977), although to a lesser extent Tuma and Hallinan (1979) further report a positive relationship between similarity of children's level of academic achievement and stability of friendship choice. Clearly, however, these are broad factors which act only to restrict the range of companions from which individuals' friendship choices are most likely to come. Any notions of identifying factors which determine children's friendships have proved to be quite unrealistic.

The third research tradition identified by Hallinan is perhaps the one with the most obvious direct implications for schools as it focuses on the relationship between contextual or situational variables and the pattern of relationships developing within a group. In one study Hallinan (1976) compared the patterns of sociometric nominations emerging in classrooms organized along traditional lines, to those emerging in classrooms of an 'open' type where children were organized in groups, and a much greater degree of interaction was encouraged. She found that friendship choices were more evenly spread amongst the group in the open classrooms. Choices were more polarized in the traditional ones, with greater numbers of very popular and very isolated children being apparent. Mutual friendship choices were also more stable in open classrooms. It would seem, therefore, that the way in which a teacher organizes the classroom has a significant effect on the nature of the peer relationships experienced by the pupils, with organizing and teaching along 'open' lines creating a more flexible and less exclusive type of social structure. Teachers should clearly take this into account when planning their teaching programmes. The methods used have broader implications than might often be assumed. Hallinan and Tuma (Hallinan 1981) also demonstrated the influence which teachers' patterns of classroom organization can have on pupils' friendships. They found that assignment to the same small group for instruction had a positive effect on the formation and stability of friendship choice. They also found that close friendships were more stable and more likely to develop if pupils were allowed to determine the membership of their work groups. Again the implications for teachers are clear.

Gender has been considered as a contextual variable, bearing in mind the very strong tendency for children to form friendships with peers of their own sex. Eder and Hallinan (1978) found that girls tend to form smaller and more exclusive 'cliques', whereas boys tend to develop a more open type of group structure. This accords with the earlier findings of Waldrop and Halverson (1975), who found that 8-year-old girls had more 'intensive' patterns of friendship in that they reported having fewer friendships but with a greater contact and commitment.

It is perhaps this third and most recent tradition of sociometric research which has proved to be the most promising application of the methodology. New developments of the method are allowing researchers to identify particular types of social structure and 'cliques' within larger groups. If teachers can develop a clear picture of the social dynamics of their own classes, then social groupings can be organized to facilitate co-operative work, making sensitive use of individual preferences. Furthermore, changes in the overall social structure of the class might be fostered through an alteration in teaching methods, although the extent to which this can be achieved remains to be determined.

Models of the development of children's friendships

Whilst much of the sociometric research could be criticized for being atheoretical and lacking a developmental perspective, more recently researchers have increasingly sought to put the consideration of children's relationships into a developmental framework.

One fertile theoretical model for the study of how friendships develop has been Harry Stack Sullivan's 'Interpersonal Theory of Psychiatry'. Sullivan (1953) proposed a theoretical progression for the development of children's friendships, based on the central premise that it is through such close peer relationships that children develop the ability to empathize and sympathize with other individuals.

Sullivan's model has four main stages: in the first stage (ages roughly 2 to 5), children are dependent on adults and not able to maintain peer relationships without adult intervention. The child will simply play with whoever is next to him or whoever he is directed at.

In the second stage, (ages 4 to 8) children have regular playmates, independent of any adult support. These relationships are still essentially self-centred, in that children have no commitment to maintaining them if they are not serving their immediate needs at that time.

176

Friendship is seen as a transitory phenomenon which has no in-built stability.

In the third stage (ages *c*. 7 to 12) intimacy and reciprocity appear in the relationship and friendships become correspondingly more intense. This is the stage of 'pre-adolescent chumship'. At this time, Sullivan argues, the child is rapidly developing real sensitivity to what matters to another person. The child becomes concerned to anticipate the friend's thoughts and feelings and so act in a way which will please the friend, thus further reinforcing their relationship. Friendships now have a much greater commitment from their participants who will seek actively to make and maintain lasting relationships of this type.

At the adolescent stage Sullivan focuses on the shift in attention from relationships with same sex peers to heterosexual relationships, arguing that the new challenge becomes that of translating some of the characteristics of chumships (loyalty, mutual support, and so on) to the context of relationships which also involve sexual dynamics. Friendships also continue to develop, however, with an increasingly sophisticated sensitivity to the needs, feelings, attitudes and beliefs of the other and with a greater emphasis on loyalty and emotional self-disclosure. In many respects the adolescent's friendships act as supports for their first dangerous forays into the world of heterosexual relationships.

Whilst Sullivan's developmental model is structured around the emergence of the ability to empathize and sympathize with others, Selman (1976, 1981) has proposed an alternative developmental stage model based on the classical Piagetian stages and founded on the premise that the development of friendships is intimately linked with the emerging cognitive abilities of the child in non-social contexts.

Selman presents four stages, at stage 0, corresponding to the early pre-operational stage of Piaget (age *c*. 3 to 6), friends are said to be merely 'momentary physicalistic companions', with there being no real relationship beyond the here and now. At this stage a close friend is simply someone with whom one is playing at the time. Friends at this stage, Selman says, are more accurately described as playmates.

At stage 1 (ages 4 to 9: Piaget's late pre-operational stage) there is the beginning of a relationship but it is mainly one way. The child sees the friend as one who provides assistance but does not appreciate any obligation to do so in return. Thus the friend is seen as someone who does things for one, and the notion of 'close' friendship is understood by the child as simply indicating that one has a better knowledge of the friend's likes and dislikes.

At stage 2 (ages 6 to 12: Piaget's stage of concrete operations) reciprocal obligations emerge but there is only 'fair weather' co-operation which easily breaks down when conflict arises. When conflicts do arise these tend to lead to a total breakdown of the relationship with there being no understanding of the possibility of a relationship continuing in spite of minor differences of opinion on specific issues.

It is only at stage 3 (ages 9 to 15: Piaget's stage of formal operations) that intimate and mutually-shared relationships are established with each partner recognizing a long-term commitment and a need to compromise and negotiate to resolve conflict positively. Friends now share problems and appreciate the importance of friendship as personal support on a mutual basis. These relationships can transcend conflicts but there is said to be an over-emphasis on jealously-guarded two-person cliques arising from anxiety about the difficulty of forming new friendships of this type.

At stage 4 (ages 12 to adulthood) the balance is redressed; the need for each partner in a friendship to establish relationships with others is recognized. There is still dependence on the relationship for support but there is also a degree of independence and autonomy which makes such relationships less intensely cliquey.

Both Sullivan's and Selman's models lay out a similar course of developmental progression over a similar time-scale. Whilst focusing on different aspects of social cognitive development, both also acknowledge a subtle interplay between developing cognitive constructs and social behaviour such that friendship plays a key role in providing a context which facilitates progress.

Two further studies also complement, and in some way support, the developmental progression described above. These studies are both based on the analysis of how children responded when asked to describe their friends. Bigelow and La Gaipa (1980) found that children in the early school years (*c.* age 6 to 9) described friends as being people who do the same things as them or live near to them or simply as people who were 'nice to them'. From the ages of about 8 to 12 the emphasis of their descriptions altered to a focus on character admiration, although this would tend to be in terms of fairly overt characteristics rather than personality or psychological traits. From the age of 12 onwards, however, notions such as loyalty, commitment, genuineness, intimacy and acceptance dominate the descriptions with a recognition also of the importance of common interests. Berndt (1981) also describes a similar progression from definitions of friends in terms of common play, association and pro-social behaviour in early childhood, towards definitions in terms of intimacy, trust and loyal support as adolescence approaches. Berndt differs from the previous authors, however, in that he sees the development of concepts about friendship as being a gradual, cumulative elaboration of a construct system, with many of the features of earlier stages being retained in later stages in some form (rather than a stage-by-stage progression in which each stage transforms the previous one and renders its concepts redundant).

Overall, with regard to children's descriptions of friends and their understanding of friendship at a level which they can articulate out of context, there seems to be considerable consensus about the general course of development. This consensus can be broadly summarized in terms of three stages of progression:

1. At the pre-school and early infant stages most children's thinking about friends is predominantly egocentric with only a superficial awareness of the friend as a person and relatively low commitment to the relationship.
2. In the middle primary years a greater awareness of the personal characteristics and viewpoints of others develops, and the child accordingly becomes more committed to friendships and shows more selectivity with regard to friends. In parallel with this, more complex forms of co-operative play develop.
3. By the latter years of primary schooling further levels of intensity have entered friendships, and concepts of loyalty and commitment have come to be of central importance in the context of a relationship which involves much self-disclosure, intimacy and meshing of views, opinions and values.

Developmental studies of children's behaviour with friends

The models of friendship development discussed in the last section were largely based on verbal or written evidence from children of various ages, acquired through interviews or structured tasks. Some researchers have attempted to follow this up with studies of how children actually behave with their friends in an attempt to see whether or not children's friendship behaviour, as observed in natural or experimental settings, supports the validity of these developmental models. The evidence from studies of this type suggests that children may actually display higher levels of friendship development in the context of their real-life behaviour with friends than these developmental models of children's thinking about friendship may suggest.

Vandell and Mueller (1980), looking at peer relationships amongst children of only two years of age, found evidence of lasting friendships, with the partners tending, mutually, to seek each other out in preference to other children and with a higher quality of interaction being evident between the partners. They contrast this finding with Selman's stage zero (age range three to six years) which describes friends as merely momentary, physicalistic companions.

William Maxwell

Howes (1983) studied groups of infants (median age 10 months), toddlers (median age 20 months) and pre-schoolers (median age 42 months). She found stable friendships, defined in terms of mutual preference, mutual enjoyment, and the ability to engage in skilful, reciprocal interaction in all these groups, although infant social exchanges were relatively short and generally object-centred, whilst older children become increasingly verbal and focused on fantasy and pretend play.

Rubin and Pepler (1980) report further observations of interactions between pre-school friends which seem significantly in advance of what would be expected on the basis of the cognitive developmental models. They suggest a downward revision of Selman's age bands is necessary if they are to reflect children's actual performance in the context of real friendships rather than their ability to articulate in the abstract.

What seems to be happening is that children first advance the sophistication of their relationships with friends in the immediate context of their day to day social interaction. They do not immediately acquire the ability to stand back and talk about friendship outside the immediate context with the same level of insight. Their understanding of relationships is, at first, context bound, and only later do they develop more generalized concepts which they can articulate in a more abstract setting. Furthermore, it may be the case that particular advances in general cognitive development, established through interaction with the world of objects in non-social contexts, are necessary before certain types of friendship behaviour or abstract concepts about friendship can appear. Thus, progress in the ability to imagine and co-ordinate views of an object from different physical perspectives may lay the groundwork for the ability to appreciate the differing desires or motives of a friend and reconcile them with one's own. There is clearly a complex interplay going on between general cognitive development, behaviour in social contexts and social cognition.

With regard to older children, Sullivan's stage of pre-adolescent chumship has stimulated research, particularly with regard to his contention that the development of a close relationship of this nature results in an enhanced tendency to empathize and sympathize with others. McGuire and Weisz (1982) compare children with close chums to those without, on a measure of altruistic behaviour. They found, as predicted, that the group with close chums performed more altruistically. Children with close chums were also better at imagining the feelings of another child in a different situation from themselves. Mannarino (1976) produced similar results using an adaptation of the prisoners' dilemma game and a questionnaire. Again pre-adolescents with close friends performed more altruistically than those without.

There does appear, therefore, to be a real relationship between having a close friend and greater social sensitivity to the needs and feelings of others, although the direction of causality has not been clearly established. It is interesting to note, furthermore, that McGuire and Weisz found no significant association between sociometric popularity and altruism or affective perspective-taking skill. The importance of distinguishing between friendship and popularity is again emphasized in that the benefits of close friendship do not necessarily accrue to children who are popular but only have relatively superficial relationships with their associates. For close friendships to develop, with their associated benefits in the development of empathy and social sensitivity, children need opportunities to interact frequently and intensively with their friendship partners, in a context which encourages mutual co-operation in joint activity. In so far as teachers seek to develop empathy and social sensitivity, therefore, they should plan opportunities for their pupils to interact with their friends in this way.

Models of individual differences in children's friendship patterns

Whilst the sociometric method has produced a significant body of research, its most appropriate use is at the level of measuring the social structure of a group, or identifying cliques within a group, rather than at the level of identifying and comparing the friendships of individual children.

When used as a basis for the identification or comparison of individuals' friendships, sociometric methods have a number of severe limitations.

First, there is no guarantee that sociometric nominations will be reflected in real substantive relationships in the playground. Children may make nominations based on wishful thinking rather than reality, or on the basis of a very short-term view of who they were playing with that day rather than whom they tend to relate to in the longer term. There is much scope for spurious nominations. This is particularly problematic amongst pre-school and early schoolage children (Hymel 1983). With children of this age individual nominations are only very weak evidence that a relationship exists. This problem has led researchers to concentrate on observational methods for the identification of relationships amongst pre-schoolers (for example, Clark *et al.* 1969), and there is some evidence that high levels of association can be taken as an indication of a significant relationship existing (Hinde *et al.* 1985). However, it is also true that association measures, taken alone, can be highly misleading in individual cases.

Second, models of popularity or sociometric status fail to take account of a crucial dimension along which peer relationships differ both between and within individuals, and that is the dimension of 'closeness' or 'strength' of the relationship.

Many authors, in recent years, have drawn attention to the importance of clearly distinguishing between the concepts of friendship and popularity in considering children's peer relationships (Foot *et al.* 1980; Hayes *et al.* 1980; Rubin 1980; McGuire and Weisz 1982; Serafica 1982). The two concepts are clearly distinct. To say that a child is more or less popular tells you little or nothing about the closeness or strength of the friendships. A child may be generally unpopular whilst still maintaining a close friendship which is satisfying and rewarding. Bearing this in mind, it is clearly naive to consider popularity or high sociometric status to be either a necessary or sufficient condition for social 'success'. Rubin (1980) warns against the uncritical promotion of popularity as a desirable end in itself as this may lead to an emphasis on superficial relationships and an unhealthy competitive atmosphere amongst children.

A significant friendship, to adopt a consensus definition derived from a number of sources, is a dyadic relationship which involves mutual positive affect and mutual preference such that the two friends prefer each other as interaction partners. Children who are not popular may none the less develop deep and rewarding friendships with one or two others, effectively providing them with high quality peer interaction, whilst children who are popular could none the less lack any friendships of such quality. The functions proposed for close, reciprocal friendships of this nature are usually similar to those proposed for peer relationships in general, only more so. Thus, the ongoing stability of the friendship is generally thought to be facilitating higher quality peer interaction which in turn leads to more efficient acquisition of social skills, enhanced social-cognitive development, personal identity formation and socialization.

The validity of distinguishing between close friendships of this type and more casual acquaintanceship is supported by a study by Hayes, *et al.* (1980). They found that pre-schoolers used different concepts when describing why they liked friends with whom they had reciprocal friendships from those they used to describe friends with whom they had only a unilateral relationship (that is, acquaintances with whom they would like to be friends but currently are not). Cognitively more advanced concepts seemed to come into play in describing reciprocated friendships. Howes (1983) also reports some findings which support the notion that, even at the pre-school age, close best friendships provide a context which facilitates the development of more sophisticated levels of social interaction between peers. She found that, over the course of a year, pre-schoolers in stable friendship pairs showed greater increases in the complexity of their interaction than those without such relationships.

Maxwell (1984) also reported similar findings. He found that pre-schoolers with reciprocal best friendships engaged in higher frequencies of co-operative play with their friends than they did with other children.

A proper description of a child's pattern of peer relationships, there-fore, has to take account of a number of factors and draw on a number of sources of evidence. As well as considering the number of friends with whom the child interacts and his/her best friend, it is also necessary to consider the strength of these relationships, and to what extent they are reciprocated. Maxwell (1984) provides an example of a system of analysis using a combination of sociometric and observational data which leads to a classification of pre-schooler's friendship patterns into one of three types: (i) children with a reciprocated best friendship, that is, a strong best friendship which seems to be of special importance to both partners; (ii) children with an unreciprocated best friendship, so a strong relationship does not, in fact, exist; and (iii) children with a pluralistic friendship pattern. These children seem uninterested in forming intense best friendships but prefer having a range of regular play companions none of whom is especially important or significant to them. There is some evidence from previous research (Waldrop and Halverson 1975) that a tendency to form either close best friendships on the one hand, or pluralistic patterns of relationships on the other, are relatively stable individual characteristics from pre-school to early school years. An increasing association with gender also seems to become apparent with sociable girls tending to develop close best friendships whilst the more sociable boys tend towards pluralistic friendship patterns.

Overall, a complex picture emerges. Whilst there is a clear tendency for children to develop stronger, more stable friendships through the pre-school and primary years (Horrocks and Thompson 1946) there are also individual differences and differences between the sexes, in the extent to which one special friendship will tend to dominate the children's pattern of relationships. These individual differences have to be taken account of over and above the general developmental trends. Whilst some developmental advantages seem to accrue in children who develop stable, reciprocated best friendships with peers, there may be other advantages associated with maintaining a more pluralistic pattern of relationships. The least advantaged group, socially, are those who have neither pattern properly established.

Summary and implications for educational practice

This chapter has reviewed a wide range of studies often coming from disparate research traditions but, viewed overall, a coherent picture begins to emerge. A number of general points can be made, each of which may have implications for educational practice.

A great deal of important learning and development results from interactions occurring within the context of children's friendships. Through their experiences with friends, children learn to manage social relationships, understand and accommodate the feelings and actions of others, and relate to social rules and routines. Clearly then, if one of the main aims of school is to encourage the development of pupils into well-adjusted, socially-competent adults, then the social life of the classroom has to be given consideration by teachers. Consideration should include fostering appropriate relationships within the group and facilitating constructive group activity between friends, and the rooting of educational experiences designed to promote social or moral under-standing in the context of children's day-to-day social experience with their own friends.

With regard to the first consideration, it is clearly inappropriate to be too prescriptive about how teachers might foster particular relationships between pupils. A variety of more or less informal approaches could be taken depending on the circumstances. In general, however, it is clear that much might be done by planning class activities based on friendship pairings or groupings. The important point is that these activities should encourage co-operation on equal terms towards joint goals, and involve the exploration of the feelings, views and personality of friends at an appropriate age level. Much classwork could be adapted to serve these purposes whilst also serving more conventional academic aims.

With regard to the second consideration, planning for promotion of social and moral development in pupils should include engaging them in structured group work focused on their relationships with friends rather than presenting them with parables or tales with a moral message set in contexts to which they cannot directly relate. As in other areas of the curriculum, learning will be more efficient when it is rooted in practical activity in a real life context with personal relevance to the child. What better, more personally salient context, than the children's own friendships in which they invest so much energy and importance?

Recent sociometric work has demonstrated that teaching style and classroom management can affect the social structure of a class. Teachers cannot avoid affecting the friendships of their charges in that decisions they make about teaching have consequences in that respect. Group-based teaching methods and encouraging children to have greater autonomy in choosing who they work with seems to have positive pay-offs in terms of more evenly spread and stable friendships within the group. A better understanding of the social dynamics of a class will enable teachers to use group-based teaching methods more effectively. Although this is an under-researched area, there will be advantages in grouping children on social rather than academic lines, at least for some purposes. To take an example, co-operative story-writing might be more productive between two friends of differing individual attainments than between non-friends of the same academic level. Similarly, practical problem-solving activities may be accomplished more effectively. (The increased quality of social interaction evident between friends as opposed to non-friends suggests that this will be so.)

Many teachers will be concerned about how best to help pupils in their care who are clearly failing to develop appropriate friendships within the class. Unfortunately the research reviewed provides no easy answers in this respect. It does, however, provide a framework within which to analyse the problem. The teacher should first consider whether or not the child simply lacks an appropriate repertoire of social skills with which to introduce him/herself to potential friends, maintain constructive interaction, and resolve conflicts. If the problem is not simply lack of knowledge of appropriate strategies which might be taught and practised, then the teacher will need to address the nature of the child's social aims or goals and what the child is seeking to get out of interacting with peers. In such cases a long-term dialogue will need to be established with the child to increase awareness of alternative ways of behaving with friends whilst helping to control and reduce the types of behaviours which interfere with friendship-making. As an element in any such programme, the teacher may also wish to harness the co-operation of parents as the child's behaviour may be more clearly understood and more effectively helped with the added insight and support thus gained.

The importance of distinguishing between popularity and friendship should also be taken into account. It is important to recognize that a high degree of popularity is not necessary for a child to have access to a close friendship with its associated benefits of more sophisticated interaction and the development of sensitivity to the feelings of others. Teachers should encourage their pupils to value and respect friendship with its enhanced developmental potential, rather than promoting the importance of popularity which can, in itself, be a very superficial achievement. Whilst there are individual differences in the extent to which children develop close friendships and with respect to the range of friends with whom they regularly associate, there are also general developmental trends towards closer friendships as children proceed through the primary years. All children can benefit from close friendships at their own appropriate level.

With regard to the broad developmental progression in children's concepts of friendship, there does seem to be considerable consensus. The insights provided should inform teaching practice at all levels but they also have less obvious implications for the ways in which teachers deal with class management. With pre-adolescents, for example, it is important to recognize the significance of loyalty to friends before asking one child to inform on another. With younger children loyalty is not a salient concept in this regard, and with older children it may be possible for them to appreciate a 'greater loyalty' to the social group at large. At the pre-adolescent stage loyalty between friends is crucial and absolute, not tempered by higher order considerations of justice. To force such a child to inform on a friend will consequently have very serious adverse implications. Applying knowledge of children's social development in this way, teachers may be able to deal more sensitively with potentially difficult situations.

Observational research on children's behaviour with friends should encourage teachers to pick up on instances of more advanced friendship behaviour between pupils, even though the children involved may not be able to articulate concepts of friendship at an equivalent level of sophistication. As in so many areas of development the ability to articulate concepts seems to lag behind their use in real-life situations. It is important, therefore, not to underestimate children's friendship behaviour on the basis of a limited ability to articulate concepts out of context.

In many respects personal and social development has been the 'cinderella' area of the primary curriculum in that it is only given the broadest and most unstructured type of consideration in educational planning. Perhaps, with a greater understanding of the nature of children's friend- ships emerging from the literature, a more central position will be given to this area of children's progress.

References

Asher, S.R. and Renshaw, P.D. (1981) 'Children without friends', in S.R. Asher and J.M. Gottman (eds) *The Development of Children's Friendships*, Cambridge: Cambridge University Press.

Asher, S.R., Renshaw, P.D., Geraci, R.L. and Dor. A.K. (1979) 'Peer acceptance and social skill training', paper presented at biennial meeting of the Society for Research in Child Development, San Francisco, USA.

Bandura, A. (1977) *Social Learning Theory*, Englewoods Cliffs, NJ: Prentice-Hall.

Berndt, T.J. (1981) 'Relations between social cognition, non-social cognition and social behaviour: the case of friendship', in J.H. Flavell and L.D. Ross (eds) *Social Cognitive Development*, New York: Cambridge University Press.

Bigelow, B.J. and La Gaipa, J.J. (1980) 'The development of friendship values and choice', in H.C. Foot, A.J. Chapman and J.R. Smith (eds) *Friendship and Social Relations in Children*, Chichester: Wiley.

Brooks-Gunn, J. and Lewis, M. (1978) 'Early social knowledge: the development of knowledge about others', in H. McGurk (ed.) *Issues in Childhood Social Development*, London: Methuen.

Clark, A.H., Wyon, S.M. and Richards, M.P.M. (1969) 'Free play in nursery school children', *Journal of Child Psychology and Psychiatry* 10: 205–16.

Damon, W. (1981) 'Exploring children's social cognition on two fronts', in J.H. Flavell and L. Ross (eds) *Social Cognitive Development*, Cambridge: Cambridge University Press.

Damon, W. (1983) *Social and Personality Development*, New York: W.W. Norton.

Eder, G. and Hallinan, M. (1978) 'Sex differences in children's friendships', *American Sociological Review* 43: 237–50.

Erikson, E.H. (1968) *Identity, Youth and Crisis*, New York: W.W. Norton.

Foot, H.C., Chapman, A.J. and Smith, J.R. (1980) 'Patterns of interaction in children's friendships', in H.C. Foot, A.J. Chapman and J.R. Smith (eds) *Friendship and Social Relations in Children*, Chichester: Wiley.

Furth, H.G. (1978) 'Young children's understanding of society', in H. McGurk (ed.) *Issues in Childhood Social Development*, London: Methuen.

Gottman, J.M., Gonso, J. and Rasmussen, B. (1975) 'Social interaction, social competence and friendship in children', *Child Development* 46: 709–18.

Gottman, J.M., Gonso, J. and Schuler, P. (1976) 'Teaching social skills to isolated children', *Journal of Abnormal and Social Psychology* 4: 179–97.

Hallinan, M.T. (1976) 'Friendship patterns in open and traditional classrooms', *Sociology of Education* 49: 254–65.

Hallinan, M.T. (1981) 'Recent advances in sociometry', in S.R. Asher and J.M. Gottman (eds) *The Development of Children's Friendships*, Cambridge: Cambridge University Press.

Hartup, W.W. (1978) 'Children and their friends', in H. McGurk (ed.) *Issues in Childhood Social Development*, London: Methuen.

Hartup, W.W., Glazer, J.A. and Charlesworth, R. (1967) 'Peer reinforcement and sociometric status', *Child Development* 38: 1017–24.

Hayes, D.S., Gershman, E. and Bolin, L.J. (1980) 'Friends and enemies: cognitive bases for preschool children's unilateral and reciprocal relationships', *Child Development* 51: 1276–9.

Hinde, R.A., Titmus, G., Easton, D. and Tamplin, A. (1985) 'Incidence of "friendship" and behaviour towards strong associates versus nonassociates in preschoolers', *Child Development* 56: 234–45.

Horrocks, J.E. and Thompson, G.G. (1946) 'A study of the friendship fluctuations of rural boys and girls', *Journal of Genetic Psychology* 69: 189–98.

Howes, C. (1983) 'Patterns of friendship', *Child Development* 54: 1041–53.

Hymel, S. (1983) 'Preschool children's peer relations: issues in sociometric assessment', *Merrill-Palmer Quarterly* 29: 237–60.

Hymel, D. and Asher, S.R. (1977) 'Assessment and Training of Isolated Children's Social Skills', paper presented at the biennial meeting of the Society for Research in Child Development, New Orleans, USA.

Kutnick, P.J. (1988) *Relationships in the Primary School Classroom*, London: Chapman.

Ladd, G.W. (1981) 'Effectiveness of a social learning method for enhancing children's social interaction and peer acceptance', *Child Development* 52: 171–8.

McDavid, J.W. and Harari, H. (1966) 'Stereotyping of names and popularity in grade school children', *Child Development* 37: 453–9.

McGuire, K.D. and Weisz, J.R. (1982) 'Social cognition and behaviour correlates of pre-adolescent chumship', *Child Development* 53: 1478–84.

Mannarino, A.P. (1976) 'Friendship patterns and altruistic behaviour in pre-adolescent males', *Developmental Psychology* 12: 555–6.

Marshall, H.R. and McCandless, B.R. (1957) 'Relationships between dependence on adults and social acceptance by peers', *Child Development* 28: 413–19.

Maxwell, W.S. (1984) 'Patterns of friendship and interaction style in young children', unpublished PhD thesis, Edinburgh University.

Mead, G.H. (1934) *Mind, Self and Society*, Chicago: University of Chicago Press.

Moore, S.G. and Updegraff, R. (1964) 'Sociometric status of preschool children as related to age, sex, nurturance giving and dependency', *Child Development* 35: 519–24.

Moreno, J.L. (1934) *Who Shall Survive?*, Washington: Nervous and Mental Disease Publishing Company.

O'Connor, R.D. (1969) 'Modification of social withdrawal through symbolic modelling', *Journal of Applied Behaviour Analysis* 2: 15–22.

O'Connor, R.D. (1972) 'Relative efficacy of modelling, shaping and the combined procedures for modification of social withdrawal', *Journal of Abnormal and Social Psychology* 79: 327–34.

Oden, S. and Asher, S.R. (1977) 'Coaching children in social skills for friendship making', *Child Development* 48: 495–506.

Peery, J.C. (1979) 'Popular, amiable, isolated, rejected: a reconceptualisation of sociometric status in preschool children', *Child Development* 50: 1231–4.

Piaget, J. (1932) *The Moral Judgement of the Child*, New York: Free Press.

Plowden Report (1967) *Children and their Primary Schools*, 2 vols, Report of the Central Advisory Council for Education in England: HMSO.

Potashin, R. (1946) 'A sociometric study of children's friendships', *Sociometry* 9: 48–70.

Pullantz, M. and Gottman, J.M. (1981) 'Social skills and group acceptance', in S.R. Asher and J.M. Gottman (eds) *The Development of Children's Friendships*, Cambridge: Cambridge University Press.

Renshaw, P.D. and Asher, S.R. (1983) 'Children's goals and strategies for social interaction', *Merrill-Palmer Quarterly* 29: 353–74.

Rubin, Z. (1980) *Children's Friendships*, London: Fontana.

Rubin, K.H. and Pepler, D.J. (1980) 'The relationship of child's play to social-cognitive growth and development', in H.C. Foot, A.J. Chapman and J.R. Smith (eds) *Friendship and Social Relations in Children*, Chichester: Wiley.

Scottish Education Department (1965) *Primary Education in Scotland (The Primary Memorandum)*, Edinburgh: HMSO.

Selman, R.L. (1976) 'Towards a structural analysis of developing interpersonal relations concepts: research with normal and disturbed preadolescents', in A.D. Pick (ed.) *Minnesota Symposium on Child Psychology*, vol. 10, Minneapolis: University of Minnesota Press.

Selman, R.L. (1981) 'The child as a friendship philosopher', in S.R. Asher and

J.M. Gottman (eds) *The Development of Children's Friendships*, Cambridge: Cambridge University Press.

Serafica, F.C. (1982) 'Conceptions of friendship and interaction between friends: an organismic-developmental perspective', in F.C. Serafica (ed.) *Social-Cognitive Development in Context*, London: Methuen.

Singleton, L.C. and Asher, S.R. (1977) 'Peer preference and social interaction amongst third grade children in an integrated school district', *Journal of Educational Psychology* 69: 330–6.

St John, N. and Lewis, R. (1975) 'Race and the social structure of the elementary classroom', *Sociology of Education* 48: 346–68.

Sullivan, H.S. (1953) *The Interpersonal Theory of Psychiatry*, New York: Norton.

Tuma, N. and Hallinan, M. (1979) 'The effects of sex, race and achievement in school on children's friendships', *Social Forces* 57: 1265–85.

Vandell, D.L. and Mueller, E.C. (1980) 'Peer play and friendships during the first two years', in H.C. Foot, A.J. Chapman and J.R. Smith (eds) *Friendship and Social Relations in Children*, Chichester: Wiley.

Waldrop, M.F. and Halverson, C.F. (1975) 'Intensive and extensive peer behaviour: longitudinal and cross-sectional analysis', *Child Development* 46: 19–26.

Chapter eleven

Sex roles in the primary classroom

Paul Croll and Diana Moses

Editors' introduction

The last decade or so has seen a notable increase in the amount of research attention directed at the issue of gender differentiation within the school. As Croll and Moses point out here, it is clear that within society generally one's gender has a critical impact upon one's life chances. It is natural to assume that school reflects and is, at least, partially responsible for these differences.

At the start of the decade clear differences existed in the 16+ age range, and while these differences are subject to change they are clearly still significant. Croll and Moses' task here is to assess available evidence with a view to establishing the role of the primary school in this. As will be seen, their conclusion is that while differences between boys and girls clearly do exist at primary school, the evidence suggests that girls are not educationally disadvantaged by their experiences there.

Croll and Moses suggest that researchers need to pay closer attention to an examination of the links between experiences in the primary school and later developments at secondary level. No adequate account of these links currently exists, but factors related to self-esteem and motivation are likely to prove significant. The reader is therefore asked to consider the case made out here together with the issues discussed by Schunk and Rogers (Chapters 5 and 6).

Croll and Moses also argue that studies picking out gender differences may be influenced by the different levels of special educational needs and disruptive behaviour found in boys and girls. The reader is also, therefore, directed specifically to Chapters 12 and 13 on special needs and co-operative group work.

Introduction

The focus of attention of this chapter is an exploration of the differences between the educational experiences of boys and girls in their primary schools. Are girls and boys treated differently from one another and do they have different educational experiences in the early years of schooling? If so, what significance and consequences does such differentiation have? Do boys and girls develop different skills and attitudes, for example, and do any differences between classroom experiences and educational attitudes and achievements which emerge in the primary school years have implications for later educational performance and in the adult world of work?

As we shall see later in this chapter, there is evidence that girls flourish in the primary school. They at least hold their own on measures of academic attainment compared with boys and they are much less likely to experience problems, either in connection with their academic performance or with their behavioural and emotional adjustment to school. On the other hand we know that, later in life, females are most unlikely to enjoy the same degree of occupational success and financial rewards as their male peers. In Britain in the 1980s women still do not enjoy the same occupational opportunities as men. They earn considerably less on average and, even within the same occupational groups, tend to have lower incomes. Much of the work done exclusively or virtually exclusively by women is particularly poorly paid. Women are underrepresented at the top of all occupations, even those such as nursing and primary school teaching which have traditionally been the preserve of women and in which they still predominate numerically (see Equal Opportunities Commission 1987, for a summary of some of the relevant statistical information on the economic situation of women).

The question naturally arises of whether, despite the apparently satisfactory performance of girls at primary level, they are, nevertheless, in some way being prepared to be second best to boys. A number of writers have suggested that the educational system is, in various ways, implicated in the disadvantages females appear to suffer in later life (for example, Acker 1984, 1988). Related to such arguments is the suggestion put forward by Sara Delamont that schools do not simply reflect the different sex roles and gender differentiation of the wider society but exaggerate and amplify such distinctions (Delamont 1980, 1983). Delamont argues that schools operate as a conservative force in which traditional female roles are emphasized and exaggerated and in which females suffer discrimination greater than that prevailing elsewhere.

In this chapter we shall attempt to summarize the available information on various aspects of the different school experiences, attainments and responses of girls and boys in British primary schools. First we shall consider the extent of gender differentiation in the everyday experience of the primary classroom. This analysis will be extended to look at possible disadvantaging features of classroom life, especially those related to teacher–pupil interaction. We shall then examine the learning outcomes for pupils, comparing the attainments in academic subjects and the extent of academic and related difficulties experienced by girls and boys. Finally we shall consider evidence on differences between female and male pupils' attitudes to and perceptions of school and differences in the ways that teachers perceive male and female pupils. Following the presentation of the empirical evidence on gender differences in the experience of primary education, we shall return to the question of the link between early educational experience and later occupational and financial disadvantage, and also consider whether schools exaggerate gender differentiation compared with that existing in the wider society.

Gender differentiation in the classroom

Gender differentiation is a prominent feature of this and other societies and it is not surprising that differentiation between boys and girls should be a feature of schools. Schools cannot exist in a vacuum and by the time they come to school, and then alongside their school experience, children have learnt and continue to learn a great deal about the world from their parents, their peers, books, comics, television and other sources. When they come to school at the age of four or five the child will have a clear image of her/himself as a boy or girl. The great majority of given names are specific to males or females, similarly, the clothes children wear are often gender specific. Boys and girls are likely to have been treated rather differently from the time that they were born and, for instance, given different toys to play with. Evidence on sex differences in pre-school play is given by Serbin (1983).

Studies such as those of King (1978) have documented the routine pattern of gender differentiation in a variety of school routines and activities. Teachers also automatically used gender as an organizing category within the classrooms in his study. Boys' and girls' names were listed separately on the register, coats were hanged up separately, record cards were in different colours for boys and for girls, histograms containing data from the children were done separately for girls and boys and so on. King notes that a significant feature of these practices was that they were 'taken for granted' and not regarded as in any way problematic by the teachers who did not think they needed explaining, still less justifying. In a study of a Scottish primary school Hartley (1985) describes the predominance of organizational practices based on gender and also notes that children's friendships tend to be same-sex specific. Another feature of the classrooms described by King was the use of competition between boys and girls both as a strategy for control and as an organizational feature of the classroom. Contrasts between the behaviour of the groups were made by teachers and 'gender-inappropriate' behaviour commented on. Task were sometimes divided between boys and girls with a competitive element introduced.

However, gender differentiation is not always a feature of descriptions of classrooms. As Delamont (1980) points out, the British observational studies of classrooms conducted before that of King made no reference at all to gender. Later studies have not generally seen gender as central although studies such as those of Hartley (1985) consider gender differences. Pollard (1985) considers gender as an issue but concludes that other differentiating characteristics of children are more relevant for his analysis of the social experience of schooling. He writes of '... the close similarity in the perspectives of boys' and girls' friendship groups regarding school which led me to focus primarily on the goody, joker and gang distinction as having more analytic power than that of gender' (Pollard 1985: 195). King, who is one of the researchers to put most emphasis on gender differentiation, also stresses that this is only one of the differentiating factors in the classroom and not the most important of these (King 1978).

What emerges from these studies is that primary classrooms are, in a commonsense fashion, heavily gender differentiated. Primary classes are made up of little boys and little girls rather than little children and reference to this and the use of it for organization, control and class management is a routine feature of teaching in the primary school. Such differentiation is probably the most obvious single feature of primary classrooms and the lack of reference to it in many discussions of teaching is an indication of its 'taken-for-granted' nature. This is different, however, from saying that gender differentiation is the most important feature of primary classrooms or, in particular, that it operates in a way that disadvantages one or other of the sexes. Some possible ways in which the different experiences of the primary classrooms may in fact be disadvantaging, in particular to girls, will be considered below.

Teacher–pupil interaction in the classroom

One possible difference in the classroom experience of boys and girls which has received recent attention is that girls may be disadvantaged in the classroom by receiving less attention from the teacher than is given to boys. Some fairly extreme claims about this gender imbalance have been made, especially by writers approaching the issue from a feminist perspective. Perhaps the best-known work in this tradition is that of Spender who writes of boys receiving '... so much more attention from teachers than do girls...' (Spender 1982: 54). Spender also claims that gender imbalances are so routinized and expected in classrooms that even when teachers are trying to equalize attention girls get only just over a third of the teacher's time (Spender 1982). However, no details are given of the basis of these assertions.

Similarly, Stanworth (1981), reporting on a study of pupil perceptions of classroom interactions, shows pupils reporting boys as twice as likely to seek teacher attention and four times as likely to offer contributions to discussion. Buswell (1981: 196) writes of lessons in which female pupils took no part at all and that there were '...many more classes [in which] girls received only minimal attention compared with boys'.

Some of these assertions come from studies of classrooms using a qualitative observational methodology. Other studies of classrooms using such an approach do not report such differences. As was shown above, Pollard (1985), in an extensive observational study of primary schools, made little use of gender as an explanatory category. Similarly, gender differences do not emerge from the observations in infant classrooms reported by Sharp and Green (1975). King (1978) and Hartley (1985) both focus on gender differences in their studies of primary classrooms but do not report differences in levels of teacher interaction.

The obvious way to establish whether boys get more attention than girls in the primary classroom is to observe in a substantial sample of classrooms and to count or time in a systematic fashion the number of teacher interactions which are directed to boys and girls and see if they differ. If we wish to go beyond statements about the relative number of interactions and say something about the type of interaction it will also be necessary to distinguish between different types of interaction in the counting or timing procedure. Data relevant to this issue come from the many studies which have conducted systematic observation in classrooms.

Systematic observation provides a method of getting precise quantitative data on aspects of interaction and behaviour in classrooms. Observations are made by using a predetermined set of categories and a precise timing system. For example, a very simple system relevant to the present discussion would be one where an observer focused observation on a teacher and every ten seconds noted whether or not the teacher was involved in a one-to-one interaction with a pupil and, if so, whether this was with a boy or a girl. Such an observation system allows a precise estimate to be given of the amount of teacher interaction with male and female pupils. Clearly such a system could be made more sophisticated and could also allow the categorization of type of interaction such as curriculum-related or non-curriculum-related, or whether the teacher or the pupil had initiated the interaction. A full account of this kind of classroom research can be found in Croll (1986).

A large number of studies using systematic observation have been conducted in school classrooms, most of them in the United States, but also in British classrooms. Although the issue of differential attention to boys and girls has not usually been the main focus of these studies, many of them provide data on such differences. Alison Kelly has recently published a meta-analysis of 81 research studies which provide quantitative data on the relative amount of teacher interaction received by boys and girls in classrooms (Kelly 1988). Meta-analysis is a technique for summarizing the results of different studies to give an overall estimate of an effect (Kelly 1986). In addition to data on overall differences in teacher interactions with boys and girls, Kelly also retrieves information about different aspects of the interactions from many of the studies.

The analysis of overall differences in the amount of teacher interaction with boys and with girls derived from the meta-analysis shows that girls receive 44 per cent of all classroom interactions and boys receive 56 per cent. The type of interactions in which girls were least well represented were those involving criticism by the teacher. Girls received only 35 per cent of criticisms and only 32 per cent of criticisms directed at behaviour. However, the underrepresentation of girls cannot be accounted for simply by the boys being more heavily criticized: girls received 44 per cent of questions, 44 per cent of response opportunities, and 48 per cent of praise. The analysis also shows that the underrepresentation of girls in classroom interactions does not arise from an unwillingness to participate as girls were more likely than boys to volunteer or put their hands up (52 per cent). They were, however, less likely than boys to call out answers (41 per cent). Another result to emerge from the study was that when children were divided into those having desirable characteristics (high ability, good behaviour, and so on) and those having undesirable characteristics (low ability, poor behaviour), the sex bias was more pronounced among the 'desirable' group than among the 'undesirable' group.

The studies analysed by Kelly covered a variety of age ranges and not just the primary years. Relatively few of the studies were conducted in Britain and over 80 per cent of them were American. A breakdown of the estimates from different groups of studies shows that in those conducted by British authors the sex bias was very slightly less (45 per cent). Studies conducted on 6- to 11- year-olds also show a slightly lower sex bias (46 per cent) although the sex bias in studies of children under 6 is much greater (41 per cent).

This sort of meta-analysis provides a very valuable overall estimate from a wide range of studies, but it is not possible to derive from it specific estimates for British primary schools. Moreover, a number of recent major studies of British primary schools were not included in the analysis. For these reasons, and also because it is interesting to locate estimates of interaction differences in specific identifiable studies, a number of researches using systematic observation in British primary school classrooms will be discussed below. There are five studies published within the last ten years which give quantifiable data on teacher–pupil interactions in a large sample of English primary school classrooms, and which allow distinctions to be made between interactions with male and female pupils. These are: the ORACLE research which provides observational data on 120 classrooms across the junior age range (Galton *et al.* 1980), the *One in Five* study (Croll and Moses 1985) which provides data on 34 second year junior classes, the NFER study (National Foundation for Educational Research 1987) giving data on 59 third and fourth year junior classrooms, the Inner London Education Authority (ILEA) study (Mortimore *et al.* 1988) giving data on 50 Inner London junior classrooms, and the Thomas Coram study (Tizard *et al.* 1988) based on observation on 30 infants' classrooms. Of these studies only the ORACLE research was included in the meta-analysis described above (Kelly 1988, Appendix 1), probably because the others were published too recently for the information to be available.

The ORACLE research (Galton *et al.* 1980) was the first large-sale observational study to be conducted in British classrooms. Gender differences were not a feature of the main analysis which concentrated on the impact of different teaching approaches and the consequences for classroom interaction of a predominantly individualized approach to teaching. It showed how, even when teachers interacted mainly with individual pupils, the main contact with the teacher of pupils in the class was as a member of the whole class audience. This clearly has implications for differences between boys and girls in the amount of teacher attention they received. In the data derived from observations of individual pupils and describing the amount of teacher interaction they received, boys were observed to receive more individual attention than girls. In the terms used by Kelly, boys received 54 per cent of the teachers' attention to individuals while the girls received 46 per cent. But when all interactions, including whole class interactions, are included in the analysis, girls are involved in over 49 per cent of interactions compared with 46 per cent of individual interactions.

The research reported in *One in Five* (Croll and Moses 1985), and in a subsequent analysis of these data (Croll 1986), was mainly concerned with children with special educational needs, but also included observational data on the classroom interactions of a control sample of other children in second year junior classrooms. These data provide a very similar picture of sex differences in pupil–teacher interaction to those of the ORACLE study. Girls receive 46 per cent of individual teacher interactions and boys 54 per cent. As in the ORACLE study, the great majority of teacher–pupil interactions were whole class interactions where there were no sex differences.

The ILEA junior school project followed the progress and school experiences of 2,000 children as they went through 50 Inner London junior schools and observed children in second and third year junior classes. This research found that 'Teachers contributed more at an individual level with boys than with girls...' (Mortimore *et al.* 1988: 167). Expressed in terms comparable with those used in the Kelly analysis, girls received 46 per cent of the teachers' individual attention in the second year classroom and 42 per cent in the third year classrooms. The major difference between boys and girls was that boys received more comments, both critical and neutral, about their behaviour, but this did not completely account for the gender imbalance.

These three projects all found sex differences in levels of teacher interaction with boys and girls. The final two studies, however, found no such differences. A project conducted by the National Foundation for Educational Research used the ORACLE observation system to observe language and mathematics lessons in 59 3rd and 4th year junior classes (NFER 1987). This study found no differences in the amount of teacher attention to boys and to girls in either mathematics lessons or language lessons.

Finally, research conducted by the Thomas Coram Research Centre observed pupils in 30 classes in ethnically mixed Inner London infant schools (Tizard *et al.* 1988). This study also reported no differences in overall levels of teacher interactions with boys and girls.

A consideration of Kelly's meta-analysis and of the five British studies discussed above shows that there is a consistent tendency for girls, on average, to receive slightly less individual teacher attention than boys although this is not invariably so in either individual classrooms or in all studies. The studies reviewed by Kelly range from those which show no differences in interaction to those showing girls receiving less than 40 per cent of interactions. Averaged across all the studies girls received 44 per cent of interactions. Of the five recent large-scale British studies, three showed lower levels of interaction with girls of an extent broadly comparable to Kelly's results while two showed no differences. No study has shown girls receiving more individual teacher attention than boys. The studies which show boys getting more attention almost invariably show that this is in part due to boys receiving substantially more behavioural criticism, but the studies also show that this does not account for the overall differences in levels of interaction. Compared with the claims reported above about the discrepancies in teacher attention across the sexes, the differences reported here are not large but, as Kelly (1988) points out, over a school career they amount to a considerably lower level of direct contact with the teacher for individual girls.

Various explanations have been put forward for this pattern of inequality in teacher interaction. Some authors have suggested that sexist bias is so prevalent in society that male dominance is 'natural' and effectively invisible (for example Megarry 1981; Spender 1982). Kelly (1988) suggests that the emphasis that teachers put on working with children as individuals and responding to their individual needs may mean that lack of equality between groups such as males and females is not apparent or not important to them. An observation originally made by French and French (1984) is that there is not a general pattern of higher levels of interaction with all boys but rather a tendency for a few boys to get more attention than other pupils generally. This explanation was tested by Croll (1986) in an analysis of classroom interaction in 34 2nd year junior classes. The hypothesis that the increased attention to boys occurs because teachers regard a much higher proportion of boys than girls as having special educational needs was also investigated. The results of this analysis suggest that to some extent the increased attention to boys is a result of a higher proportion of boys having special educational needs. Both boys and girls, identified as having special needs received very much above average levels of teacher attention which were equal across the sexes. This matches the result reported in Kelly's meta-analysis that sex imbalances were greatest among pupils having 'desirable' characteristics and least among pupils having 'undesirable' characteristics. However, these differences did not entirely account for the imbalance of attention to boys and girls and the suggestion put forward by French and French was also supported. In these classrooms a few boys, who were not identified as having special needs, nevertheless were involved in very high levels of teacher interaction in a way that was not true of girls.

If it is the case that there is not a general pattern whereby all or most boys get slightly more attention than all or most girls, but rather a pattern whereby a few boys get very much more attention than all other pupils, then the gender imbalance is best seen as a problem of classroom management rather than necessarily a problem of sexist bias. Such a pattern would also explain both the overall similarity between studies and the pattern of variation in results whereby in some classrooms there is no sex bias and in others there is a bias towards boys, but no studies report a bias towards girls. If the imbalance reflects poor classroom management strategies or poor class control then this is something which we should expect to vary considerably between teachers and possibly between schools and types of schools. Such a view also offers an explanation of the way that some qualitatively-based studies claim very much greater levels of inequality than are reported in any of the systematic observation studies. The qualitative studies by their nature are focused on very few classrooms and may chance upon classrooms where problems of management are greatest. It is also likely that a few incidents involving very high levels of attention to certain boys can come to dominate the researcher's perception of the classroom and disguise the similar levels of attention given to most boys and most girls.

Other aspects of classroom behaviour

Teacher interaction is one of the most contentious areas for looking at differences in the classroom experiences of boys and girls, but there are other areas where differences may arise. The ORACLE study gives the most detailed account of classroom behaviour and interactions of primary-aged pupils and, as in the case of teacher interaction, differences in other types of behaviour are small, although girls have slightly higher total work involvement than boys (Galton *et al.* 1980). The study of infant classrooms by Tizard *et al.* (1988) found very similar patterns of classroom experience and, for example, the same level of time-on-task for boys and girls. One difference which did emerge in this study was that white boys in the sample spent more time engaged on mathematics tasks and this seemed to reflect teacher allocation rather than pupil choice (Tizard *et al.* 1988).

One aspect of classroom interaction which is apparent from the ORACLE research and from other studies is the marked tendency for girls to interact with other girls and boys to interact with other boys. In the ORACLE study same-sex seating pairs were observed to interact twice as frequently as opposite sex pairs. In mixed sex groups interaction is twice as likely to be with a pupil of the same sex and the grouping pattern with the highest levels of pupil–pupil interaction were same sex groups. In all, over 80 per cent of pupil–pupil interactions were with members of the same sex and this clearly arose, for the most part, from pupil choice rather than from teacher grouping arrangements (Galton *et al.* 1980). In respect of pupil interactions, gender differentiation in the primary classroom is imposed by the pupils themselves through their social behaviour. These results are in accord with those of researchers such as Hartley (1985) who reports a strong tendency to same-sex friendship choices in the primary school.

Sex differences in academic achievement

Perhaps the central issue in any consideration of the consequences of sex differences and gender differentiation in the primary school is in the area of educational achievement. Academic achievement, especially in the areas of reading, language and mathematics, is central to the aims of primary schoolteachers (Ashton *et al.* 1975) and predominates in the content of the primary curriculum (Galton *et al.* 1980). If there are sex role differences in primary schools and, in particular, if differentiation works to the disadvantage of girls, differences in patterns of achievement, if they occur, would be the most serious manifestation of these differences.

An important source of evidence for levels of achievement in the primary school is the work of the Assessment of Performance Unit (APU). Surveys of achievement among 11-year-olds in language, mathematics and science were conducted by the APU in the late 1970s and early 1980s. The 1979 survey of language (APU 1981a) showed no significant differences between the performance in reading of boys and girls but found that girls were ahead in writing skills. A survey a year later found that girls were ahead in both reading and writing. These differences were statistically significant but in absolute terms were small (APU 1982a). Surveys of mathematics achievement were made in 1978, 1979 and 1980 (APU 1980, 1981b, 1982b). In all of these studies there were sex differences between the various subcategories of mathematics achievement tested, with girls scoring higher in some and boys in others. However, in all three surveys boys received higher scores in the majority of the subcategories. The survey of achievement in science made in 1981 showed no overall differences in performance between girls and boys. However, boys performed better at measures of science concepts while girls performed better at measures concerned with representing information. The report suggests that boys were performing better at the specifically scientific aspects of the assessments (APU 1981c).

The research conducted in infant classrooms in London by Professor Tizard and her colleagues at the Thomas Coram Research Centre provides evidence on the achievements of a group of children at an early stage in their primary school careers (Tizard *et al.* 1988). At the end of the children's time at nursery school, through the infant school, and in the first year of the juniors, a variety of tests measuring reading, writing and number skills were administered. The results at the end of the nursery school show that at this stage there were few sex differences in performance although the girls had better writing skills. In reading girls and boys made about the same progress up to the middle infants but girls made slightly more progress in their year in the top infants. In the first year junior girls were ahead on reading. In writing girls maintained but did not increase their lead over boys through the infant school. Writing was not tested in the junior schools. In mathematics boys had made more progress than girls by the top infants and were ahead in the first year juniors.

Recent studies of the attainments of junior-aged children include the ORACLE research (Galton and Croll 1980), the ILEA study (Mortimore *et al.* 1988), and the *One in Five* study (Croll and Moses 1985). The ORACLE research showed an overall identical level of performance by girls and boys. Within this overall figure was a slight advantage to boys in the mathematics test and a slight advantage to girls in the language test. Performance on the reading test was identical for boys and girls (Galton and Croll 1980). The ILEA study followed 2000 children through their four years in the junior school. The test results showed a general pattern of somewhat higher attainments for girls. Girls had higher levels of attainment at each of the assessment points for both reading and writing. However, the higher attainments in each of these subjects at the end of the junior school years were no more than would have been predicted from the girls' higher level of attainments at the beginning of junior school: progress, as opposed to level of attainment, was the same for boys and girls. In the case of mathematics there was little difference in attainment or progress between boys and girls, although girls made more progress during the third year of the junior school. No sex differences were found in performance on tests of oral skills (Mortimore *et al.* 1988). The *One in Five* study assessed both second year and fourth year juniors on tests of reading and non-verbal reasoning. Girls were found to be slightly ahead on both these measures (Croll and Moses 1988).

The APU surveys and the primary school research projects described above have broadly comparable results to those of a much earlier study of children's attainments, the Medical Research Council longitudinal study reported in *Home and School* (Douglas 1964). This research replicated earlier results in indicating that girls are more successful than boys at primary school. In this study girls performed better on tests of verbal and non-verbal intelligence, tests of sentence completion and tests of arithmetic than boys. The girl's advantage was noticeably greater in the sentence completion tests than in the arithmetic tests. The study conducted during the time of selection for secondary education at 11+, also showed that girls were more likely than boys to be selected for grammar school education (Douglas 1964).

All of these studies are in broad agreement that girls perform at least as well and generally slightly better than boys during the primary school years. They also agree that the relative performance of girls and boys differs across subjects and, to some extent across different aspects of a subject. Girls consistently do better on language-related aspects and relatively less well on mathematical aspects of assessments, although in some of the studies they still do as well as or better than boys at mathematics.

At the time of Douglas's research, although girls were outperforming boys at primary school and were more likely to be selected for grammar school, far fewer girls than boys were successfully completing 16+ and 18+ examinations and continuing to higher education. The possibility needs to be considered that even though the recent studies show girls doing as well or better than boys at primary school they are, nevertheless, in some way being prepared for failure later in their school careers and their equality or advantage will disappear in the secondary school. The most recent data relevant to secondary school performance of boys and girls comes from the 1987 edition of the Department of Education and Science statistics (DES 1987). The figures given here relate, for the most part, to the academic year 1985–6 when children in the ORACLE study and in some of the APU survey were entering post-compulsory education

These figures suggest that there is no longer an increasing underachievement of girls as they pass through the school system. As an indication of performance at 16+ the DES statistics give the proportion of boys and girls leaving school with 'O' levels at grade C or above or Grade 1 in GCSE (irrespective of any 'A' levels obtained). Of the girls, 58 per cent had at least one such grade compared with 52 per cent of boys. This performance is also reflected in the way that a higher proportion of girls than boys in the 16-18 age group remain in post-compulsory education, 34.9 per cent compared with 30.5 per cent of boys. Of those remaining in the school sector of post-compulsory education there was again a slightly higher proportion of girls, 18.1 per cent, compared with 17.2 per cent of boys (DES 1987).

A comparison of the 'A' level performances of boys and girls for the 1985–6 school year shows a very similar pattern in overall performance. An identical proportion of girls and boys, 18.5 per cent, left school with at least one 'A' level. Fractionally more boys than girls, 14.9 per cent compared with 14.3 per cent, left school with two or more 'A' levels. This equality is not sustained into higher education, however. Among the 19 to 20-year-old age group, for example, 13.3 per cent of males were in higher education compared with 11.8 per cent of females. And in 1985, 56 per cent of those receiving first degrees were male (DES 1987).

Although the overall level of secondary school achievement is similar for boys and girls, the achievements in different subjects differ considerably. The direction of this difference reflects in an exaggerated form differences which had begun to be apparent at primary school. At 16+ 46 per cent of girls received an 'O' level pass or CSE Grade 1 in English compared with 35 per cent of boys. In contrast, 35 per cent of boys achieved this result in mathematics compared with 30 per cent of girls. In post-compulsory education this tendency has become much stronger: 55 per cent of boys with two or more 'A' levels included mathematics in their results compared with 32 per cent of girls, while 51 per cent of girls with two or more 'A' levels passed 'A' level English compared with 27 per cent of boys (DES 1987).

As has been apparent from the measures of academic achievement presented above, there is no straightforward way in which girls can be regarded as academically disadvantaged in the primary school. Their overall performance is at least as high as that of boys and in most studies is rather higher. Measures of achievement and participation rates in secondary school also show that girls achieve equally with boys. It is not until entry into higher education that the disadvantages women suffer in occupations and in the wider society appear in their educational experiences. This makes it unlikely that the primary school can be regarded as in some way preparing females to fail despite their apparent equal or higher achievement compared with males.

The question of subject bias in achievement is more complex. It is plain that girls' higher levels of achievement manifest themselves most clearly in aspects of achievement related to language and reading. In mathematics and science girls are generally either not ahead of boys or performing slightly less well. This polarization of achievement is only very marginal at primary level, especially with regard to girls' underachievement. At secondary school, however, the polarization of achievement and subject choice between linguistic/humanities-orientated subjects and mathematical/scientific subjects is very apparent. The consequences of this polarization are more difficult to establish. At primary level reading achievement is the single most important academic aim for teachers (Ashton *et al*. 1975). Reading is central to primary classrooms as a medium for instruction and a criteria for assessment, and dominates the judgements teachers make of children's academic ability (Croll and Moses 1985). At this level it is certainly not a less highly-valued skill than scientific and mathematical achievements.

Special educational needs

Although the difference between the average attainment of boys and girls in the primary school is relatively small, it is boys who are far more likely than girls to have special educational needs. Several studies have found that, over the whole range of special needs, boys outnumber girls by approximately two to one. This was the conclusion reached by the epidemiological studies of Rutter *et al*. (1970) and Pringle *et al*. 1966).

More recently, in a study of teachers' views of special educational needs, Croll and Moses (1985) found that twice as many boys as girls were regarded as having special educational needs by their class teachers. The research showed that, overall, teachers of junior-aged pupils thought that 24.4 per cent of boys in their classes had special educational needs but only 13.2 per cent of the girls. When various kinds of educational needs are considered interesting differences emerge. Learning difficulties were attributed to 19.5 per cent of the boys and

11.1 per cent of the girls and behavioural problems to 10.9 per cent of boys and 4.5 per cent of girls. Although, in total, relatively few children were regarded as being discipline problems, boys outnumbered the girls by nearly four to one (boys 6.4 per cent and girls 1.7 per cent). These boys were not simply indulging in boisterous 'boylike' behaviour that was a nuisance to the teacher but expected and accepted. Virtually all the boys who were regarded as discipline problems were also thought to have emotional and behavioural difficulties which were creating problems for the child as well as being a nuisance to the teacher. Behaviour problems were also associated with learning difficulties, and many more boys than girls experienced this complex of special needs.

As we have seen, there are only small differences between the average scores of boys and girls on reading tests but there are many more boys than girls who experience problems with reading in the primary school. Croll and Moses (1985) compared the reading ages of boys and girls in 34 second year junior classrooms and found that nearly twice as many boys as girls had a reading age two years or more behind their chronological age (6.7 per cent of boys and 3.6 per cent of girls). The proportion of boys scoring between one and two years behind their real ages was half as great again as the proportion of girls (17.6 per cent of boys and 11.8 per cent of girls). These figures are a clear indication that more boys have reading difficulties, and it is not surprising that the 428 junior class teachers interviewed by Croll and Moses described 9.5 per cent of the girls in their classes as 'poor readers' compared with 17.5 per cent of the boys. However, a comparison of test scores with teacher assessments suggested that, when performance is taken into account, teachers tended to underestimate the extent to which girls had reading difficulties compared with their estimation of the reading difficulties of boys.

Previous discussions of the relationship between teachers' views of their pupils and the pupils' actual performance have tended to concentrate on the possible advantages accruing to children who are favourably regarded by their teachers and the disadvantages of being less well regarded. Concern with the effect of teacher expectations and with 'self-fulfilling prophecies' has led researchers to concentrate on the positive aspects of being favourably regarded by teachers and the possible unfairness this involves to the other children in the class. If we take this view then the advantage is overwhelmingly in favour of the girls. Nevertheless, there is little solid evidence for such processes (see Boydell 1978 and Croll 1981 for a review of some of the relevant evidence). It is, at least on the face of it, at least as plausible that a child may be disadvantaged by not having her or his difficulties recognized as that such a recognition will become self-fulfilling.

Attitudes to school among girls and boys

There is evidence that girls express more positive attitudes towards school than do boys. The ORACLE study found that girls scored higher than boys on a measure of contentment at school and on intrinsic motivation to do well at school (Croll and Willcocks 1980) and the ILEA research reported that girls had higher scores on a scale of attitude towards school and also had more positive self-concepts in relation to school (Mortimore *et al.* 1988). However, there is also evidence that girls have higher levels of anxiety (Croll and Willcocks 1980). Tizard *et al.* (1988) report that among infant school children boys are more likely than girls to rate themselves as above average on academic tasks although their performance did not justify this. Evidence on aspects of pupil attitudes with regard to particular curriculum areas can be found in the Assessment of Performance Unit (APU) surveys. In mathematics there was no difference in expressed levels of enjoyment between boys and girls, a result also reported in the ILEA study (ILEA 1988). There were also no differences in their perceptions of the usefulness of mathematics. However, boys had more confidence in their own mathematical ability than did girls (APU 1980). In the case of science boys were more positive than girls about the experimental aspects of science and rated these more highly than the non-experimental aspects in a way that was not true of girls (APU 1981c).

It seems that in their overall view of school girls are rather more positive and motivated than boys. However, there is some tendency for girls to be more anxious and for boys to be more self-confident about school work.

Teacher perceptions of girls and of boys

There is ample evidence that teachers perceive boys' classroom behaviour as being more problematic than that of girls. When considering special educational needs we saw that teachers were much more likely to describe boys as having behaviour problems and as posing discipline problems in the classroom. Earlier studies such as that of Douglas (1964) also report teachers as being much more critical of boys than of girls. The ILEA research and the London infant school survey also showed that boys were more likely than girls to be described as having behavioural difficulties (Mortimore *et al.* 1988; Tizard *et al.* 1988). In his detailed case study of a primary school Hartley (1985) reports that teachers have more positive views of girls and regard boys as noisy and disruptive. A similar study in infant classrooms by King (1978) reports that boys were reproved more and that teachers had more favourable assessments of girls' behaviour.

It is less clear if these perceptions have any wider consequences for the classroom experiences of boys and girls. Boys are more likely to be seen by teachers as having learning difficulties than girls (see above), but this still only applies to a minority of boys. However, Douglas shows that at the time of the 11+ examination teachers were more likely to think that girls rather than boys should be given grammar school places, even though there was little difference in their test scores (Douglas, 1964). The ILEA research reports that primary records are more favourable to girls than to boys (Mortimore *et al.* 1988), and King (1978) found that in the infant classrooms he studied boys were typified by teachers as making less progress than girls.

For the most part these differences in teacher perceptions almost certainly reflect real differences in pupil behaviour and attainment. The poorer behaviour of boys and their greater likelihood of having learning difficulties are mirrored in their teachers' views. It should also be noted that, as King (1978) points out, the most important typification teachers make of pupils is as individuals. Although King describes the different perceptions teachers had of boys and of girls, he emphasizes that such generalizations were of limited importance compared with the teachers' stress on each child's individuality.

Discussion

The studies discussed above have pointed to aspects of both difference and similarity in the educational experiences of girls and boys at primary level. In many respects sex roles are highly differentiated in the primary classroom. Children are differentiated by their names, their clothes and some of the activities they engage in. Gender groupings are also an important aspect of the way classrooms are managed and most of the children's own social and work interactions are with pupils of the same sex. However, in other respects boys' and girls' educational experiences are very similar: they have broadly similar levels of academic achievement, broadly similar attitudes towards school and broadly similar levels of interaction with the teacher. Where differences emerge in these areas the extent to which they can be regarded as disadvantaging either girls or boys varies. Boys get rather more individual attention from the teacher, are slightly more confident and sometimes perform better at mathematics; girls like school more and are more motivated, perform slightly better, especially in the area of language, and are considerably more favourably regarded by their teachers. However, in all these respects differences within gender groups are very much more important than differences between them.

The research reviewed here cannot be regarded as supporting the thesis that gender differentiation in the primary school contributes in any substantial fashion to the disadvantages females suffer in the outside world and, in particular, in the world of employment. Not only do girls succeed in the primary school, they continue to perform equally with boys throughout secondary schooling. If the primary school is preparing them for failure, it takes a long time for this effect to make itself felt. It has sometimes been argued that it is the failure of girls to choose and to do well in mathematical and scientific subjects which in part accounts for their disadvantaged occupational position (for example, Deem 1978). The beginnings of this process can be identified in some of the studies of primary schools although the underachievement of girls, even where it occurs, is small. What is ignored in this argument however, is that boys who study the subjects in which girls excel are not disadvantaged in employment.[1]

A further issue to be considered is whether schools go beyond gender differentiation in society as a whole and impose a more rigid division into traditional sex roles. Sara Delamont argues that schools are essentially conservative institutions in which prevailing sex stereotypes are not only not challenged but are exaggerated (Delamont 1980, 1983). This is an important and carefully stated argument, but while we accept that schools do not in general challenge prevailing societal assumptions about sex roles and gender divisions (Acker 1988), the extent to which they can be seen as exaggerating them is far less clear. Examples of exaggerated gender divisions include rules about clothing, separate registers, separate games, and so on. Other examples, however, could include equal levels of achievement, equal (or higher) representation in high achieving streams, equal access at the primary level to virtually all of the curriculum and all its central aspects, and equal regard for their achievements by teachers. Although these features seem so obviously right that they are not worth commenting on, it should be noted that such equality does not generally prevail in society. These are also the aspects of school which are central to their purpose. It is in these areas where schools are most distinctive that they are also more equal than society at large. Although girls are differentiated at primary school the evidence suggests that they are not disadvantaged.

Note

1 It is commonly suggested that the disadvantages women experience in employment can be attributed to the fact that they are less likely than men to have studied mathematical and scientific subjects at school and in higher education. Deem writes:

> Once these patterns of subject choice are established, public examination entries and pass rates reflect them, and may serve to stop girls from ever going beyond the *narrow occupational confines of arts*

Paul Croll and Diana Moses

disciplines whether they enter a job immediately after leaving or go on to higher or further education first.

(Deem 1978: 71, emphasis added)

As we have seen above, a third of girls taking 'A' levels pass maths compared with just over half of the boys, so the subject differences are not so great as the above quotation suggests. More importantly, however, there is no reason to suppose that the large number of males taking arts 'A' levels and graduating in arts disciplines are occupationally disadvantaged compared with those from science and mathematical backgrounds. Elite positions in British society are largely dominated by men from non-scientific and technical backgrounds. This is true of government, both Parliament and the civil service, financial institutions, boardrooms and the media. Even in industry there are frequent complaints that senior positions are not held by technical experts. If scientific and mathematical training is not an advantage to men, why should its lack be disadvantaging to women?

References

Acker, S. (1984) 'Sociology, gender and education' in S. Acker *et al.* (eds) *World Yearbook of Education: Women and Education*, London: Kogan Page.
Acker, S. (1988) 'Teachers, gender and resistance', *British Journal of Sociology of Education* 9(3): 307–22.
Ashton, P., Kneen, P., Davis, F. and Holley, B.J. (1975) *The Aims of Primary Education*, London: Macmillan.
Assessment of Performance Unit (APU) (1980) *Mathematical Development: Primary Survey Report 1*, London: HMSO.
Assessment of Performance Unit (APU) (1981a) *Language Performance in Schools: Primary Survey Report 1*, London: HMSO.
Assessment of Performance Unit (APU) (1981b) *Mathematical Development: Primary Survey Report 2*, London: HMSO.
Assessment of Performance Unit (APU) (1981c) *Science in School Age 11*, London: HMSO.
Assessment of Performance Unit (APU) (1982a) *Language Performance in School: Primary Survey Report 2*, London: HMSO.
Assessment of Performance Unit (APU) (1982b) *Mathematical Development: Primary Survey Report 3*, London: HMSO.
Boydell, D. (1978) *The Primary Teacher in Action*, London: Open Books.
Buswell, C. (1981) 'Sexism in school routines and classroom practices', *Durham and Newcastle Research Review*, 9:195–200.
Croll, P. (1981) 'Social class, pupil achievement and classroom interaction', in B. Simon and J. Willcocks (eds) *Research and Practice in the Primary Classroom*, London: Routledge & Kegan Paul.
Croll, P. (1986) *Systematic Classroom Observation*, Lewes: Falmer Press.
Croll, P. and Moses, D. (1985) *One in Five: The Assessment and Incidence of*

Special Educational Needs, London: Routledge & Kegan Paul.

Croll, P. and Willcocks, J. (1980) 'Personality and classroom behaviour', in M. Galton and B. Simon (eds) *Progress and Performance in the Primary Classroom*, London: Routledge & Kegan Paul.

Deem, R. (1978) *Women and Schooling*, London: Routledge & Kegan Paul.

Delamont, S. (1980) *Sex Roles and the School*, London: Methuen.

Delamont, S. (1983) 'The conservative school? Sex roles at home, at work and at school', in S. Walker and L. Barton *Gender Class and Education*, Lewes: Falmer Press.

Department of Education and Science (DES) (1987) *Statistics of Education 1987*, London: HMSO.

Douglas, J.W.B. (1964) *The Home and the School*, London: MacGibbon & Kee.

Equal Opportunities Commission (1987) *Women and Men in Britain: A Statistical Profile*, London: HMSO.

French, J. and French, P. (1984) 'Gender imbalances in the primary classroom: an interactional account', *Educational Research*, 26(2): 127–36.

Galton, M. and Croll, P. (1980) 'Pupil achievement and progress', in M. Galton and B. Simon (eds) *Progress and Performance in the Primary Classroom*, London: Routledge & Kegan Paul.

Galton, M., Simon, B. and Croll, P. (1980) *Inside the Primary Classroom*, London: Routledge & Kegan Paul.

Inner London Education Authority (ILEA) (1988) *The Junior School Project*, vols 1-3, London: ILEA.

Hartley, D. (1985) *Understanding the Primary School*, London: Croom Helm.

Kelly, A. (1986) 'A method to the madness? Quantitative research reviewing', *Research in Education*, 35: 25–41.

Kelly, A. (1988) 'Gender differences in teacher-pupil interactions: a meta-analytic review', *Research in Education*, 39: 1–23.

King, R. (1978) *All Things Bright and Beautiful?* Chichester: Wiley.

Megarry, J. (1981) *Sex, Gender and Education*, Glasgow: Jordanhill College of Education.

Mortimore, P., Sammons, P., Stoll, L., Lewis, D. and Ecob, R. (1988) *School Matters: The Junior Years*, Wells: Open Books.

National Foundation of Educational Research (NFER) (1987) *Teaching Styles and Pupil Performance at the Primary Level*, NFER mimeo.

Pollard, A. (1985) *The Social World of the Primary School*, London: Holt, Rinehart & Winston.

Pringle, M.L.K., Butler, N. and Davie, R. (1966) *Eleven Thousand Seven Year Olds*, London: Longman.

Rutter, M., Tizard, J. and Whitmore, K. (1970) *Education, Health and Behaviour*, London: Longman.

Serbin, L. (1983) 'The hidden curriculum: academic consequences of teacher expectations', in M. Marland (ed.) *Sex Differentiation and Schooling*, London: Heineman.

Sharp, R. and Green, A. (1975) *Education and Social Control*, London: Routledge & Kegan Paul.

Spender, D. (1982) *Invisible Women: the Schooling Scandal*, London: Writers and Readers Publishing Cooperative.

Stanworth, M. (1981) *Gender and Schooling: a Study of Sexual Divisions in the*

Classroom, London: Women's Research and Resources Centre.
Tizard, B., Blatchford, P., Burke, J., Farquhar, C. and Plewis, I. (1988) *Young Children at School in the Inner City*, Hove and London: Lawrence Erlbaum Associates.

Chapter twelve

Interaction with children with special educational needs

David Galloway

Editors' introduction

Pupils with special needs in the primary classroom are a major concern of teachers and the subject draws upon many of the themes of this volume. Estimates range from 20 to 40 per cent of pupils presenting some form of special need during their schooling career. A very sizeable minority of school children, most of whom have special needs, will be identified and given attention in the classroom. Galloway, who has undertaken much research in this area, places special needs in a decidedly social context. Teachers make judgements of special needs through social comparisons with 'normal' pupils. A vast majority of pupils labelled as having special needs are found in ordinary classrooms and will form an understanding of themselves through the social context in which they interact and the quality of learning (or curricular) treatment that they are offered. Teachers are central to the development of all children in their charge though the socio-emotional climate created in the classroom, the relationships that are structured for learning, and the interpretation of curriculum assigned to each child.

Themes that have arisen in this volume and which are discussed in greater detail here include: the creation of individual identities and self-efficacy through the interactions and social comparisons in which the special needs child participates; the understanding that the presentation of the curriculum to the child provides an orientation to bring together or divide the class; friendships based on perceptions of similarity (and legitimated by the teacher) may not allow for the integration of special needs children unless active efforts are made to enhance children's social skills and ability to work with others; the central role of teachers in structuring the social and curricular experiences of their charges.

There is much 'food for thought' in this chapter as it relates to special needs and 'normal' classroom experience. The chapter is strongly based in past and current legislation. It offers terms for practical consideration that includes moral climate, co-operative groupings and individual differences. The chapter describes happenings in classrooms where children with special needs are integrated without their social needs being catered for, and directs the reader to a number of alternative processes through which the teacher can make their integration more successful.

Introduction

According to the Warnock Committee, children with learning difficulties would need either special means of access to the curriculum, a special or modified curriculum, or 'special attention to the social structure or emotional climate in which learning takes place' (DES 1978a). With the dubious wisdom of hindsight, the problem here is not that this distinction is inappropriate, but rather that it failed to address some of the most pressing issues in provision for special educational needs. The Warnock Committee is widely believed by teachers to have encouraged integration of children with special educational needs into the mainstream classroom. The arguments for integration are at least as concerned with opportunities for children with special needs to interact socially with their peers in the mainstream, as with opportunities for them to experience the mainstream curriculum.

Historically, provision for children with special needs had been based on special or modified curricula. This was provided either in full-time special schools or classes, or in the withdrawal groups and remedial classes of mainstream schools. More than ten years after the Warnock Report it is not clear how far this has changed. In a majority of local education authorities (LEAs) withdrawal groups for extra help with reading and numeracy are the most prevalent means of helping primary children with learning difficulties. These frequently consist of activities which have only an indirect relationship to work the children have been doing in their regular class. Thus backward readers are more likely to find themselves doing new and different activities than to receive help which gives them a feeling of competence in classroom tasks on which they are currently failing.

This chapter is concerned with social interactions among primary children for whom access to social and curricular experiences of the ordinary class is a realistic goal. In practice, this refers to a vast majority of the 20 per cent of children considered by Warnock to require some form of special educational treatment at some stage in their school careers. This group includes children with physical or sensory disabilities not associated with severe learning difficulties. It also includes children currently placed in schools for pupils with moderate learning difficulties, for whom the educational benefits of integration have been extensively documented (for example, the review in Galloway and Goodwin 1987). Not least it also includes those children defined as disruptive or having emotional or behavioural difficulties. In passing it is tempting to ask whether as many as 20 per cent of school leavers would *not* have benefitted at some stage in their school careers from 'special attention to the social structure or emotional climate' in which learning took place. It is hard to see how the Warnock Committee could have regarded this as other than a thinly-veiled argument for the removal of children whose behaviour teachers found difficult or disturbing. Yet the evidence from school effectiveness research suggests clearly and consistently, that interactions within the school play the major part in the origin of such problems (see Galloway *et al.* 1989).

My argument, then, will be that many of the social problems created and experienced by children with special educational needs derive from lack of effective access to the mainstream curriculum. I shall start by considering the purpose of integration as regards children's social development and will then identify some of the conflicting pressures which may reduce the quality of social interaction for children with special needs. Finally, I will argue that teachers' understanding of social interaction in their classes is illuminated by their understanding of individual differences.

The purpose of integration

Internationally, the movement for integration, or mainstreaming, seems to have acquired its own momentum in which ideology and personal values are as important as empirical evidence. The problem with movements that acquire their own momentum is that their goal comes to be seen as an end in itself rather than a means to an end. There would be no point in integration if the quality of social and learning experiences was not developmentally more appropriate for the children concerned than alternative provision in a special school. Hence we must consider what social experiences we are trying to provide. A starting point is to ask how learning in an ordinary class can benefit the social development of children with special needs.

In most classes social development probably depends largely on vicarious learning, by enhancing opportunities for modelling age-appropriate behaviour, or by increasing the frequency of chance interactions. The quality and range of a child's social skills depend largely on the stimulation provided (Strain 1984). The less stimulation provided, the more limited will be the children's social skills. I recently saw an example of this in a special school for children with very severe physical and intellectual impairments. The children were seated on three sides of a large table. The teacher and two welfare assistants showed each child individually the various stages of mixing the ingredients for bacon omelette. When talked to directly each child responded to the adult, albeit in a limited way. Yet for over 85 per cent of the lesson each child was sitting on his or her own. The adults were occupied with other children and no attempt was made to facilitate social interactions between the children, if only at the simple level of 'look what Simon is doing'. For most of the lesson the children's opportunities for social interaction were virtually non-existent.

This incident took place in a special school class that had previously been held up as an example of good practice by the head teacher and by a college tutor. It illustrated vividly the importance of planning social interactions for children with special needs. Yet while the importance of planning is perhaps most evident in special school settings, there can be no justification for assuming that similar problems do not exist for children with special needs in the mainstream or, for that matter, for all other children.

The 'opportunities' for social interaction with non-handicapped peers may be illusory if the ethos of the mainstream school and classroom does not facilitate co-operative activities. As the Joint Council for the Education of Handicapped Children had argued before the Warnock Report was published, isolation in a large community can be far worse than the loneliness of the small community. When special schools operate as small self-contained communities children can easily feel cut off from their mainstream peers, but the effects of this loneliness can be mitigated by the support provided within the community. If adequate attention is not paid to the curriculum and social climate, children in the mainstream may feel equally cut off, without the mitigating support. This may explain why some, though not all, evaluation studies have found that children with moderate learning difficulties appear to be socially better adjusted in special schools than in the mainstream.

Leaving to chance or osmosis the social development of children with special needs, may not only be disastrous for the children concerned but also poor social education for their peers in the mainstream. Hence, if modelling is to facilitate the social development of children with special needs, much will depend on the kind of model to which they are exposed. In other words, there may be a need not only for a more actively interventionist approach towards the children themselves, but also for attention, as Warnock put it, to the underlying social structure and emotional climate of the (mainstream) classroom. Indeed, the presence of children with special needs may actually enable teachers to identify tensions in this area. If every child's progress and social adjustment appeared satisfactory, there would be little incentive to review current practice. Thus, if the jerk-jerk chatter inanities of Dick and Dora had captured all children's imagination, providing the background to a self-reinforcing love of reading, teachers would have had little incentive to seek more imaginative and stimulating materials.

Even when integration appears to be facilitating the social adjustment of a child with special needs, a closer look at the child's interactions with peers may be revealing. Guralnick (1981) has argued that when allowed a free choice children tend to choose friends from other children who have similar cognitive ability to themselves, are high in social status in their own peer group, and adopt a control-and-demand orientation, behaving towards their developmentally-delayed peers as though they were adults and their peers with special needs were children. This may foster leadership qualities in the children with high social status, and may also have some educational value for children with special needs. It may be unlikely, though, to encourage them to develop the skills needed for active participation in their peer groups. By implication, a structured programme may be needed if children with special needs are to acquire the social skills needed for participation with mainstream peers.

Whether this kind of relationship develops between high status children and peers with emotional and behavioural difficulties or with mild learning difficulties is unclear. It seems improbable that they will interact as equals. Whether the relationship is characterized by control-and-demand orientation or by a helping, co-operative one may depend less on the children themselves than on the 'moral climate', or ethos which the teacher has established in the classroom. Nevertheless, it is clear that children's consciousness of social status increases with age, and is likely to have an increasingly powerful influence on how children with special needs perceive their own position in their peer group.

On an INSET course, a group of 70 teachers took less that five minutes to produce a list of more than 70 derogatory labels in current use in their own schools when pupils were referring to peers regarded as slow learners (for example, 'divvy', 'remmo', 'spas'). This problem may be less acute and less pervasive in primary schools, but interactions at this stage may well provide the basis for more destructive labelling later. Even in the infant school children are sensitive to their teacher's attempts to group them by ability, recognizing promotion or demotion to a higher, or lower table. Many parents can recall their infant school children talking about being moved 'up' or 'down' a table.

While it is clear that the social development of children with special needs may at times be the object of direct intervention in the mainstream classroom, the limitations of such intervention should be acknowledged. Strain (1984) has demonstrated the value of social skills training with nursery school children with autistic symptoms, but his conclusion may not hold true for older children nor for the less handicapped children with whom this chapter is concerned. The teacher's task is to create a climate which accepts and respects individual differences. At times this will require explicit attention to the social problems of individual children, but the impact of any individualized programme is likely to be limited. There are four problems:

1. Much of the rhetoric of special needs has focused on identifying and meeting *individual* needs. In the United States, for example, Public Law 94–142 required Individual Educational Programmes for handicapped children as well as introducing into Federal Legislation the concept of the 'least restrictive alternative'. In Britain, the 1981 Education Act provides an elaborate machinery for assessing individual needs. This individualized focus may have done teachers and children a disservice. Teachers may legitimately feel that 'experts' have failed to recognized the practical difficulties in implementing individual programmes in a class consisting of thirty individuals. Both on practical and theoretical grounds, the problem lies in finding ways to meet individual needs by means of group activities.

2. Quite apart from the practical problems in implementing individualized programmes in a mainstream classroom, there is the theoretical point that children's – and adult's – sense of personal identity develops in a social context (Hargreaves 1983). After the family, the principle influence is that of the school. Programmes which focus on the individual as an individual rather than as a contributing member of a group may inadvertently restrict the child's personal development. This is particularly true in the mainstream class where children with special needs are more viable and more vulnerable than in a separate special class.

3. Developing the last point, the hidden curriculum is likely to exert a more profound as well as a more subtle influence on children's social development than any teacher-directed programme. If the hidden curriculum fosters a climate in which all children expect, and are expected, to contribute to the work of the class, then the need for programmes focusing explicitly on the social development of individual children will be greatly reduced. If the hidden curriculum does not foster such a climate, then an individualized programme will be operating in opposition to tensions in the social structure of the school or classroom.

4. Even at the pre-school stage, children with moderate learning difficulties benefit from opportunities for observational learning in mainstream classes. As they progress through primary school, they become increasingly sensitive to the negative implications inherent in individual programmes, namely that the aim is to remedy their defects. Their peers also become sensitive to the negative

implications, and the effect is seen in the derogatory labels referred to earlier.

Conflicting pressures on teachers and children

National developments

Until recently, education in Britain was seen as a three-way partnership between the Department of Education and Science (DES), LEAs and schools. The 1988 Act, however, accelerated a trend evident in the earlier Acts of 1980 and 1986, shifting power away from teachers and LEAs to central government and, to a lesser extent, parents. These changes seem likely to exert a far-reaching influence on the social climate in schools as well as on the educational climate. The 1988 Act attracted opposition from virtually all professional groups involved in education (Haviland 1988), and particularly from special educators. It is not, however, clear that their fears are justified. In this section I shall address one of the most controversial aspects of the Act, the National Curriculum and its associated attainment targets for particular age groups.

The desirability of a National Curriculum was seriously contested only by professional educationalists. Fears were expressed that it would lead to a narrowing of the curriculum for children with special needs (for example, Brennan 1987). There were also fears that the imposition of attainment targets would encourage not only a narrowly academic pedagogy, but also attempts by head teachers to gain exemption from the National Curriculum's requirements for children whose learning or behavioural difficulties threatened the progress of stability of the rest of the class. Further, publication of the results of national testing would, it was alleged, damage the self-esteem of lower attaining pupils.

These are not groundless fears but they do conveniently overlook the damaging consequences of the curricular arrangements replaced by the 1988 Act. In particular, the lack of any agreed National Curriculum and of associated attainment targets placed enormous responsibility on teachers' professional judgement. It led to the widespread adoption of alternative, low-status curricula, for 'non-examination' classes in secondary schools. The social consequences were at least as severe as the educational. Individually, most teachers were catering as effectively as they could for their academically less able pupils, but they were constrained by a system which promoted the needs of an academic elite. The 1988 Act does at least require that all pupils should have access to the National Curriculum except in specified, and restricted, circumstances. Potentially, this could encourage head teachers and governors to take the needs of their 'special' pupils more seriously than before. Yet it may also encourage them to refer pupils for formal assessment under the 1981 Act, not in order to obtain a clearer picture of their needs, but in order to gain their exemption from the requirements of the National Curriculum. More seriously, there are already signs that the National Curriculum itself may legitimize differential curricula based on perceived pupil ability. This concern comes from the Science Working Party's decision to accept pressure from the Secretary of State to recommend a two-tier curriculum in which an elite of pupils will receive more science teaching than the rest (DES 1988a). The fact that this results from the national shortage of science teachers should not obscure the likelihood that it will perpetuate a second-class curriculum for second-class pupils, at least in the eyes of the pupils themselves, their parents and many of the teachers who teach both groups.

Whether the National Curriculum will, as some critics maintain, encourage a formal teaching style with a narrow focus on attainment targets and minimal interaction between pupils, will depend on how the various subject working groups define their task. They are, however, under pressure for a narrow and formal curriculum from the Secretary of State, as illustrated by his demand for more grammar following the report of the English Working Group (DES 1988b). Nevertheless, the trend throughout the 1980s has consistently been towards a more inter-active relationship between pupils and between pupils and teachers. In the primary sector this was recommended as far back as the Plowden Report (1967). In the secondary sector it is evident in the group work required in many GCSE curricula, pupil involvement in records of achievement, and the range of developments in 14–19 education.

In the primary sector the impact of the policy changes has not always been clear. Superficially, the insistence on teachers developing subject specialities, first raised in the Her Majesty's Inspectors (HMI) Primary Survey (DES 1978b), maintained in successive DES circulars (for example, DES 1984) and reflected in the subject divisions of the National Curriculum, strikes at the heart of the post-Plowden primary ethos with its emphasis on teaching the 'whole child' through theme, topic and project work. Research, however, suggests that this ethos has never been reflected in what actually happens in the majority of primary school classrooms. Rather, as HMI have repeatedly insisted, the evidence suggests that class teachers have great difficulty in covering the whole range of the curriculum effectively. Moreover, if primary teachers are to have full-time responsibility for a class, then it is essential for the school to contain a member of staff with expertise in each area. The focus on subject specialisms may well lead to a defensive retreat into formal subject teaching in some schools, but this is not inevitable. One could equally well argue that it should facilitate rather than impede the development of cross-curricular approaches and teaching methods that encourage pupils' active participation. These are presumably the trends that HMI is seeking to encourage, since lack of pupils' involvement in their own learning is one of their most frequent criticisms of primary schools, as of secondary. A more realistic assessment, though, may be that the National Curriculum and associated pressures to develop subject specialisms will polarize the profession. A minority of schools will develop further their existing interactive approaches, while others, perhaps a majority, will feel justified in resorting to ever-increasing formality. The children who suffer most from the passivity induced by increasing formality will be those with special needs. Schools which resort to this kind of strategy may find themselves caught up in a vicious circle in which pupil behaviour deteriorates as the curriculum and pedagogy becomes more restrictive.

Influences on classroom behaviour

It is important to see the impact of recent developments dictated by central government and/or by HMI in the context of other research on children's learning. Doyle (1985) identified two principal tasks for class teachers: keeping order and facilitating learning. In practice these are interlinked. An unprepared lesson encourages a range of disruptive behaviours, and careful preparation is of little avail if the teacher lacks basic classroom management skills.

The interlinked tasks of keeping order and facilitating learning are themselves subject to developmental influences which deserve more attention than they have so far received. It seems probable that pupils' perception of teachers shifts as they progress through the stages of compulsory education from that of facilitator to that of disciplinarian. Kutnick (1983) observed that junior school teachers were much more controlling than infant teachers, and this was associated with a concomitant extension of children's understanding of teachers. Yet although children become increasingly likely to see their teachers in disciplinary roles as they get older, it does *not* follow that they themselves become less amenable or co-operative. In most secondary schools a minority of teachers rely on excessive note-taking, 'chalk and talk' or 'death by a thousand work-sheets'. Most secondary pupils acquiesce in the tedium induced by these approaches for most of the time. In junior schools they would lead almost invariably to open disruption and in infant schools to pandemonium. In other words, the infant teacher's survival depends on active teacher–pupil and pupil–pupil interaction to an extent which, perhaps regrettably, is not true in secondary schools.

Primary and secondary school teachers are, nevertheless, subject to many of the same pressures and many of them adopt similarly self-defeating strategies. In concluding that up to 20 per cent of children would require some form of special educational treatment at some stage in their school career, the Warnock Committee drew on research on the epidemiology of learning and behavioural difficulties. The research on learning difficulties used tests of cognitive and educational attainment which were designed to ensure that responses from a large sample would fit the normal distribution. The research on behavioural difficulties used screening instruments in which items were selected at least partly on the basis that they would be familiar to teachers, thus ensuring that a substantial minority could be identified as 'deviant or 'maladjusted'. The problem does not lie in the research itself which provided a much-needed overview of the epidemiology of learning and behavioural difficulties, but rather in the way it has been used to encourage too narrow a focus on the alleged needs of individual children.

There is no great difficulty in constructing clinical instruments which provide pseudo-scientific 'proof' of what a teacher already knows, for example, that a hostile child is high on the hostility scale of Stott's (1971) Bristol Social Adjustment Guide. The objection lies in the implication that the problem is in the child rather than in interactions which occur in a particular social context. There is no great difficulty in finding research evidence in support of this view. If the problem lay principally in the child one would not expect to find major differences in pupil behaviour between schools, provided one controlled for pupil intake, or between classes in one school. Yet recent school effectiveness research demonstrates that schools vary widely in the behaviour of their pupils, and there is a similarly wide variation between classes within a school (Mortimore *et al*. 1988). Further, the differences are not attributable only to variations in the pupils' social and educational backgrounds. Within an entirely different research tradition, Berger (1982) has drawn attention to the problem of transfer in classroom behaviour modification studies. The evidence suggests that behaviours acquired in one context will not transfer to other contexts unless transfer is explicitly built into the programme. In other words, classroom behaviour is context specific.

This brings us back to Hargreaves' (1983) point that personal identity is established in a social context. The study of social interaction in the classroom reveals ways in which children obtain recognition, acceptance and friendship. One can do this within a behaviourist paradigm, though many behaviourists might regard these as unacceptably nebulous contacts. Thus analysis of the behaviour of a child regarded as the 'class clown' by his teacher may demonstrate that the child consistently receives reinforcement from the teacher and/or his peers for the unwanted behaviours. Other paradigms lead to equally plausible and not dissimilar explanations. Sociologists and social psychologists might invoke the concept of secondary deviance to describe the same situation (for example, Hargreaves *et al.* 1975), arguing that the clown's status in the classroom had changed as a result of the teacher's irritation early in the school year.

It is one thing for social psychologists to study interaction at the 'micro' level of the classroom, but quite another to show how interaction at this level is influenced by changes at 'macro' level in the state education system. Yet this is arguably the more interesting and more important question. The nature and quality of social interaction will reflect the ethos or moral climate of the school and of the class (Pring 1984). The moral climate refers to the climate of social expectations that influence relationships between pupils, between a teacher and pupils and, outside the classroom, between teachers. It is also reflected in the teacher's order of priorities and in the value ascribed to the achievements of particular pupils or groups of pupils.

The ethos or moral climate of a school is, however, as much a political construct as an educational one. One person's ideal 'moral climate' will emphasize attributes such as obedience, conformity and competition between pupils. Another person's will emphasize the development of pupil autonomy, co-operation and independent critical questioning of school and societal policies (the range is from Summerhill to Eton). Successive Education Acts since 1980 have extended parents' rights to information about their schools, as well as restricting LEA freedom to limit entry to popular schools. For better or worse, schools are now in the market-place and survival will depend on their ability to attract pupils, or rather to attract pupils' parents. In this context, any heads who respected the traditional classroom autonomy of primary teachers could be charged with having an irresponsibly *laissez-faire* attitude to their school's future. With the introduction of local management of schools, class teachers will increasingly find themselves held accountable to the head, and through the head to governors for the progress and motivation of their class. How this will affect responses to pupils with special needs in unclear. The pessimistic view is that teachers will increasingly seek individualized explanations for problems of group interactions. This would result in more frequent use of formal assessment under the 1981 Act in order to gain exemption from the requirements of the National Curriculum. The more optimistic view is that a developing sense of mutual accountability within a school's staff, as well as of partnership with parents and governors, will encourage attempts to identify special needs in terms of problems in pedagogy and in group interaction rather than in terms of supposed deficits in individual children. What is not in dispute is that attempts to find individual solutions to all of Warnock's 20 per cent with special needs, let alone Sir Keith Joseph's under-achieving 40 per cent, are doomed to failure. Yet this does not mean we can ignore individual differences.

David Galloway

Social interaction and individual differences

Psychologists often find it easier to urge teachers to encourage co-operative learning in their pupils than to learn from each other. Just as clinical and educational psychologists sometimes underestimate the relevance of contextual influences in the school or classroom when assessing the needs of individual children, social psychologists sometimes seem oblivious to the relevance of individual differences. In theory, the 1981 Education Act requires educational psychologists to assess children's needs without reference to how or where they should be met, since the decisions on placement and resources are a matter for the Chief Education Officer (DES 1983). The distinction may make sense to a tidy bureaucratic mind, but fails to recognize, not only that children fail in a particular setting, but also that professional and parental responses to their failure will be influenced by a variety of factors, including perceptions about the availability of resources.

Trying to assess special needs without reference to how and where they should be met is like trying to assess the ability to drive a car by giving applicants a test on the Highway Code. Whether candidates know the Highway Code is probably important, but their performance on the road is a great deal more important. Similarly, psychometric information may reveal some useful information on a child's special needs, but without additional information about the classroom context and about the child's responses, it will be, to say the least, of limited use.

How a child performs in a particular classroom, then, is the product of a complex interaction between the child, the teacher and other pupils. Two children may respond to the same experience in totally different ways. Hargreaves (1983) describes the development of antiauthority subculture in secondary schools in terms of the pupils' attempt to maintain their self-respect in the face of low status dictated by the school's official policies. From a different perspective Willis (1977) had earlier noted the pride with which the 'lads' in his research valued their ability to flout school rules. This kind of response is not confined to secondary schools, but has origins in the pressure which much younger children exert on each other in matters such as dress, speech and behaviour in the classroom or in the playground. The question is not whether some children adopt strategies of which teachers and parents disapprove in order to maintain their sense of self-worth. Clearly some do. The more interesting question concerns the range of strategies adopted by children with special needs in response to feelings of educational and/or social inadequacy.

Craske (1988) has reviewed studies indicating that motivation to defend a sense of self-worth by avoiding effort, as proposed in different ways by Hargreaves and Willis, is more prevalent amongst boys than girls. The reverse is true of the 'learned helplessness' response in which pupils perform increasingly poorly following failure. Girls, in other words, are more likely to attribute their educational failure to lack of ability, whilst boys are more likely to attribute it to a 'boring' curriculum.

Craske's own work suggested that learned helpless children can be innoculated against the negative effects of failure by a training programme which encourages them to attribute success and failure to effort or lack of effort respectively, rather than to lack of ability. In contrast, training did not have the same potentially beneficial effects with the self-worth group. These children continued to attribute failure to lack of ability in spite of the attribution retraining programme. Consequently it seemed likely that they would continue to rationalize their lack of success in the curriculum by making little effort. How far teachers can innoculate children against learned helplessness as part of their everyday classroom work, without resorting to a structured programme, is not clear. Nor is there adequate information on whether improvements observed in structured programmes generalize to the classroom, or if so, for how long. Similarly, there is a dearth of evidence not only on the origins of self-worth motivation, but also on ways in which teachers may encourage children in this group to develop a sense of self-worth based on effort as well as ability (Beery 1975).

Conclusions

Contrary to popular belief, the commitment to integration in the 1981 Act was decidedly lukewarm (see Galloway and Goodwin 1987). The Act managed to give a sympathetic nod to the groundswell of international opinion in favour of integration, while acknowledging the many practical problems that such a policy would create. The Act has nevertheless encouraged greater attention than ever before to pupils with special needs, especially those remaining in ordinary schools. This attention has coincided with the government's often-repeated concern about the alleged under-achievement of a large minority of pupils. Education is essentially a social process, and the learning difficulties of an arbitrally defined minority of pupils are a product of that process.

At the earliest stage of identification teachers define a child as having special needs because they find the child's behaviour, relationships with other children or educational progress disturbing. This is neither a criticism nor a value judgement, merely an example of how a child's perceived need results from a process of interaction. The pressure on teachers, and hence the frequency of identification, may increase as a result of recent legislation, though this is less self-evident than some critics would have us believe. In contrast, there can be little doubt that pressures will increase to integrate children who would previously have been placed in special schools, and that the progress and adjustment of academically less able pupils will continue to exercise the interest of politicians.

Given this scenario, it would be tempting for teachers and educational psychologists to seek 'special' teaching and learning strategies for use in mainstream lessons. This would probably be a futile search. The reason is that the teaching and learning strategies which benefit 'special' pupils are precisely those which also benefit the majority. Teachers vary in their effectiveness, but the evidence suggests that they vary in their effectiveness with all pupils; those who are effective in teaching able pupils are also effective in teaching pupils with learning and adjustment difficulties and vice versa. The task for teachers and educational psychologists, then, is to identify strategies for utilizing available resources in ways which promote the teacher's interaction with all pupils, not just those whose behaviour or progress is at one or other end of the continuum. The strategies in question are neither new nor particularly controversial. Research on school and teacher effectiveness indicates the importance of 'open' questioning techniques, matching the task to the pupil's ability, a rigorous awareness of the effects of negative labelling, encouraging children to monitor their own performance, involving them in formulating and maintaining the school's disciplinary system, and insisting that all children contribute, and are seen to contribute, to the life and work of the school. What all this underlines, though, is that children with special needs benefit from the same teaching strategies as all other children. We should emphasize what they have in common with their peers, not the relatively minor differences.

References

Beery, R. (1975) 'Fear of failure in the student experience' *Personnel and Guidance Journal* 54: 190–203.

Berger, M.M. (1982) 'Applied behaviour analysis in education: a critical assessment and some implications for training teachers', *Educational Psychology* 2: 289–300.

Brennan, W. (1987) 'Once more into the core', *Special Children* XIV (October): 14–15.

Craske, M.L. (1988) 'Learned helplessness, self-worth motivation and attribution retraining for primary school children', *British Journal of Education Psychology* 58: 152–64.

Department of Education and Science (DES) (1978a) *Special Educational Needs* (The Warnock Report), London: HMSO.

Department of Education and Science (DES) (1978b) *Primary Education in England: a survey by HM Inspectors of Schools*, London: HMSO.

Department of Education and Science (DES) (1983) *Assessments and Statements of Special Educational Needs*, (Circular 3/83), London: DES.

Department of Education and Science (DES) (1984) *Initial Teacher Training: Approval of Courses* (Circular 3/84), London: DES.

Department of Education and Science (DES) (1988a) *Science for Ages 5–16*, London: DES.

Department of Education and Science (DES) (1988b) *English for Ages 5–11: Proposals of the Secretary of State for Education and Science and the Secretary of State for Wales* (The Cox Report), London: DES.

Doyle, W. (1985) 'Classroom organisation and management', in M.C. Wittrock (ed.) *Handbook of Research on Teaching*, 3rd edn, New York: Macmillan.

Galloway, D. and Goodwin, C. (1987) *The Education of Disturbing Children: Pupils with Learning and Adjustment Difficulties*, London: Longman.

Galloway, D., Mortimore, P. and Tutt, N. (1989) 'Enquiry into discipline in schools: evidence from the Departments of Educational Research and Social Administration, University of Lancaster', in N. Jones (ed.) *School Curriculum and Pupil Behaviour*, Lewes: Falmer (in press).

Guralnick, M.J. (1981) 'The social behaviour of pre-school children at different developmental levels: effects of group composition', *Journal of Experimental Child Psychology* 31: 115–30.

Hargreaves, D.H. (1983) *The Challenge for the Comprehensive School: Culture, Curriculum and Community*, London: Routledge & Kegan Paul.

Hargreaves, D.H., Hestor, S.K. and Mellor, F.J. (1975) *Deviance in Classrooms*, London: Routledge & Kegan Paul.

Haviland, D. (1988) *Take Care, Mr Baker*, London: Fourth Estate.

Kutnick, P. (1983) *Relating to Learning*, London: Allen & Unwin.

Lemert, E.M. (1967) *Human Deviance: Social Problems and Social Control*, Englewood Cliffs, NJ: Prentice-Hall.

Mortimore, P., Sammons, P., Stoll, L., Lewis, D. and Ecob, R.C. (1988) *School Matters: The Junior Years*, Wells: Open Books.

Plowden Report (1967) *Children and their Primary School*, 2 vols, Report of the Central Advisory Council for Education in England, London: HMSO.

Pring, R. (1984) *Personal and Social Education in the Curriculum*, London: Hodder & Stoughton.

Stott, D.H. (1971) *The British Social Adjustment Guide*, London: University of London Press.

Strain, P.S. (1984) 'Social interactions of handicapped pre-schoolers in developmentally integrated and segregated settings: a study of generalization effects', in T. Field, J.L. Roopnarine and M. Segal (eds) *Friendship in Normal and Handicapped Children*, Norwood, NJ: Ablex.

Willis, P. (1977) *Learning to Labour: How Working Class Kids Get Working Class Jobs*, London: Saxon House.

Chapter thirteen

Co-operative learning

Robert E. Slavin

Editors' introduction

The final substantive chapter of the book provides an account by Robert
Slavin of the results of a considerable amount of research into
co-operative learning. The chapter has been written very much with the
school-based practitioner in mind. Slavin discusses the broad issues
involved, examines the results of evaluation research and then provides
practical guidelines for implementation. These serve as a clear invit-
ation to teachers to try it out in their own classrooms.

Slavin's research has identified three key features of successful
co-operative learning programmes. Pupils must be operating under a
regime which rewards team results, but where each individual remains
accountable for their own contribution and where each individual has an
equal opportunity of being successful. In order to ensure this, Slavin's
work involves the use of highly-structured programmes. Readers will
need to consider carefully the ways in which these might fit into their
own teaching situations.

The chapter serves a useful purpose in drawing together the various
issues explored throughout this volume. Co-operative learning brings
together considerations of social structures, personal identity and autonomy, the development and importance of friendship, the enhancement
of motivation and the essentially social nature of the activity of learning.
Slavin's chapter clearly implies that to maximize the positive effects of
all of this, teachers need to be prepared to undertake some form of social
engineering. *Laissez-faire* groupings or highly individual approaches
are unlikely to suffice. While Slavin's approach has limited applic-
ability (it can only be strictly implemented in situations where pupils'
work can be assessed in a relatively straightforward right or wrong
manner) it provides an interesting and challenging example of the
application of social psychological principles and theory.

Introduction

'Class,' said Ms James, 'Who remembers what part of speech are words such as *it, you*, and *he*?'.

Twenty hands shoot up in Ms James's top end junior class. Another ten pupils try to make themselves small in hopes that Ms James won't call on them. She calls on Eddie.

'Proverb?'

The class laughs. Ms James says, 'No, that's not quite right'. The pupils (other than Eddie, who is trying to sink into the floor in embarrassment) raise their hands again. Some of them are halfway out of their seats, calling 'me! me!' in their eagerness. Finally Ms James calls on another child 'Elizabeth, can you help Eddie?'.

Think about the scene being played out in Ms James's class, a common sequence of events at every level of schooling, in every subject, in all sorts of schools. Whether or not she is conscious of it, Ms James has set up a competition between the children. The children want to earn her approval, and they can only do this at the expense of their classmates. When Eddie fails, most of the class is glad; pupils who know the answer now have a second chance to show it, while others know that they are not alone in their ignorance. The most ironic part of the vignette is when Ms James asks if Elizabeth can 'help' Eddie. Does Eddie perceive Elizabeth's correct answer as help? Does Elizabeth? Of course not.

What is wrong with the competitive situation Ms James has established? If properly structured, competition can be a healthy, effective means of motivating individuals to perform. However, competition in the classroom is typically of a less positive nature. Consider what is going on below the surface of Ms James's class. Most of the class is hoping that Eddie (and also Elizabeth) will fail. Their failure makes their classmates look good. Because of this, over time pupils begin to express norms or values opposed to doing too well academically. Pupils who try too hard are 'teacher's pets', 'nerds', 'grinds', and so on. Pupils are put in a bind; their teachers reward high achievement, but their peer group rewards mediocrity. As children enter adolescence, the peer group becomes all-important, and except for a few very talented individuals, most pupils accept their peers' beliefs that doing more than what is needed to get by is for suckers. Research on secondary schools clearly shows that academic success is not what gets children accepted by their peers.

Typical classroom competition can also be detrimental for another reason. Recall the ten pupils who tried to make themselves invisible when Ms James asked her question. For low achievers, a competitive situation is both a poor motivator and, for some, almost constant psychological torture. Children enter any class with widely divergent skills and knowledge. Low-achieving pupils may lack the prerequisites to learn new material. For example, children may have difficulty learning long division because they never learned to subtract well. For this and other reasons, success is difficult for may pupils, while it comes easily for others. Success is defined on a relative basis in the competitive classroom. Even if low achievers learn a great deal, they are still at the bottom of the class if their classmates learn even more. Day in, day out, low achievers get negative feedback on their academic efforts. After a while they learn that academic success is not in their grasp, so they choose other avenues in which they may develop a positive self-image. Many of these avenues lead to anti-social, delinquent behaviour.

How can teachers avoid the problems associated with classroom competition? How can pupils help one another learn and encourage one another to succeed academically?

Think back to Ms James's class. What if Eddie and Elizabeth and two other pupils had been asked to work together as a team to learn parts of speech, and the teams were rewarded on the basis of the learning of all team members? Now the only way for Eddie and Elizabeth to succeed is if they make certain that they have learned the material and that their team-mates have done so. Eddie and Elizabeth are now motivated to help one another and to encourage one another to learn. Perhaps most importantly, they are rooting for one another to succeed, not to fail.

This is the essence of co-operative learning (Slavin 1983 a,b). In co-operative learning methods pupils work together in four member teams to master material initially presented by the teacher. For example, in a method called Student Teams-Achievement Divisions or STAD (Slavin 1986b), a teacher might present a lesson on map-reading, and then give children time to work with maps and answer questions about them in their teams. The teams are heterogeneous, made up of high, average and low achievers, boys and girls, and students of any ethnic groups represented in the class. After having a chance to study in their teams, pupils take individual quizzes on map-reading. The individual quiz scores are added up. All teams whose average scores meet a high criterion receive special recognition, such as fancy certificates or having their team picture posted in the classroom.

The idea behind this form of co-operative learning is that if pupils want to succeed as a team, they will encourage their team-mates to excel and will help them to do so. Often, pupils can do an outstanding job of explaining difficult ideas to one another by translating the teacher's language into their own.

Of course, co-operative learning methods are not new. Teachers have used them for many years in the form of laboratory groups, project groups, discussion groups, and so on. However, recent international research has created systematic and practical co-operative learning methods intended for use as the main element of classroom organization, has documented the effects of these methods, and has applied them to the teaching of a broad range of curricula. These methods are now being used extensively in every conceivable subject, from infant level to college level, and in all kinds of schools throughout the world.

Co-operative learning methods

While social psychological research on co-operation dates back to the 1920s (see Slavin 1977), research on specific applications of co-operative learning in the classroom did not begin until the early 1970s. At that time four independent groups of researchers began to develop and research co-operative learning methods in classroom settings. At present there are researchers all over the world studying practical applications of co-operative learning principles, and there are many co-operative learning methods available. This chapter focuses on the methods that have been most extensively researched and used in primary and secondary classrooms.

Student team learning

Student team learning methods are co-operative learning techniques developed and researched at Johns Hopkins University, USA. More than half of all studies of practical co-operative learning methods involve student team learning methods.

All co-operative learning methods share the idea that pupils work together to learn and are responsible for one another's learning as well as their own. In addition to the idea of co-operative work, student team learning methods emphasize the use of team goals and team success which can only be achieved if all members of the team learn the objectives being taught. That is, in student team learning the students' tasks are not to do something as a team but to learn something as a team.

Three concepts are central to all student team learning methods: team rewards, individual accountability and equal opportunities for success. In these techniques teams may earn certificates or other team rewards if they achieve above a designated criterion. The teams are not in competition to earn scarce rewards; all (or none) of the teams may achieve the criterion in a given week. Individual accountability means that the team's success depends on the individual learning of all team members. This focuses the activity of the team members on tutoring one another and making sure that everyone on the team is ready for a quiz or other assessment which they will take without team-mate help. Equal opportunities for success means that pupils contribute to their teams by improving over their own past performance. This ensures that high, average and low achievers are equally challenged to do their best, and the contributions of all team members will be valued.

Research on co-operative learning methods (summarized below) has indicated that team rewards and individual accountability are essential elements for producing basic skills achievement (Slavin 1983a,b, 1988). It is not enough simply to tell pupils to work together. They must have a reason to take one another's achievement seriously. Further, research indicates that if pupils are rewarded for doing better than they have in the past, they will be more motivated to achieve than if they are rewarded on the basis of their performance in comparison to others, because rewards for improvement make success neither too difficult nor too easy for students to achieve (Slavin 1980).

Four principal student team learning methods have been extensively developed and researched. Two are general co-operative learning methods adaptable to most subjects and grade levels: Student Teams-Achievement Divisions, or STAD, and Teams-Games-Tournament, or TGT. The remaining two are comprehensive curricula designed for use in particular subjects at particular grade levels: Team Assisted Individualization (TAI) for mathematics in grades 3 to 6 (approximately 8- to 12-year-olds) and Co-operative Integrated Reading and Composition (CIRC) for reading and writing instruction in grades 3 to 5 (approximately 8- to 11-year-olds). These four methods all incorporate team rewards, individual accountability, and equal opportunities for success, but in different ways.

Student Teams-Achievement Divisions (STAD)

In STAD (Slavin 1978, 1986b) children are assigned to four-member learning teams that are mixed in performance level, sex, and, where appropriate, ethnicity. The teacher presents a lesson, and then pupils work within their teams to make sure that all team members have mastered the lesson. Finally, all pupils take individual quizzes on the material, at which time they may not help one another.

Children's quiz scores are compared to their own past averages, and points are awarded based on the degree to which they can meet or exceed their own earlier performance. These points are then summed to form team scores, and teams which meet certain criteria may earn certificates or other rewards. The whole cycle of activities, from teacher presentation, to team practice, to quiz usually takes three to five class periods.

STAD has been used in every imaginable subject, from mathematics to language arts, to social studies, and has been used from age 7 to college students. It is most appropriate for teaching well-defined object-ives with single right answers, such as mathematical computations and applications, language usage and mechanics, geography and map skills, and science facts and concepts.

The main idea behind Student Teams-Achievement Divisions is to motivate children to encourage and help each other to master skills presented by the teacher. If pupils want their team to earn team rewards, they must help their team-mates to learn the material. They must encourage their team-mates to do their best, expressing norms that learning is important, valuable, and fun. Pupils work together after the teacher's lesson. They may work in pairs and compare answers, discuss any discrepancies, and help each other with any learning problems. They may discuss approaches to solving problems, or they may quiz each other on the content they are studying. They teach their team-mates and assess their strengths and weaknesses to help them succeed on the quizzes.

Although children study together, they may not help each other with quizzes. Every pupil must know the material. This individual account-ability motivates children to do a good job tutoring and explaining to each other, as the only way for a team to succeed is if all team members have mastered the information or skills being taught. Because team scores are based on children's improvement over their own past records (equal opportunities for success), all of them have the chance to be the team 'star' in a given week, either by scoring well above their past record or by getting a perfect paper, which always produces a maximum score regardless of past averages.

A detailed guide to the use of STAD appears at the end of this chapter.

Teams-Games-Tournament (TGT)

Teams-Games-Tournament (DeVries and Slavin 1978; Slavin 1986b) was the first of the Johns Hopkins co-operative learning methods. It uses the same teacher presentations and team work as in STAD, but replaces the quizzes with weekly tournaments in which pupils compete with members of other teams to contribute points to their team scores. Children compete at three-person 'tournament tables' against others with similar past records in mathematics. A 'bumping' procedure keeps the competition fair, that is, the winner at each tournament table brings six points to his or her team, regardless of which table it is; this means that low achievers (competing with other low achievers) and high achievers (competing with other high achievers) have equal opportunities for success. As in STAD, high performing teams earn certificates or other forms of team rewards.

TGT has many of the same dynamics as STAD, but adds a dimension of excitement contributed by the use of games. Team-mates help one another prepare for the games by studying worksheets and explaining problems to one another, but when pupils are competing their team-mates cannot help them, ensuring individual accountability.

Team-Assisted Individualization (TAI)

Team-Assisted Individualization (Slavin, Leavey and Madden 1986) shares with STAD and TGT the use of four-member mixed ability learning teams and certificates for high-performing teams. But where STAD and TGT use a single pace of instruction for the class, TAI combines co-operative learning with individualized instruction. Also, where STAD and TGT apply to most subjects and age levels, TAI is specifically designed to teach mathematics to pupils in grades 3 to 6 (approximately 8- to 12-year-olds) or older pupils not ready for a full alegbra course.

In TAI, children enter an individualized sequence according to a placement test and then proceed at their own rates. In general, team members work on different units. Team-mates check each others' work against answer sheets and help one another with any problems. Final unit tests are taken without team-mate help and are scored by pupil monitors. Each week teachers total the number of units completed by all team members and give certificates or other team rewards to teams which exceed a criterion score based on the number of final tests passed, with extra points for perfect papers and completed homework.

Because pupils take responsibility for checking each others' work and managing the flow of materials, the teach can spend most classtime presenting lessons to small groups of children drawn from the various teams who are working at the same point in the mathematics sequence. For example, the teacher might call up a decimals group, present a lesson on decimals, and then send the children back to their teams to work on decimal problems. Then the teacher might call the fractions group, and so on.

TAI has many of the motivational dynamics of STAD and TGT. Children encourage and help one another to succeed because they want their teams to succeed. Individual accountability is assured because the only score that counts is the final test score, and pupils take final tests without team-mate help. Children have equal opportunities for success because all have been placed according to their level of prior knowledge; it is as easy (or difficult) for a low achiever to complete three subtraction units in a week as it is for a higher-achieving classmate to complete three long-division units.

Unlike STAD and TGT, TAI depends on a specific set of instructional materials. These materials cover concepts from addition to an introduction to algebra. Although designed for use in grades 3 to 6 (approximately 8- to 12-year-olds), they have been used for primary instruction in grades 2 to 8 (approximately 7- to 14-year-olds), and as remedial instruction in secondary schools. The TAI materials include specific concept lesson guides that suggest methods of introducing mathematical ideas by using demonstrations, manipulatives, and examples. The curricular emphasis in TAI is on rapid, firm mastery of algorithms in the context of conceptual understanding and on applications of mathematical ideas to solution of real-life problems.

Co-operative Integrated Reading and Composition (CIRC)

The newest of the student team learning methods is a comprehensive programme for teaching reading and writing in the upper elementary grades called Co-operative Integrated Reading and Composition or CIRC (Madden, Stevens and Slavin 1986; Stevens, *et al.* 1987). In CIRC teachers use basal readers and reading groups, much as in traditional reading programmes. However, pupils are assigned to teams composed of pairs of pupils from two different reading groups. While the teacher is working with one reading group, pupils in the other groups are working in their pairs on a series of cognitively engaging activities, including reading to one another, making predictions about how narrative stories will come out, summarizing stories to one another, writing responses to stories, and practising spelling, decoding and vocabulary. Children work in teams to master main ideas and other comprehension skills. During language arts periods children engage in writing drafts, revising and editing one another's work and preparing for 'publication' of team books.

In most CIRC activities, pupils follow a sequence of teacher instruction, team practice, team pre-assessments and quiz. That is, they do not take the quiz until their team-mates have determined that they are ready. Team rewards are certificates given to teams based on the average performance of all team members on all reading and writing activities. Because pupils work on materials appropriate to their reading levels, they have equal opportunities for success. Pupils' contributions to their teams are based on their quiz scores and final independently written compositions, which ensures individual accountability.

Other co-operative learning methods

Jigsaw

Jigsaw was originally designed by Elliot Aronson and his colleagues (Aronson, *et al.* 1978). In Aronson's Jigsaw method, children are assigned to six-member teams to work on academic material which has been broken down into sections. For example, a biography might be later divided into early life, first accomplishments, major setbacks, later life and impact on history. Each team member reads his or her section. Next, members of different teams who have studied the same sections meet in 'expert groups' to discuss their sections. Then pupils return to their teams and take turns teaching their team-mates about their sections. Since the only way pupils can learn sections other than their own is to listen carefully to their team-mates, they are motivated to support and show interest in one another's work.

A modification of Jigsaw developed at Johns Hopkins University as part of the student team learning programme is called Jigsaw II (Slavin 1986b). In this method, children work in four- or five- member teams as in TGT and STAD. Instead of each child being assigned a unique section, they all read a common narrative, such as a book chapter, a short story or a biography. However, each individual receives a topic on which to become an expert. Those with the same topics meet in expert groups to discuss them, after which they return to their teams to teach what they have learned to their team-mates. Then pupils take individual quizzes, which result in team scores based on the improvement score system of STAD. Teams which meet preset standards may earn certificates.

Learning together

David and Roger Johnson at the University of Minnesota developed the Learning Together model of co-operative learning (Johnson and Johnson 1987). The methods they have researched involve pupils working in four- or five- member heterogeneous groups on assignment sheets. The groups hand in a single sheet, and receive praise and rewards based on the group product.

Group Investigation

Group Investigation, developed by Shlomo Sharan at the University of Tel-Aviv (Sharan and Sharan 1976), is a general classroom organization plan in which pupils work in small groups using co-operative inquiry, group discussion, and co-operative planning and projects (Sharan and Sharan 1976). In this method pupils form their own two- to six- member groups. After choosing subtopics from a unit being studied by the entire class, the groups further break their subtopics into individual tasks, and carry out the activities necessary to prepare group reports. Each group then makes a presentation or display to communicate its findings to the entire class.

Research on co-operative learning

Co-operative learning methods are among the most extensively evaluated alternatives to traditional instruction in use in schools today. More than seventy high-quality studies have evaluated various co-operative learning methods over periods of at least four weeks in regular primary and secondary schools; sixty-three of these have measured effects on pupil achievement (see Slavin 1988). These studies all compared effects of co-operative learning to those of traditionally-taught control groups on measures of the same objectives pursued in all classes. Teachers and classes were either randomly assigned to co-operative or control conditions, or they were matched on pre-test achievement level and other factors.

Academic achievement

Overall, of sixty-three studies of the achievement effects of co-operative learning, thirty-six (57 per cent) have found significantly greater achievement in co-operative than in control classes. Twenty-six (41 per cent) found no differences, and in only one study did a control group out-perform the experimental group. However, the effects of co-operative learning vary considerably according to the particular methods used. As noted earlier, two elements must be present if co-operative learning is to be effective: group goals and individual accountability (Slavin 1983a,b, 1988). That is, groups must be working to achieve some goal or earn rewards or recognition, and the success of the group must depend on the individual learning of every group member. In studies of methods of this kind (for example, STAD, TGT, TAI, CIRC), effects on achievement have been very consistently positive; thirty-four out of forty-one such studies (83 per cent) found significantly positive achievement effects. In contrast, only four of twenty-two studies (18 per cent) lacking group goals and individual accountability found positive effects on student achievement. Two of these positive effects were found in a study which compared four co-operative learning methods to a competitive control group in a Nigerian junior high science classes (Okebukola 1985). This study found greater learning in Learning Together and Jigsaw classes (co-operative learning methods lacking group goals and individual accountability) than in competitive control classes, but the STAD and TGT classes learned considerably more than did the other co-operative methods (or the control method). The other two successful studies of co-operative learning methods lacking group goals evaluated Group Investigation in Israel (Sharan *et al*. 1984; Sharan and Shachar 1986). In Group Investigation, pupils in each group are responsible for one unique part of the group's overall task, ensuring individual accountability. Then, the group's overall performance is evaluated. Even though there are no specific group rewards (as are used in STAD, TGT, TAI and CIRC), the group evaluation probably serves the same purpose.

Why are group goals and individual accountability so important? To understand this, consider the alternatives. In many forms of co-operative learning pupils work together to complete a single worksheet or to solve one problem together. In such methods there is little reason for more able pupils to take time to explain what is going on to their less able group-mates or to task their opinions. When the group task is to do something, rather than to learn something, the participation of less able pupils may be seen as interference rather than help.

In contrast, when the group's task is to ensure that every group member has learned something, it is in the interests of every group member to spend time explaining concepts to their group-mates. Research on pupils' behaviour within co-operative groups has consistently found that those who gain most from co-operative work are those who give and receive elaborated explanations (Webb 1985). What group goals and individual accountability do is to motivate children to give such explanations, to take one another's achievement seriously.

Co-operative learning almost never has negative effects on achievement, so teachers can reap the social benefits of co-operation by simply allowing pupils to work together or by giving them problems to solve as a group. However, if they wish to use co-operative methods to accelerate pupil achievement, the research evidence is clear that they must set up co-operative activity so that their groups are rewarded (for example, with certificates, recognition, a small part of their grades) based on the individual achievement of every group member. Usually this means that pupils study together in their groups and then have their scores on individual quizzes averaged to form a team score.

Do co-operative learning methods work equally well for all types of children? In general, the answer is yes. While occasional studies find particular advantages for high or low achievers, boys or girls, and so on, the great majority find equal benefits for all types of children. Sometimes a concern is expressed that co-operative learning will hold back high achievers. The research provides absolutely no support for this claim; high achievers gain from co-operative learning (relative to high achievers in traditional classes) just as much as do low and average achievers.

Intergroup relations

Classroom studies of co-operative learning have found quite consistently that children express greater liking for their classmates in general as a result of participating in a co-operative learning method (see Slavin 1983a). This is important in itself. Liking among pupils is especially important, however, when they come from different ethnic backgrounds. Anyone who has spent much time in a racially-mixed secondary school in the USA knows that white children associate mostly with white children, black children with black children, and so on. There is substantial evidence that, left alone, ethnic separateness in schools does not naturally diminish over time (Gerard and Miller 1975).

Social scientists have long advocated inter-ethnic co-operation as a means of ensuring positive intergroup relations in a desegregated setting, emphasizing, however, that positive intergroup relations would arise from school desegregation if, and only if, pupils were involved in co-operative, equal-status interaction sanctioned by the school (see Allport 1954; Slavin 1985a).

The research on co-operative learning methods has borne out the expectations. Co-operative learning methods embody the requirements of co-operative, equal-status interaction between children of different ethnic backgrounds sanctioned by the school (Slavin 1985a). In most of the research on intergroup relations, children were asked to list their best friends at the beginning of the study and again at the end. The number of friendship choices children made outside their own ethnic groups was the measure of intergroup relations. Positive effects on intergroup relations have been found for STAD, TGT, TAI, Jigsaw, Learning Together, and Group Investigation models (Slavin 1985b). Two of these studies, one on STAD (Slavin 1979), and one on Jigsaw II (Ziegler 1981) included follow-ups of intergroup friendships several months after the end of the studies. Both found that children who had been in co-operative learning classes still named significantly more friends outside their own ethnic groups than did children who had been in control classes.

Integration and special needs

Although ethnicity is a major barrier to friendship, it is not so large as the one between physically or mentally handicapped children and their normal-progress peers. Since 1975 the integration movement in the United States has created an unprecedented opportunity for handicapped children to take their place in the mainstream of society by integrating such children in regular classrooms. It has also created enormous practical problems for classroom teachers, however, and it often leads to social rejection of the handicapped children. The situation is similar in the UK (Hegarty, *et al.* 1981). Because co-operative learning methods have been successful in improving relationships across the ethnicity barrier – which somewhat resembles the barrier between integrated and normal-progress pupils – these methods have also been applied to increase the acceptance of the newly-integrated child.

The research on co-operative learning and integration has focused on the academically-handicapped child. In one study STAD was used to attempt to integrate children performing two years or more below the level of their peers into the social structure of the classroom. The use of STAD significantly reduced the degree to which the normal-progress children rejected their integrated classmates, and increased the academic achievement and self-esteem of all children, integrated as well as normal-progress (Madden and Slavin 1983). Similar effects have been found for TAI (Slavin, Madden and Leavey 1984), and other research using co-operative teams has also shown significant improvements in relationships between integrated academically-handicapped pupils and their normal-progress peers (Ballard, *et al.* 1977; Cooper, *et al.* 1980). In addition, one study in a self-contained school for emotionally disturbed adolescents found that the use of TGT increased positive interactions and friendships among participants (Slavin 1977). Five months after the study ended, these positive interactions were still found more often in the former TGT classes than in the control classes. In a study in a similar setting, Janke found that the emotionally-disturbed children were more on-task, better behaved, and had better attendance in TGT classes than in control classes (Janke 1978).

Perhaps the most important fact about co-operative learning methods in the integrated classroom is that these techniques are not only good for the handicapped children, but they are among the very few methods for helping these children that also have a clear benefit for all pupils in terms of academic achievement.

Self-esteem

One of the most important aspects of a child's personality is his or her self-esteem. Many people have assumed that self-esteem is a relatively stable attribute of a person that schools have little ability to change. Several researchers working on co-operative learning techniques have found, however, that teams do increase childrens' self-esteem. Children in co-operative learning classes have been found to have more positive feelings about themselves than do those in traditional classes. These improvements in self-esteem have been found for TGT and STAD (Slavin 1983a), for Jigsaw (Blaney, *et al.* 1977), and for the three methods combined (Slavin and Karweit 1981). Improvements in pupil self-concepts have also been found for TAI (Madden, Slavin and Leavey 1984). Why does this occur? First, it has been consistently found that TGT and STAD pupils report that they like others and feel liked by others more than control pupils do (Slavin 1983a). Liking of others and feeling liked by others are obvious components of feeling worthwhile. Second, it seems probable that pupils feel (and are) more successful in their school work when they work in teams than when they work independently. This can also lead to an increase in self-esteem. Whatever the reason, the effect of co-operative learning methods on self-esteem may be particularly important with regard to the long-term effects on mental health. A child who has had a co-operative, mutually supportive experience in school may be less likely to be antisocial, withdrawn or depressed in later life. In fact, a remarkable study in the Kansas City (Missouri) schools found that lower socio-economic-status children at risk of becoming delinquent, who worked in co-operative groups in the sixth grade (approximately 12 year-olds), had better attendance, fewer contacts with the police, and higher behavioural rating by teachers in the seventh through eleventh grades (approximately 13- to 16-year-olds) than did control children (Hartley 1976).

Other outcomes

In addition to effects on achievement, positive intergroup relations, greater acceptance of integrated children, and self- esteem, effects of co-operative learning have been found on a variety of other important educational outcomes. These include liking of school, development of peer norms in favour of doing well academically, feelings of individual control over the child's own fate in school, and co-operativeness and altruism (see Slavin 1983a). TGT (DeVries and Slavin 1978) and STAD (Janke 1978; Slavin 1978) have been found to have positive effects on pupils' time on-task.

Conclusion

The positive effects of co-operative learning methods on a variety of outcomes are not found in every study or for every method, but the overall conclusion to be drawn from this research is that when the classroom is structured in a way that allows pupils to work co-operatively on learning tasks, they benefit academically as well as socially. The greatest strength of co-operative learning methods is the wide range of positive outcomes that has been found for them in the research. Although there may be many ways to improve relationships between children of different ethnic backgrounds or between integrated and normal-progress pupils, few can also help improve pupil achievement. And although there are certainly many ways to accelerate pupil learning in one or more subjects or age levels, few apply equally well in almost all subjects and age levels; and fewer still can document improvements in learning and also show improvements in pupils' social relationships, self-esteem, liking of school, and other outcomes.

Other special features of all the co-operative learning methods are their inexpensiveness and their ease of use. In their simplest form, all these methods require is that the teacher assign pupils to small teams, give them material to study together, assess pupil learning, and give the teams some kind of recognition or reward based on the average of the team members' scores. Teachers need minimal training to use these techniques. Detailed teacher's manuals are available for TGT, STAD and Jigsaw II (Slavin 1986b), TAI (Slavin, Leavey and Madden 1986), and CIRC (Madden, Stevens and Slavin 1986). Books describing the original Jigsaw (Aronson, *et al.* 1978), the Learning Together model (Johnson and Johnson 1987), and Group Investigation (Sharan and Sharan 1976) are also available. Thousands of teachers have successfully used these methods, especially STAD and TGT, with nothing more than the manuals and books, and thousands more have done so after a one-day workshop. Once teachers know how to use them, the methods require little or no additional preparation time.

Because of their effectiveness, their practicality, and perhaps most importantly, the fact that teachers and pupils simply enjoy using them, co-operative learning methods are being used more and more widely throughout the United States and in several other countries.

In sum, the research on co-operative learning methods supports the usefulness of these strategies for improving such diverse outcomes as pupil achievement at a variety of age levels and in many subjects, intergroup relations, relationships between integrated and normal-progress pupils and pupil self-esteem. Their widespread and growing use demonstrates that in addition to their effectiveness, co-operative learning methods are practical and attractive to teachers. The history of the development, evaluation, and dissemination of co-operative learning is an outstanding example of educational research resulting in directly useful programmes that have improved the educational experience of many children and will continue to affect many more.

Student team-achievement divisions

A practical guide

Student Teams-Achievement Divisions or STAD, is among the simplest and most adaptable of the co-operative learning methods. It can be used at any primary school level, and in any subject area in which there are single right answers, such as mathematics, language, science and much of social studies. STAD can be used all year in a given subject, but it is most often used for six to eight week units at various points during the school year.

Assigning students to teams

Teams in STAD have four or five members. Four is preferable; make five-member teams only if the class is not divisible by four. To assign pupils to teams, rank them from top to bottom on some measure of academic performance (for example, past grades, test scores) and divide the ranked list into quarters, with any extra pupils in the middle quarters. Then put one pupil from each quarter on each team, making sure that the teams are well balanced in sex and ethnicity. Extra (middle) pupils may become fifth members of teams.

Determining initial base scores

In STAD, the points children contribute to their teams are based on the degree to which their quiz scores exceed their past performance. This makes it equally difficult for all children to contribute to their team scores. Each child gets a base score which represents his or her past average. If you are starting STAD after you have given at least three quizzes or tests, average these scores to determine base scores. Otherwise, use other suitable scores.

Preparing materials

Make a worksheet and a short quiz for each unit you plan to teach.

Schedule of activities

STAD consists of a regular cycle of instructional activities, as follows:

Teach: Present the lesson.
Team study: Pupils work on worksheets in their teams to master the material.
Test: Pupils take individual quizzes.
Team recognition: Team scores are computed on the basis of team members' improvement scores, and a class newsletter or bulletin board recognizes high-scoring teams.

Descriptions of these activities follow.

Teach

Each lesson in STAD begins with a class presentation. The lesson should take one to two class periods.

Robert E. Slavin

Team Study

During team study (one or two class periods) the team members' tasks are to master the material themselves and to make sure that their team-mates have done so. Pupils have worksheets and answer sheets they can use to practise the skill being taught and to assess themselves and their team-mates. Only two copies of the worksheets and answer sheets are given to each team, to force team-mates to work together. After teaching a lesson, introduce team study to your class using the following steps:

Read off team assignments.

Have team-mates move their desks together or move to team tables, and allow pupils about ten minutes to decide on a team name.

Hand out worksheets and answer sheets (two of each per team).

Tell pupils on each team to work in pairs or threes. If they are working on problems (as in mathematics), each pupil in a pair or three should work on the problem, and then check with his or her partner(s). If anyone missed a question, that pupil's team-mates have a responsibility to explain it. If pupils are working on short-answer questions, they may quiz each other, with partners taking turns holding the answer sheet or attempting to answer the questions.

Emphasize to pupils that they are not finished studying until they are sure all their team-mates will score full marks on the quiz.

Make sure that pupils understand that the worksheets are for studying – not for filling out and handing in. That is why it is important for pupils to have the answer sheets to check themselves and their team-mates as they study.

Have pupils explain answers to one another instead of just scoring each other against the answer sheet.

When children have questions, have them ask a team-mate before asking you.

While pupils are working in teams, circulate through the class, praising teams that are working well, sitting in with each team to hear how they are doing, and so on.

Test

After pupils have had adequate time to study as a team (one period is usually sufficient), distribute the quiz. Do not let pupils work together on the quiz; at this point they must show what they have learned as individuals. Have them move their desks apart if this is possible. Either allow pupils to exchange papers with members of the other teams, or collect the quizzes to score after class. Test scores should be expressed in terms of percentage correct.

Calculating individual improvement scores

As soon as possible after each quiz you should calculate individual improvement scores and team scores and award certificates or other rewards to high-scoring teams. If at all possible, the announcement of team scores should be made in the first period after the quiz.

Pupils earn points for their teams based on the degree to which their quiz scores exceed their base scores, as follows:

Quiz score	Improvement points
More than 10 points below base score	0
10 points below to 1 point below base score	10
Base score to 10 points above base score	20
More than 10 points above base score	30
Perfect paper (regardless of base score)	30

Calculating team scores

Calculate team scores by adding up the improvement points earned by the team members and dividing the sum by the number of team members present on the day of the quiz.

Recognizing team accomplishments

There are two levels of awards given based on average team scores, as follows:

Criterion (average team score)	Award
18–22	GREATTEAM
23 or above	SUPERTEAM

Note that all teams can achieve the awards; teams are not in competition with one another. The criteria are set to make success difficult but not impossible for all teams. If the criteria turn out to be too easy or too difficult for your pupils, you may change them.

Provide some sort of recognition or reward for achieving at the GREATTEAM level and a larger or fancier award for SUPERTEAMS. For example, you might give small certificates to GREATTEAMS and larger ones for SUPERTEAMS; let SUPERTEAMS line up for lunch and break first, GREATTEAMS second; post photographs of SUPERTEAMS and GREATTEAMS on notice boards, and so on. Your own enthusiasm about team scores and a communication that you value co-operation and success as a team are as important as any other factor in the success of STAD.

Changing teams and revising base scores

After five or six weeks of STAD, reassign pupils to new teams. This gives pupils who were on low-scoring teams a new chance, allows them to work with other classmates, and keeps the programme fresh. Also, revise pupils' base scores at this time, computing new averages using pupils' quiz scores from the previous five to six weeks.

Notes

1 This chapter was written under a grant from the Office of Educational Research and Improvement, US Department of Education (no. OERI-G-86-0006). However, any opinions expressed are mine and do not represent OERI policy. Sections of this chapter are adapted from earlier articles by Slavin (1986a, 1987).

2 For a more detailed description of STAD and other Student Team-Learning methods, a teacher's manual (Slavin 1986b) can be obtained from the Johns Hopkins Team Learning Project, 3505 N. Charles Street, Baltimore, Maryland, 21218, USA.

References

Allport, G. (1954) *The Nature of Prejudice*, Cambridge, Mass.: Addison-Wesley.

Aronson, E., Blaney, N., Stephan, C., Sikes, J. and Snapp, M. (1978) *The Jigsaw Classroom*, Beverly Hills, Cal.: Sage.

Ballard, M., Corman, L., Gottlieb, J. and Kauffman, M. (1977) 'Improving the social status of mainstreamed retarded children', *Journal of Educational Psychology* 69: 605–11.

Blaney, N.T., Stephan, S., Rosenfeld, D., Aronson, E. and Sikes, J. (1977) 'Interdependence in the classroom: a field study', *Journal of Educational Psychology* 69: 121–8.

Cooper, L., Johnson, D.W., Johnson, R. and Wilderson, F. (1980) 'Effects on cooperative, competitive and individualistic experiences in interpersonal attraction among heterogeneous peers', *Journal of Social Psychology* 111: 243–52.

DeVries, D.L. and Slavin, R.E. (1978) 'Teams-Games-Tournament (TGT):

review of ten classroom experiments', *Journal of Research and Development in Education* 12: 28–38.

Gerard, H.B. and Miller, N. (1975) *School Desegregation: A Long-range Study*, New York: Plenum.

Hartley, W. (1976) 'Prevention outcomes of small group education with school children: an epidemiologic follow up of the Kansas City School Behavior Project', unpublished manuscript, University of Kansas Medical Center.

Hegarty, S., Pocklington, K. and Lucas, D. (1981). *Educating Pupils with Special Needs in the Ordinary School*, Windsor: NFER-Nelson.

Janke, R. (1978) *The Teams-Games-Tournament (TGT) Method and the Behavioral Adjustment and Academic Achievement of Emotionally Impaired Adolescents*, paper presented at the annual convention of the American Educational Research Association, Toronto, (April).

Johnson, D.W. and Johnson, R.T. (1987) *Learning Together and Alone*, (2nd edn), Englewood Cliffs, NJ: Prentice-Hall.

Madden, N.A. and Slavin, R.E. (1983) 'Cooperative learning and social acceptance of mainstreamed academically handicapped students', *Journal of Special Education* 17: 171–82.

Madden, N.A., Slavin, R.E. and Leavey, M. (1984) 'Combining cooperative learning and individualized instruction: effects on student mathematics achievement attitudes and behaviors', *Elementary School Journal* 84: 409–22.

Madden, N.A., Stevens, R.J. and Slavin, R.E. (1986) *A Comprehensive Cooperative Learning Approach to Elementary Reading and Writing: Effects on Student Achievement*, Baltimore, Md: Center for Research on Elementary and Middle Schools, The Johns Hopkins University, report no. 2.

Okebukola, P.A. (1985) 'The relative effectiveness of cooperative and competitive interaction techniques in strengthening students' performance in science classes', *Science Education* 69: 501–9.

Sharan, S., Kussell, P., Hertz-Lazarowitz, R., Bejarano, Y., Raviv, S. and Sharan, Y. (1984) *Cooperative Learning in the Classroom: Research in Desegregated Schools*, Hillsdale, NJ: Erlbaum.

Sharan, S. and Shachar, C. (1986) 'Cooperative learning effects on students' academic achievement and verbal behavior in multi-ethnic junior high school classrooms in Israel, unpublished paper, University of Tel Aviv, Israel.

Sharan, S. and Sharan, Y. (1976) *Small-group Teaching*, Englewood Cliffs, NJ: Educational Technology Publications.

Slavin, R.E. (1977) 'A student team approach to teaching adolescents with special emotional and behavioral needs', *Psychology in the Schools* 14 (1): 77–84.

Slavin, R.E. (1978) 'Student teams and achievement divisions', *Journal of Research and Development in Education* 12: 39–49.

Slavin, R.E. (1979) 'Effects of biracial learning teams on cross-racial friendships', *Journal of Educational Psychology* 71: 381–7.

Slavin, R. E. (1980) 'Effects of individual learning expectations on student achievement', *Journal of Educational Psychology* 72: 520–4.

Slavin, R.E. (1983a) *Cooperative Learning*, New York: Longman.

Slavin, R.E. (1983b) 'When does cooperative learning increase student achievement? *Psychological Bulletin* 94: 429–45.

Slavin, R.E. (1985a) 'Cooperative learning: applying contact theory in desegregated schools', *Journal of Social Issues* 41: 45–62.

Slavin, R.E. (1985b) 'Team-assisted individualization: a cooperative learning solution for adaptive instruction in mathematics', in M. Wang and H. Walberg (eds) *Adapting Instruction to Individual Differences*, Berkeley, Calif: McCutchan, pp. 236–53.

Slavin, R.E. (1986a) 'Learning together', *American Educator*: 6–13.

Slavin, R.E. (1986b) *Using Student Team Learning*, (3rd edn). Baltimore, Md: Center for Research on Elementary and Middle Schools, The Johns Hopkins University.

Slavin, R.E. (1987) *Cooperative learning: Student Teams*, (2nd edn). Washington, DC: National Education Association.

Slavin, R.E. (1988) 'Cooperative learning and student achievement', in R.E. Slavin (ed.) *School and Classroom Organization*, Hillsdale, NJ: Erlbaum.

Slavin, R.E. and Karweit, N. (1981) 'Cognitive and affective outcomes of an intensive student team learning experience', *Journal of Experimental Education* 50: 29–35.

Slavin, R.E., Leavey, M.B. and Madden, N.A. (1986) *Team-Accelerated Instruction – Mathematics*, Watertown, Mass.: Mastery Education Corporation.

Slavin, R.E., Madden, N.A. and Leavey, M.B. (1984) 'Effects of Team-Assisted Individualization on the mathematics of academically handicapped and nonhandicapped students', *Journal of Educational Psychology* 76: 813–19.

Stevens, R.J., Madden, N.A., Slavin, R.E. and Farnish, A.M. (1987) 'Cooperative Integrated Reading and Composition: two field experiments', *Reading Research Quarterly* 22: 433–54.

Webb, N. (1985) 'Student interaction and learning in small groups: a research summary', in R.E. Slavin, S. Sharan, S. Kagan, R. Hertz-Lazaraowitz, C. Webb and R. Schmuck (eds) *Learning to Cooperate, Cooperating to Learn*, New York: Plenum, 148–72.

Ziegler, S. (1981) 'The effectiveness of cooperative learning teams for increasing cross-ethnic friendship: additional evidence', *Human Organization* 40: 264–8.

Chapter fourteen

Individuals, groups and interventions

Colin Rogers and Peter Kutnick

Readers who have taken the unusual step of reading the book from start to finish in the order that we, as editors, have judged to be appropriate, will have been rewarded by concluding with the reading of the chapters by Galloway and Slavin, both of which make strong calls for collective and interventionist approaches. While they each get to these conclusions from rather different starting points, and while their conclusions differ in respect to a number of points of detail, each of them has drawn attention to matters of fundamental importance for a social psychology of education and its future.

Written from a British perspective in 1989, it is not surprising to find Galloway concerned with the implications of the 1988 Act, the National Curriculum and all that. It is important, though, to notice that Galloway's main concerns, writing from the vantage point of a special needs specialist, are not with the National Curriculum itself, or even with its associated testing, but more with the introduction of 'market forces' into the education system. The shift away from a centrally funded, locally planned system, to one that is dominated by central regulation subject to local forces of supply and demand, has considerable potential significance. It is, at present, far too early to assess just what the impact of the Local Management of Schools (LMS), the right to 'opt out' of Local Education Authority control, open enrolment and the increased power of governing bodies will turn out to be. Galloway's discussion of these issues serves to remind us, however, of two important features of these changes.

First, it is clear that teachers are to be placed in a position of greater but perhaps, more importantly, different forms of accountability. While the changes in the pressures that this will bring to bear upon teachers will be important in their own right, it is the recognition of the existence of pressures and constraints *per se* that has the greater significance for the further development of the social psychology of education. Several of the contributors to this volume have addressed themselves to the need to develop the autonomy of the individual pupil, so as to create independent learners. However, autonomous learners are less likely to be produced within a system that places external constraints and pressures upon their teachers. Galloway addresses this within the particular context of those pupils with identified special needs, but his point is one that has a general application. Social psychologists need to attend more closely to the links between educational policy and classroom practice, both in terms of drawing out policy implications from social psychological theory, but also in terms of assessing the implications of policy within a framework provided by such theory.

Second, from the outset it appears clear that any consideration of educational issues cannot be conducted exclusively at the level of the individual. Again Galloway makes the point most clearly with respect to the pupil with special needs arguing that the nature of the relationship between pupils in a class will be determined more by the 'moral climate' or ethos of the class than by the characteristics of the children themselves. This is a point that social psychologists would readily concede, recognizing as it does the essentially social nature of human life.

Slavin's work also represents a recognition of the importance of a collective or group approach to education rather than one that is based solely upon the activities of the individual. For present purposes, however, the more important aspect of Slavin's work is his advocacy of a strongly interventionalist approach. For Slavin, it is clear that the benefits of group-based work in school classrooms will not simply come about by teachers asking pupils to work together. Co-operative teaching and learning techniques are presented as a highly systematic, carefully controlled and monitored strategy.

The teacher's interventions, however, are aimed not at the individual, nor directly at the activities of the group. Rather the aim of the enterprise is to establish sets of conditions that will then generate activity on the part of the pupil that will further development. As such, Slavin can be seen to be unashamedly advocating a form of social engineering.

Slavin's approach can also be seen as a very pragmatic one. Systematic research has revealed techniques which work, and techniques which appear to be less successful. This systematic approach has also enabled him to identify critical elements within the process such as equal opportunity scoring, individual accountability and team rewards. The point that we would wish to emphasize here is that these clearly implicate the importance of the individual pupil developing strategies to deal with the conditions thus established, and thereby coming to behave in a manner which appears to be more conducive to a higher level of learning.

Individuals within a social context

The idea of pupil strategies is not a new one (Woods 1980) and a number of the chapters within this volume have discussed this aspect of classroom life. Galton draws attention to the demands imposed upon pupils by various forms of group work. Pupils find themselves in situations in which they are required to establish strategies that enable them to obtain a sense of ownership over the work they are undertaking, while at the same time not wishing to be seen to be accepting responsibility for work that might be judged to be substandard by their peers. A group, or collectively-based classroom, is one in which a high proportion of the pupils' activities become public. Added to the appraisal of the teacher is the appraisal of the peer group. While it is generally accepted that peer appraisal is likely to be of greater significance for the older, secondary school pupil, it is clear that it is already an issue for the primary child.

In developing classroom practices which place a greater emphasis upon the work carried out by groups, teachers need to be mindful that they are sensitive to the needs of the individuals that comprise them. A group focus does not imply a neglect of the individual, but rather a focus upon the individual as a group member. Group strategies will have their effects via the influence they exert upon individual members. Just as the individual pupil needs to interpret teacher actions (and bases his or her response upon the interpretation rather than the action itself) so too must the pupil interpret, and thereby respond to, the actions of the group.

Both Rogers and Schunk have discussed some of the burgeoning literature dealing with the cognitions of individuals in social settings and the effects that these cognitions will have upon the motivations and self-esteem of the pupil. While this work does not lead directly to instructional techniques in the way that Slavin's work does, it does provide a broad theoretical perspective which has a potential for application in a wide variety of settings. If teachers are to be able usefully to anticipate the strategies adopted by pupils in a variety of different educational contexts, then they need to have a clear perspective on the nature of those strategies and the educational consequences of the adoption of any one of the range available. The concerns addressed by Galton provide one clear example of potential application.

A consistent theme of the work written for this volume has been the requirement for teachers to adopt a clearly interventionist role in the way in which they approach their work with pupils. A child-centred, 'progressive' education is not seen as one in which the child is left to discover themselves in whatever context that happens to be available. Rather it is seen to be one in which the teacher takes a proactive role designed to foster the skills of the child that make pupil progress more likely to take place. The group is utilized as a device in this procedure, partly out of recognition of the near impossibility of dealing directly with the needs of each individual child and partly from recognition of the group's central role in pupil learning. As demands for high educational standards grow, a positive approach to a child-centred (or, as the emphasis is on groups, children-centred) education becomes more of a necessity.

The call for a group focus, however, is not merely a pragmatic one. The work discussed here by French, Edwards, Kutnick, Wright, Smith and Maxwell illustrates in a variety of ways the degree to which the primary curriculum and the child's experience of that curriculum is by necessity social in nature. From the centrality of play, through the complexities of the development of pupil autonomy, to the social nature of the knowledge to be taught and learnt itself, the social experience of the child appears as fundamental. In their various ways each of these authors is pointing us towards the conclusion that the social aspects of primary schooling cannot be simply regarded as an optional extra to be bolted on to the National Curriculum as and when time, resources and teacher patience allow. The contents of the National Curriculum itself are to be seen as the results of social interaction, and the transmission of the same by further social process as necessary as well as desirable.

Dimensions of action

The work reported here can be considered to represent points on a number of dimensions. The remainder of this concluding chapter will seek, briefly, to illustrate the nature of these and then go on to set out some of the future requirements for a social psychology of education.

One clear view that emerges in virtually all of the writing here is that of the pupil as an active participant in the process of schooling. Pupils have their own concerns with the maintenance of peer group relations, self-identity, gender roles and so on, and each of these concerns interacts with the demands made upon the pupil by the teacher. Education is often characterized as a game in which the different participants play out their roles and seek to obtain their own objectives within an implicitly agreed and evolving set of rules. As long as it is not seen to trivialize the issues, such an analogy is a useful one. (To paraphrase the late Bill Shankly, 'Education is not a matter of life and death, it is much more important than that'.) In order for teachers to be able to keep at least one step ahead in the game plan it is necessary for a clear understanding of the nature of the pupils' active involvement to be obtained. It will not be sufficient to appreciate that a pupil strategy will exist. As work in self-esteem and motivation shows most clearly, the strategies developed by pupils are often designed to deal with short-term objectives rather than with longer-term ones. Effective short-term strategies may have less than desirable longer-term outcomes. However, attempts to alter these are likely to fail unless the suggested alternatives are also able to meet the functional requirements of the pupils' initial short-term concerns. As Galton has suggested, pupils will want to maintain face-saving strategies, and, therefore, greater educational rewards will not be sought out if the risk is perceived to be too great.

On the active–passive pupil dimension then, it is clear that current social psychological thinking firmly locates concern at the active end. In switching to the next dimension of concern, it is important to bear this prior observation in mind. The articles contained within this volume have also clearly advocated (although in various ways) an interventionist rather than a *laissez-faire* strategy on the part of teachers. Pupils may take an active role in their own development and education but this is not seen to imply that teachers need not strive to ensure that appropriate actions are taken to direct and influence that development. However, it is clear that interventions that are likely to be maximally effective are going to have to work with, and not against, the grain of the pupils' own strategies. It is worth repeating the point made above that teacher strategies will be most effectively developed by those with an understanding of the strategies being adopted by pupils.

However, it is also well understood that teachers are themselves constrained and pressured. At times of major change in the educational system and with much public questioning of the effectiveness of schools and teachers, such pressures and constraints are likely to be operating at high levels. One would be unwise to add to these by proposing an additional set of concerns and responsibilities. As has been demonstrated by Bennett *et al.* (1984), it is already the case that teachers find it very difficult to judge accurately the appropriateness of the interventions that they do make.

Given present resource levels within education (and those that could be realistically anticipated over the next decade or so), there are no easy solutions to this problem. However, the difficulties are greater when teacher interventions are exclusively conceptualized as operating at the level of the individual pupil. Research into school effectiveness (Mortimore *et al.* 1988: Smith and Tomlinson 1989) shows us that schools and individual classes within schools can make a difference to pupil performance. While there is still much to discover about the processes involved here, there is some tentative agreement that it is the ethos, style or character of the school or classroom that matters. Effective schools do not carefully direct each individual pupil along their own most appropriate path (but this is not to argue that this would be unwise if it were clearly possible), rather they would seem to create the conditions that facilitate the decision-making strategies of pupils (and presumably of teachers also) themselves. In the terminology being adopted here, the interventions of effective schools would be seen to be collective rather than individualistic. They build on the social life of the school and turn it to educational advantage. Less effective schools either fail to do this or, worse, create an ethos that actually prevents effective social intercourse from taking place.

This is not just a matter of good management leading to good behaviour and good results (although Croll and Moses in their article have argued that poor classroom management can be seen to lead to a number of unintended and often unrecognized effects). Rather it is the beginnings of a recognition that schools are essentially social places, children's learning and development are essentially social in nature, knowledge itself (and, thereby, the contents of the curriculum) cannot be separated from the effects of social life, and that good schools will therefore seek to capitalize on this.

Prospect

If the potential implicated throughout this volume for developing and improving present practice is to be realized, then it is essential that the social psychology of education develops along two closely-related yet separate tracks.

The first of these, naturally, is the continuing development of clear social scientific models and theories germane to relevant aspects of human social behaviour. Not all of this work, involving a variety of research methods and drawing upon a wide range of theory, will have a clear and immediate application to education.

For present purposes the second track is the more important one and involves the development of good planning models of social process to set aside the full-blown social scientific models. It is the development of these planning models that will move us away from looking at relevant bits of social psychology towards dealing with a social psychology of education. Such planning models need to be developed in conjunction with teachers and others with close and detailed experience of classroom practice, for they need to dwell upon the concerns of the educator as much as the concerns of the social scientist. Planning models will provide teachers with ways of applying the fruits of the social scientific study within the context of their everyday classroom concerns.

Slavin's work on co-operative learning is one of the better examples currently available. It is a model that provides ways of relating educational objectives to social scientific understanding, and enables the classroom teacher to develop her or his own applications within a framework that attempts to establish the central features of any success-ful instance of co-operative group work. It is this understanding of essential features that is important as this enables the teacher to develop practice in ways that are suited to the precise settings in which she or he has to operate. Social engineering will never be very effective if every situation has to attempt to accommodate to the exact same package.

Teachers need to be able to adapt and develop approaches to teaching within a guiding framework. The task of social psychology is to develop ways in which teachers can further develop their own understanding of the nature of classroom life in order to be able to make more systematic, sophisticated and effective judgements about the course of action to be chosen. Above all else this involves an understanding of the importance of process. It is here that Slavin's model still falls short of the ideal as it tells us too little about the critical elements of process. While his identification of key features is a necessary step along this route to a full-blown planning model, the lack of a detailed model of the dynamics of pupil response to various teaching techniques still sets a limit on the extent to which teachers are able to monitor and intervene in the process once started.

While Wright has argued that teacher–pupil equality is often to be seen as highly desirable, Edwards is right to point out that teaching and learning take place within a relationship characterized by inequality. The teacher's greater power, influence and knowledge can all be harnessed as forces for good, provided that teachers themselves have a sufficient understanding of the ways in which these operate.

References

Bennett, S.N., Desforges, C., Cockburn, A. and Wilkinson, B. (1984) *The Quality of Pupil Learning Experiences*, London: Lawrence Erlbaum Associates.

Mortimore, P., Sammons, P., Stoll, L., Lewis, D. and Ecob, R. (1988) *School Matters: The Junior Years*, Wells: Open Books.

Smith, D. and Tomlinson, S. (1989) *The School Effect*, London: Policy Studies Institute.

Woods, P. (ed.) (1980) *Pupil Strategies*, London: Croom Helm.

Author index

Subject index